*FICTION FIGHTS
THE CIVIL WAR*

FICTION FIGHTS THE CIVIL WAR

An Unfinished Chapter in the Literary History of the American People

by

ROBERT A. LIVELY

GREENWOOD PRESS, PUBLISHERS
WESTPORT, CONNECTICUT

Library of Congress Cataloging in Publication Data

Lively, Robert A
    Fiction fights the Civil War.

    Reprint of the ed. published by the University
of North Carolina Press, Chapel Hill.
    Bibliography: p.
    1. Historical fiction, American. 2. United
States--History--Civil War--Fiction--History and
criticism. I. Title.
[PS374.H5L5 1973]   813'.081   73-11751
ISBN 0-8371-7084-2

Originally published in 1957 by The University of
North Carolina Press, Chapel Hill

Reprinted with the permission of The University
of North Carolina Press

Reprinted in 1973 by Greenwood Press,
a division of Williamhouse-Regency Inc.

Library of Congress Catalogue Card Number 73-11751

ISBN 0-8371-7084-2

Printed in the United States of America

TO MOTHER AND FATHER

Acknowledgments

A MAN WRITES a book alone, but custom invites notice of the agencies that employed him, and pardoned his endeavor. I began a good many of the following pages as a Ph.D. candidate at the University of North Carolina, where Professor Fletcher M. Green, not without misgivings, befriended me, guided me, and encouraged my pursuit of a most unacademic topic. During the four years I taught at Vanderbilt University and the University of Wisconsin, research funds of those institutions supported me for four uninterrupted months at the typewriter; and I was recently granted very generous aid by the Princeton University Research Committee. Dr. Lawrence London, custodian of the Wilmer Collection of Civil War novels at the University of North Carolina, went beyond courtesy in his assistance to me, and Professor C. Hugh Holman, of the Carolina English Department, nerved me to encroach on his discipline. Dedication of the book to Matthew S. Lively and Noncie Cook Lively, my mother and father, is a token payment on the debt I owe them for rearing me in a home where books were in daily use.

Thanks are also due the authors and publishers who granted me permission to quote extensively from recently published Civil War novels: to Charles Scribner's Sons, for James Boyd, *Marching On* (1927), Stark Young, *So Red The Rose* (1934), and Joseph Stanley Pennell, *The History of Rome Hanks and Kindred Matters* (1944); to Coward-McCann, Inc., for Mackinlay Kantor, *Long Remember* (1934); to the Houghton

Mifflin Company, for Ross Lockridge, Jr., *Raintree County* (1947); to Rinehart & Company, for DuBose Heyward, *Peter Ashley* (Farrar & Rinehart, 1932), and Edgar Lee Masters, *The Tide of Time* (Farrar & Rinehart, 1937); to G. P. Putnam's Sons, for Allen Tate, *The Fathers* (1938); to Harcourt, Brace and Company, for Ellen Glasgow, *A Certain Measure. An Interpretation of Prose Fiction* (1943); to Appleton-Century-Crofts, Inc., for Molly Elliott Seawell, *The Victory* (D. Appleton & Company, 1906), and James Lane Allen, *The Sword of Youth* (The Century Company, 1915); to T. S. Stribling, for *The Forge* (Doubleday, Doran, & Company, 1931); to Andrew Lytle, for *The Long Night* (The Bobbs-Merrill Company, 1936); and to Evelyn Scott, for *The Wave* (Jonathan Cape and Harrison Smith, 1929).

PRINCETON, NEW JERSEY R. A. L.
July 8, 1956

Contents

Fiction Fights the Civil War

CRITICS, HISTORIANS,
AND CIVIL WAR NOVELS

EXAMINATION of five-hundred-odd novels about the Civil War is not an altogether serious task, nor, for that matter, a very safe one. Adventures in unclaimed territory between the historical and literary disciplines have left me in uncomfortable isolation, unsupported by my fellows, and untrained in the techniques of my new neighbors. Historians, my customary associates, have been suspicious of the work's legitimacy; and literary folk, amused at study of novels by the gross, have often been openly derisive. I cannot say that several years' labor with Civil War novels has been an unmitigated pleasure, but I must confess a still unsatiated delight with historical novels, however bad, which first led me to the study of history.

Five hundred and twelve novels have been examined in the course of this survey—the verb cannot quite be "read," for my attention to juveniles, and to many a stereotyped tale, has frequently been more hurried than thoughtful. The work has had to proceed without much help from the critics and historians to whom one looks for aid in matters of method and interpretation. Among the several observers who have undertaken general comment on the Civil War tradition in American literature, only one has presented a useful and thoughtful analysis —and his conclusions proceed from a list of books so limited that it cannot be counted representative of the whole war literature.[1] In general, the fact that historical novels are conservative in style, that they follow rather than establish dominant trends, means that they are overlooked by the literary historians whose interest is in developing technique rather than in orthodox performance. The book reviewers of newspapers and magazines to whom the task of evaluation is left can render only transient opinions, rarely informed by a consistent view of writing about the war. The plain fact is that the mass of Civil War novels flows out in that sluggish stream which has been described as "sub-literary." The book-page editor may use them to acquire, or sometimes to discourage, a volunteer reviewing staff, but he does not ask that they be taken seriously.

Historians have felt no obligation to supply what the reviewers have omitted. In their chapters on "culture," they have been impressed, like the critics, by a few outstanding novels—they cannot resist speculation about the influence of a phenomenon like *Gone with the Wind*—but they do not often relate such wonders to the traditions of the historical novel. They choose instead to treat them as revivals of something forgotten, not as a part of continuing production in the established trade of war literature. In the average general work in history, after all, there is no particular place for a survey of Civil War novels. For his treatment of the war, an historian works in the manuscripts and documents of the 1850's and 1860's; his interest is not in modern novels. When he reaches his chapter on recent cultural trends, he concentrates, with the critic, on outstanding works of art, on achievements rarely attained by authors of historical fiction. Any thorough study of war literature is usually made for some special purpose, as in Paul Buck's story of the literature of reconciliation, or in Francis Pendleton Gaines' analysis of the plantation tradition in the arts. Such a work is complete when certain elements of romance, a few

1. The comments referred to are in DeVoto, "Fiction Fights the Civil War," *Sat. Rev. Lit.*, XVII (Dec. 18, 1937), 3-4. For a careful attempt to categorize Civil War novels, and summarize plots in books of a limited period, see R. W. Smith, "The Civil War and Its Aftermath in American Fiction."

lingering traditions, are outlined and isolated for observation. It is not my intention to disparage these specialized uses of fiction as sources for history. The novels of the Civil War provide useful evidence of persistent sectional traditions, but they provide evidence also in support of practically any conclusion which may be drawn from study of the war. I have tried to see them whole and have sought, in this process, to illustrate their variety, their general tone, and their reliability as sources of knowledge about the conflict. I have proceeded on the assumption that great numbers of American readers have been dependent on these sources for their understanding of the era. Since this dependence is to a larger degree on form than on substance, much of my study has involved the exercise of literary rather than historical judgment. As a means of communication, the novel has such definite advantages over the monograph that frequent reference is made to its virtues and deficiencies as a medium for historical information.

An historian should pretend no surprise at the number of occasions on which fact and fancy have mingled to color our memories of the past. He has daily encounters with schoolboys stuffed with tales come down from Parson Weems, or he may labor as a scholar to untangle the early Christian martyrs from the clutches of General Lew Wallace and Hollywood. Should the history of the South be his field, he must have pondered on equally pervasive influences. The Connecticut lady who laid aside the description of Sherman's march in *Gone with the Wind* with an explosive "Those damn Yankees" puts in forceful context the process I seek here to analyze.[2] One cannot doubt that southern traditions of the Civil War have been more firmly fixed in the American consciousness by Miss Mitchell's best-seller than by Douglas Southall Freeman's minute examination of the career of Robert E. Lee. A famous sociologist has been reported, as a matter of fact, to hold *Gone with the Wind* to be the most important southern event since President Hayes withdrew the last Federal troops.[3]

2. The illustration is from Freeman, *The South to Posterity*, p. ix.
3. DeVoto, "Fiction and the Everlasting *If*: Notes on the Contemporary Historical Novel," *Harpers*, CLXXVII (June, 1938), 42.

Appropriation of historical materials by fiction provides the professional historian, in my opinion, with as much cause for gratification as for alarm. It is only natural that Clio's elopement with a novelist should cause concern in her guardian's house, but it is time to realize that on many occasions she has done very well for herself. Such a marriage may be quite Bohemian and may brighten the lives of a million tabloid readers; but Clio, after all, has a dignity and integrity revealed all the more clearly by the passions of the arts. Her adventure, furthermore, is not new, even if it always seems so. It was a novelist who first made a pageant of the past that historians have been imitating ever since. Long ago when history, after the fashion of Gibbon, resembled a "parthenon procession," its figures marching with little change across fourteen centuries, Sir Walter Scott showed "how not only clothes and weapons, but thought and morals vary according to the period, the province, the class, the man."[4] The romances of Scott and his followers waked in countless readers a desire for more knowledge of forgotten days and turned such men as Von Ranke to the study of history. Publication of the Waverley Novels, said Carlyle, "taught all men this truth, which looks like a truism, and yet was as good as unknown to writers of history and others till so taught: that the bygone ages of the world were actually filled by living men, not by protocols, statepapers, controversies, and abstractions of men."[5]

4. Trevelyan, "History and Fiction," *Living Age,* CCCXIII (June, 1922), 565.
5. Quoted by Speare, *The Political Novel,* p. 17. Possession by Sir Walter Scott of what Henry Seidel Canby calls the "basic patent" in historical fiction is generally recognized by literary historians. George Peabody Gooch, reviewing the work of historical novelists, gives a majority opinion with his observation that "for practical purposes we may say that [Scott] was the first as well as the greatest of the tribe, and that *Waverly* burst upon the world like Minerva from the head of Zeus." Romances of the past had appeared before Scott—George Saintsbury, casting about for the origins of the *genre,* pointed to Xenophon's *Cyropedia*—but to describe these earlier works as literature strains the term unduly. Certain broad intellectual movements necessarily preceded Scott's definition and practice of the art. The eighteenth century, under the tutelage of Hume, Robertson, and Gibbon, had paid increasing

Awareness of this debt to fiction scarcely relieves the frustration a scholar feels when he sees the impenetrable barriers of time yield suddenly at the flank to imaginative assault. His reaction to historical yarns is often colored by a measure of contempt, even though he offers no overt challenge to the validity of the form. Conscious of the danger in substituting what might have been for what was, his caution may blind him to the fact that an historical novel, like any other work of art, is no mere copy of the record. It is an independent and original creation, presented in the heat of a more direct attack on truth than can be launched by the most exhaustive summary of verifiable fact. While the historian labors to authenticate each tile for the mosaic he laboriously assembles, the novelist, with broad brush and vivid colors, may capture with a few bold strokes an impression of the age recalled.[6]

Now there is a considerable gulf between impressionistic history, the fruit of mature artistry, and a scientifically researched monograph, the pride of scholarship. A scholar can take only limited comfort in this distinction, however, for he inevitably competes with the artist for the attention of the community he seeks to inform. The community is unlikely to concern itself with matters of method; in general it asks the same service from both historian and historical novelist—a satisfactory impression of its earlier experience. Further, both artist and scholar must rely on the reading public for achievement of their ends. Each must provide images which will allow a reader to see, to experience personally, a moment from forgot-

---

attention to formal history; during this period a public was created, and the raw materials for the work of the novelist were put within his reach. The historical novel then came with the Romantic movement and proved to be an ideal medium for expression of that extravagant admiration of distant times which contrasts so sharply with the cool indifference of a Gibbon or a Voltaire. Canby, "What Is Truth?" *Sat. Rev. Lit.,* IV (Dec. 31, 1927), 481. Gooch, "Historical Novels," *Contemp. Rev.,* CXVII (Feb., 1920), 204. Saintsbury, *Essays in English Literature, 1780-1860,* p. 303.

6. For a sensible analysis of this distinction, see Taylor, "The Historical Novel as a Source in History," *Sewanee Rev.,* XLVI (Oct., 1938), 476.

ten time. Each is dependent on the reader himself for completion of the author's work, for the "past as it exists for all of us, the world of the past in our minds, is history synthesized"[7] by our own imaginations. The more vivid images of the novelists often control the fragment of memory which brings us closest to vanished reality.

For fifty-odd years the historian has had the best authority to shield him from the disturbing implications of this competition. Both his pride and confidence have been protected by experts on the art of fiction, who have been almost unanimous in their assurances that the historical novel is not worthy of his concern. The most ambitious history of American literature indexes no reference to the form; and such standard studies of the American novel as those of Carl Van Doren or Arthur H. Quinn have little to say about its methods and limits. Critics persist in regarding the historical novel as "a kind of mulelike animal begotten by the ass of fiction on the brood mare of fact, and hence, a sterile monster."[8]

This widespread contempt for the *genre,* fairly modern in origin, stems from the state of the American critical mind at the turn of the century. Romances of the past began to fall from grace in that era, when enthusiasm for empirical thought in the social sciences and naturalism in the arts fostered the mood that Ernest Bernbaum has described as a "naive confidence in the reality of phenomena." The scientific spirit, carried over to observations on the hopes and dreams of men, came close to destroying in the world of letters the reputation of the historical novel. Among guardians of our literary tradition, a touching faith in the ability of scientific historians to construct an objective and complete report of the past led to regular derogation of such tools as faith and imagination when they were employed for recapture of the national memories. The artist might serve as recorder for the society in which he

7. Butterfield, *The Historical Novel,* p. 22.
8. Hervey Allen, "History and the Novel," *Atlantic,* XLXXIII (Feb. 9, 1944), 119. Professor Leisy, in *The American Historical Novel,* avoids definitions and generalizations in his detailed analysis of plot and quality in novels depicting each era of American development.

lived, but his report was accepted only when it was based on direct observation of events within his own experience.[9] Critical demand for the artist as recorder, rather than dreamer, established the still prevalent view of the historical novelist as "a carpet-bagger—not through space, but through time,—and if his blunders be not so obvious, none the less must he blunder abundantly." Brander Matthews, who made the foregoing comment in 1898, argued that "As . . . the best novels of American life are those written by Americans, so the best novels of eighteenth-century manners, for example, are those written in the eighteenth century. . . ."[10]

A desire for photographic realism in the novel accounts for only part of the critical disdain for historical subjects at the beginning of the twentieth century. Resistance to the form was in equal part a reaction against the spate of costume romances which flooded the market of that day. To William Dean Howells, the high priest of American criticism at the century's turn, the remarkable outpouring of second-rate novels represented only bloody vulgarity.[11] A literary theory which had no room for historical fiction was thus combined with irritation at debasement of the novel by inept romancers. In subsequent years the literary theory was to change, but the note of contempt for the historical novel has remained a permanent element of the critical mood. There developed among critics a sort of double standard, which permitted notice of a good historical novel as an exceptional accident, a result of unusual talent working in a barren field. In this vein, a reviewer could give careful and thoughtful study to so excellent a work as Ross Lockridge's *Raintree County,* for instance, but he could reserve, at the same time, his strictures on the "historical novel" until such a dreary tract as *Forever Amber* permitted expression of sophisticated disdain for popular concern with the bedrooms of history.

9. Bernbaum, "Views of Great Critics on the Historical Novel," *PMLA,* XLI (1926), 428-29.
10. *The Historical Novel and Other Essays,* p. 104.
11. "The New Historical Romances," *No. Am. Rev.,* CLXXI (Oct., 1900), 935-48.

The historical novel would scarcely have survived had it required the encouragement of critics and literary historians. For its guardians and true believers, the form has had only authors and readers. These, happily, remain legion. Their devotion constitutes more formidable evidence of the vitality of tales from the past than can be argued away by critical commentary. The historical novel, according to one competent observer, has accounted for 20 per cent of the novels published during the past generation;[12] and another student concludes that it is today "the most popular form of American fiction."[13] This interest justifies, perhaps requires, a more intensive analysis of historical fiction than is now available.

The following survey takes no more than a sample, of course, from the writings of hundreds of authors, whose work through several generations has represented widely divergent concepts of the war era. I have tried to hold to a proper subordinate place the statement of intrusive theses which may illuminate minor aspects of the subject, but which only obscure a general review of the war literature. I have resisted, as best I could, the catalogues of authors, plots, and ideas that too often masquerade as evidence of fiction's content. My retreat from this particular skirmish leaves me very sympathetic with historians whose commentary on literary trends so often slips from analysis to listing and categorizing. When he faces novels by the score, an observer runs the constant risk of overlooking the most striking contributions made by fiction to understanding of the war. Generalizations, if they are valid, require the discovery of some standard quality in plot or characterization which appears with enough regularity to invite comment—but such common denominators are found, almost invariably, at a level well below the unique qualities of the best novels. The notable achievements of the novelist as historian appear when tradition is left off, when the peculiar personality, the individuality, of a given hero emerges. The literary heritage of the

---

12. Harrison Smith, "Motion Without Progress," *Sat. Rev. Lit.,* XXVII (Nov. 4, 1944), 16.
13. Leisy, *The American Historical Novel,* p. vii.

war deserves more than critical leveling designed to substitute "types" for people. To ignore the separateness joined with the sameness, to exclude the variation in favor of the type, is to abandon the additional dimension that is the novelist's advantage over the historian.

The scheme of my study reflects this constant collision of quantity with quality. In an effort to do justice to both, I have begun with proper subjects for statistical and chronological compilation and then have gradually narrowed my field of vision until the work is focused on a few of the memorable images which illustrate the validity of the art-form, and which demonstrate its usefulness to both historian and public. With so large a body of material, I have been limited to the simplest of questions. First the authors are considered—when they wrote and how much they wrote, who they were and where they came from, what determined their choice of subject and point of view, how they set about the task of writing fictional history. Next is presented a general summary of their themes and conclusions, revealing their shifting interests through the decades, and mapping the changing interpretations of the war in literature. Attention is then given to the performance of a hundred-odd authors at the task of solving a general problem common both to their work and to that of the professional historian. Through this effort the historical method of the novelist is analyzed, and his peculiar contribution to the understanding of complex issues is identified. Finally, from the best novels of the group, there is selected evidence to illustrate fiction's capture of the spirit that informed events during the war years.

From the evidence thus presented, generalizations are undertaken about the nature of the historical novel, about the competence of the novelist as historian, and about the fictional view of the Civil War. In retrospect the three-part pattern seems unduly academic—the catalogue of authors and themes, the novelist as historian, the fusion of history and fiction in art—but my control over these hundreds of books is much less confident than the simple outline suggests.

TABLE I

A SELECTION OF THE BEST CIVIL WAR NOVELS

1. James Lane Allen, *The Sword of Youth* (New York, 1915).
2. George Washington Cable, *Dr. Sevier* (Boston, 1885).
3. Stephen Crane, *The Red Badge of Courage* (New York, 1895).
4. John William De Forest, *Miss Ravenel's Conversion from Secession to Loyalty* (New York, 1867).
5. William Faulkner, *The Unvanquished* (New York, 1938).
6. Ellen Glasgow, *The Battle-Ground* (New York, 1902).
7. Caroline Gordon, *None Shall Look Back* (New York, 1937).
8. DuBose Heyward, *Peter Ashley* (New York, 1932).
9. MacKinlay Kantor, *Long Remember* (New York, 1934).
10. Ross Lockridge, Jr., *Raintree County* (New York, 1947).
11. Andrew Lytle, *The Long Night* (New York, 1936).
12. Joseph Stanley Pennell, *The History of Rome Hanks and Kindred Matters* (New York, 1944).
13. Evelyn Scott, *The Wave* (New York, 1929).
14. Allen Tate, *The Fathers* (New York, 1938).
15. Stark Young, *So Red the Rose* (New York, 1934).

OTHER REPRESENTATIVE CIVIL WAR NOVELS

1. Hervey Allen, *Action at Aquila* (New York, 1938).
2. Francis Courtenay Baylor, *Beyond the Blue Ridge* (New York, 1887).
3. James Boyd, *Marching On* (New York, 1927).
4. Roark Bradford, *Kingdom Coming* (New York, 1933).
5. Winston Churchill, *The Crisis* (New York, 1901).
6. John Esten Cooke, *Surry of Eagle's Nest: Or, The Memoirs of a Staff-Officer Serving in Virginia* (New York, 1866).
7. Virginius Dabney, *The Story of Don Miff, As Told by His Friend John Bouche Whacker: A Symphony of Life* (Philadelphia, 1886).
8. Thomas Cooper De Leon, *John Holden, Unionist: A Romance of the Days of Destruction and Reconstruction* (St. Paul, 1893).
9. Clifford Dowdey, *Bugles Blow No More* (New York, 1937).
10. Clifford Dowdey, *Where My Love Sleeps* (New York, 1945).
11. John Fox, *The Little Shepherd of Kingdom Come* (New York, 1903).
12. Harold Frederic, *The Copperhead* (New York, 1893).
13. Joel Chandler Harris, *On the Plantation: A Story of a Georgia Boy's Adventures during the War* (New York, 1892).
14. Joseph Hergesheimer, *The Limestone Tree* (New York, 1931).
15. Mary Johnston, *The Long Roll* (New York, 1911).

16. Sidney Lanier, *Tiger-Lilies; A Novel* (New York, 1867).
17. John Uri Lloyd, *Warwick of the Knobs: A Story of String-town County, Kentucky* (New York, 1901).
18. Edgar Lee Masters, *The Tide of Time* (New York, 1937).
19. Margaret Mitchell, *Gone with the Wind* (New York, 1936).
20. Silas Weir Mitchell, *In War-Time* (New York, 1885).
21. Henry Morford, *The Days of Shoddy; A Novel of the Great Rebellion in 1861* (Philadelphia, 1863).
22. Mary Noailles Murfree, *The Storm Center* (New York, 1905).
23. Thomas Nelson Page, *Meh Lady: A Story of the War* (New York, 1893).
24. Epes Sargent, *Peculiar: A Tale of the Great Transition* (New York, 1864).
25. Molly Elliott Seawell, *The Victory* (New York, 1906).
26. Thomas Sigismund Stribling, *The Forge* (New York, 1931).
27. Albion Winegar Tourgée, *Toinette: A Novel* (New York, 1874).
28. John Townsend Trowbridge, *Cudjo's Cave* (New York, 1864).
29. Augusta Jane Evans Wilson, *Macaria; Or Altars of Sacrifice* (New York, 1864).
30. Lydia Collins Wood, *The Haydock's Testimony: A Tale of the American Civil War* (London, 1907).

Further, my conclusions are at crucial points frankly subjective. The achievement of a successful artist is realized on a personal level, at a moment of intimate communion between author and reader. The reader's sense of knowing and believing is not shared uniformly among the author's public, and certainly my analysis of such moments as historical evidence can be tested only by an audience which has read the same materials. My references above to the "best" novels and to "successful" artistry depend on my own approach to the always baffling problem of literary judgment. Of the 512 novels here considered, no more than a score have added much of value to the nation's literature. Even the inclusion of the "good," as differentiated from the "best," would increase the list to no more than fifty titles. The mass of these books, assembled in romantic vein, has added little to understanding of the war, and less to any record of literary achievement. My own selection of the outstanding novels of the movement, presented in Table I, will probably meet with as many objections as there are critics; readers are therefore invited to choose their own substitutes from the representative works listed after my favorites. I have sought to reveal the nature of my own judgment through quotations from works presented as representative. Quotation may be the antithesis of analysis, but I have discovered no other means for direct demonstration of the novelists' achievements.

These introductory comments would be incomplete without mention of the collection of novels I employed. This study would scarcely have been made but for a fifty-cent bet a Yale University student made with a classmate on a summer afternoon in 1937. Richard H. Wilmer, Jr., believed that hundreds of Civil War novels had been published, and he proved his contention with remarkable diligence. His discovery of about three hundred titles in the Library of Congress Catalogue marked the beginning of a five-year effort to collect for his personal library all the novels ever published about the war.[14]

The task was out of hand by the time Wilmer entered the United States Navy as an Episcopal chaplain in 1942; his collection then included more than five hundred books. Such a load constituted too great a burden for a minister's travels, and when he was discharged from the Navy in 1946, he gave the collection to the University of North Carolina Library. The library agreed to buy new titles as they were published and to continue the search for novels long out of print. The collection is still growing under the direction of Dr. Lawrence London.

The Wilmer Collection has no great monetary value—only one of the first three hundred books purchased by the young collector cost more than four dollars.[15] He tried to restrict himself to $1.50 per volume—a sum too low, of course, for acquisition of works like the romances of John Esten Cooke, which command in the neighborhood of eight dollars, or *The Red Badge of Courage*, which brings an astronomical one hundred.

14. Wilmer, "Collecting Civil War Novels," *Colophon*, III (New Series, Autumn, 1938), 513-14.

15. The exception was a battered copy of De Forest's *Miss Ravenel's Conversion from Secession to Loyalty*, which cost eight dollars. *Ibid.*, p. 514.

His determination to have nothing but first editions made dealings with booksellers an affair of delicate diplomacy, for even a battered "Oliver Optic" had a way of becoming priceless when a bookstore received a copy of the mimeographed lists Wilmer sent in search of lost titles. The collector found his hobby an unending joy and looked with great reluctance to the time when he would abandon his quest. He wrote:

. . . I love them all, impossible juveniles, sentimental outbursts of the E. P. Roe period . . . Southern issuances from still-embattled, deeply-ingrained hearts; literature great and small, good and bad, I love it all. My collection will never be complete. Compared with fine collections, it is but a poor relative seated at the great banquet of books; and yet for all the filthy grubbing, the disappointment of finding wretched reprints, the expense, which while not great for some, has hampered me adequately—for all this, I have no regret. If my collection, which will grow and perhaps be somehow valuable for its bizarre nature, passes to someone who enjoys the having one jot as much as I have enjoyed and will continue to enjoy the collecting of it, he will be a happy person indeed.[16]

While my pleasure has been more restrained than Mr. Wilmer might hope, my studies, the first in the collection since its delivery to Chapel Hill, have more and more seemed worth undertaking. The past is an elusive abstraction, and the characters in the pages of these works are now and then as real—more real, perhaps—than figures the scholar portrays. Their earth is the one the historian seeks painfully to reconstruct; they share the passions and fates of once-living counterparts, but for the graves. I regret that I lack the art to erect to them the memorial they deserve.

16. *Ibid.*, p. 518.

2

NOVELS BY THE GROSS

I
Definitions

CRITICAL aversion to the historical novel is in one respect a virtue: the form remains unrestrained by the definitions, categories, and other scholarly paraphernalia by which the arts may be reduced to formula. This freedom from fixed rules allows me to adopt an embarrassingly generous definition of such terms as "historical novel" and "Civil War novel." Students of literary criticism tell me that my bibliography has swollen to undignified proportions; but their suggestions for limiting the number of books considered prove, on the whole, to be unconvincing.

The study might be held, for instance, to authors who have accepted the confining discipline of the true *historical novel*— the gospel according to Sir Walter Scott,[1] in which actual his-

1. Scott laid out his rules for historical fiction explicitly, and his definitions governed development of the form for a century. Although historical novels have been somewhat broadened since his time, his maxims are still basic to successful exploitation of historical materials in fiction. Primarily a realist, he attempted to give a plausible account of men's probable reactions under the pressure of accurately recorded historical situations. He sought to make his figures from the past come alive by reproduction of "all those minute circumstances belonging to private life and domestic character, all that gives verisimilitude to a narrative, and individuality to the persons introduced." Scott assumed that men's passions "are generally the same in all ranks and conditions, all countries and ages; and it follows . . . that the opinions, habits of

torical personages are always close by on the wings of the fictional stage, and in which recorded fact is used to shape the developing story to the pattern of actual circumstances. Such authors as John Esten Cooke or Mary Johnston submitted to this discipline, to the detriment of their finished works. Generally the more successful adventures in war fiction have been presented in the *period romance,* in which the tale is based on the manners and mood of the war era, but in which the author admits no obligation to give over to documented history the strings of his moving puppets. But if the period romance is to be considered, there is no valid basis for exclusion of the *costume romance,* in which there is sometimes imprisoned verifiable data, despite the aim of the novelist at the "exploitation,

---

thinking, and actions, however influenced by the peculiar state of society, must still, upon the whole, bear a strong resemblance to each other." This concept of an unchanging man, and an immutable moral order, was his point of contact between the present and the past, the bridge on which the ages could mingle, to the profit of the contemporary reader. Historical forces he illustrated by a deterministic method; his fictional characters were chips in the flood of time, at the mercy of external events. Always conscious of his primary obligation to entertain, Scott applied his historical beliefs in tales based on dramatic moments of the past—the wars of Louis XI, the Jacobite rebellion, the Elizabethan Age, or the Court of Richard the Lion-Hearted. He sought eras of deep-seated conflict, so that his creatures might be subjected to ultimate pressures, while his readers, at the same time, might find a maximum of adventuresome romance. He entertained no fear of anachronism; he assumed, indeed, that "It is necessary . . . that the subject assumed should be . . . translated into the manners, as well as the language, of the age we live in. . . ." Although he sought to avoid obvious introduction of the manners and words of origin more recent than his story, he relied on what he called "that extensive neutral ground," in which "manners and sentiments . . . must have existed alike in either state of society." From one principle, Scott never deviated; his actual personages, though always present, did not come to the reader directly. Great events and historic characters were put among the forces which controlled the hero and heroine, whose imagined story gave to the facts their dramatic color.

The "realism" accredited to Scott paled, of course, as the late nineteenth century's mania for the documented fact came on; Walter Bagehot concluded that the popularity of *Ivanhoe* resulted from description of "the Middle Ages as we should wish them to be. . . . All sensible people knew that the Middle Ages must have been uncomfortable. . . . No one knew the abstract facts on which this conclusion rested better

not the reconstruction or interpretation of the past."[2] One eagerly welcomes *the novel of character laid in the past;* though as yet only one Stephen Crane has appeared to create in this medium a Civil War story universal in its appeal, presented on a set in which the events of the 1860's are only incidental. In other words, a general description of war fiction seems to require notice of each variation on the form—the historical novel, the period novel, the costume novel, and the novel of character. Ernest E. Leisy's reference to Polonius is quite appropriate in this context: the Civil War novel has borne in comfort the "historical-pastoral, tragical-historical, tragical-comical-historical-pastoral, scene individual, or poem unlimited."

If form does not narrow the scope of the study, neither does an effort to find a limiting definition for "historical" novels. The problem of just when a novel gets to be historical has attracted varied opinion. An historian finds hard the abandonment of Brander Matthews' dictum, that the "really trustworthy historical novels are those which were a-writing while history was a-making."[3] For a classical view of the eighteenth century, we turn to Henry Fielding's *Tom Jones,* just as we

---

than Scott; but his delineation gives no general idea of the result: a thoughtless reader rises with the impression that the Middle Ages had the same elements of happiness which we have at present, and that they had fighting besides." Judged by contemporary standards, Scott's work does not seem unduly burdened by search for historical accuracy. For the attempt to be made at all in 1814, however, was a startling advance over the historical and fictional sermons which were the custom before Scott. It remained, of course, for his greatest English successor, William Makepeace Thackery, to illustrate, in *Henry Esmond,* how the manners and talk of another century might, by elaborate scholarship, be revived with real accuracy, within the limits of the historical novel. Sir Walter Scott, *Ivanhoe* (Riverside Ed., New York, 1923), pp. xxvi-xxxii. Walter Bagehot, quoted by Matthews, *The Hisorical Novel and Other Essays,* p. 104.

2. Holman, "William Gilmore Simms' Theory and Practice of Historical Fiction," p. 67. I am indebted to Professor Holman for his help in formulating the distinctions and categories noted above—as well as for his general aid, offered personally as well as in the study cited, in my effort to understand some of the ground rules for historical fiction.

3. *The Historical Novel and Other Essays,* p. 18.

accept *Vanity Fair* as an accurate report on the manners of the nineteenth. The survival of any novel, with the passage of years, depends on its "historical" qualities; and a novelist sensitive to the whole mood of his society may write a source book on its behavior for the readers of subsequent generations. Inclusion of novels written during the era described makes definition of the "historical novel" a sort of blue sky affair; but advocates of a specified time gap produce no convincing argument in support of their position. The sub-title of *Waverley* ("'Tis Sixty Years Since") provides the commonly employed illustration for the time-lag point of view, though Ernest E. Leisy once concluded that "in America—so rapid are changes here—a generation suffices to render a preceding period historical."[4]

An elaborate recent effort to illustrate the basic distinction between novels based on present and past themes led Sheldon Van Auken to the conclusion that to be historical, a novel should (1) be based on research rather than the author's experience, and (2) be "laid in a period unfamiliar to its contemporary readers."[5] He illustrated his distinction by comparison of *Gone with the Wind* with *All Quiet on the Western Front*—each a novel of war and defeat, but one the product of research, in contrast to the remembered experience of the other. One finds greater distinction in the authors' opinions of their subjects, however, and in the size of the social units described, than in the sources of their knowledge or the preparation of their readers. Margaret Mitchell only had to work harder to achieve the passions and opinions which came naturally to Erich Maria Remarque. With the passage of time either work may contain the same amount of truth about its subject.

In the long run, it is this true residue of fact or color which determines the value of a work as a report from the past. An

4. "The American Historical Novel," *Univ. Col. Studies, Ser. B*, II (Oct., 1945), 308.
5. "The Southern Historical Novel in the Early Twentieth Century," *Jour. So. Hist.*, XIV (May, 1948), 157-58.

author's qualification lies in his knowledge of the fact that "every age has had its special spiritual atmosphere, which is the sum total of its attitudes toward the unknown, supernatural, divine, as well as toward nature and mankind in general; and . . . unless a historical novel somehow conveys this it is not really a historical novel at all."[6] The fidelity of the report, rather than the circumstance of its origin, governs approaches to achievement in the form. Is it true? If so, then it is historical. For more exact limits to the definition we would require the answer to Pilate's question.

The term "Civil War novel" is here as loosely construed as the phrase "historical novel." My bibliography is composed of books which give notice to the conflict at some length, in which the war establishes or transforms the character of the society described. Even with so free a definition, dozens of works in the Wilmer Collection have been excluded, some because the war had little influence on their movement, and others because they were nearer in length to the short story than to the novel. I have not seen all the novels about the Civil War, of course; the call list with which the University of North Carolina seeks to complete its holdings includes hundreds of "lost" titles, largely in the dime novel and juvenile categories. My survey includes a majority of novels written about the war, however, and I would be very surprised to encounter variations in form or content which would alter the conclusions drawn from my sampling.

6. Gay, "The Historical Novel: Walter D. Edmonds," *Atlantic,* CLXV (May, 1940), 657.

II
Workers in the Civil War Industry

Since a report on Civil War novels cannot be limited to novels assembled according to a standard critical formula, to books published when the conflict was a memory rather than a common experience, nor to works which qualify by hauling a specified load of fact about the war years, description of the war literature must begin on a note of some dismay at the undisciplined bulk of the material at hand. A statistical view of the sources is overpowering; one is tempted to count Civil War novels by the shelf foot, or to code the manners and morals of their heroines on IBM cards. Arithmetic patterns prove helpful, as a matter of fact, in fixing the general chronology and character of this survey.

My basic categories for such analysis are illustrated in the five graphs on page 22. Perennial interest in war themes has left no decade without a substantial number of novels about the conflict, but an over-all view of their presentation indicates production in three major waves. The first peak came with the war fiction of the sixties, 1866 being the year when the most novels were published. Interest waned during Reconstruction to an all-time low in the late seventies. The theme's greatest popularity began during the middle eighties, the first of four decades when the Civil War novel appeared with astonishing frequency. The peak of this long wave was in 1903, when eighteen war novels were published, although the vogue continued until the entry of the United States into the World War in 1917. The modern Civil War novel was born in the mid-twenties, and except for a brief slackening of the flow during World War II, has continued unabated to the present time.

The record years of this latest period were 1938 and 1942, the latter year producing eleven novels. More exact dates can be assigned to early, middle, and modern production by comparison of publication dates with the themes and techniques employed by the majority of the authors. Such correlation, although it requires exceptions here and there, fixes in distinct and separate traditions the novels published from 1862 to 1884, those offered between 1885 and 1924, and the recent offerings between 1925 and the present. By decades, the novels appeared in the following quantity: 1862-69, 69; 1870-79, 17; 1880-89, 49; 1890-99, 76; 1900-9, 110; 1910-19, 59; 1920-29, 29; 1930-39, 59; and 1940-48, 53.

Contrary to general opinion, the fiction of the Civil War is not predominantly southern. The insatiable popular demand for the war themes, as the *Saturday Review of Literature* has said, may have made it "necessary to introduce the wood-pulp

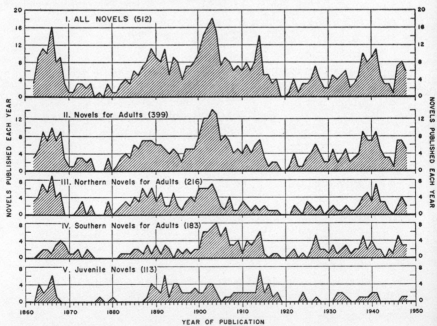

PUBLICATION DATES OF 512 CIVIL WAR NOVELS

NOVELS PUBLISHED EACH YEAR

I. ALL NOVELS (512)

II. Novels for Adults (399)

III. Northern Novels for Adults (216)

IV. Southern Novels for Adults (183)

V. Juvenile Novels (113)

YEAR OF PUBLICATION

industry to the South,"[7] but Yankee paper mills have received equal stimulation. The frequently employed generalization, that northern novels are "fewest in number,"[8] has no basis in fact. Among the 399 novels for adults included in this survey, 216 express a northern point of view, while 183 adhere to the Lost Cause. If juvenile novels are included in the tabulation, the result is 304 to 208, in the North's favor. Such division, of course, leads to some arbitrary decisions on the problem of whether a book is "southern" or "northern," for use of the divided kinsmen theme, or the story of southern unionists, might suggest a "neutral" grouping. By considering the author's background, the sectional affiliation of his hero, and the philosophical conclusions of the book, assignment to either North or South may be made with reasonable accuracy.

Southern and northern writers responded at approximately the same times to the popular demand for Civil War novels, although Graphs III and IV indicate that Southerners tended to lag behind Northerners in reaching their maximum production. The northern preponderance in numbers was won before 1900, when for four decades two novels with a pro-Federal point of view were produced to every one embodying pro-Confederate sentiment. Southerners forged ahead between 1900 and 1920, when their section was glorified by 72 novels, as compared with the North's 53. Since 1920, the sections have been about evenly balanced, there having appeared 56 pro-northern novels and 59 pro-southern.

Authors have usually taken their sectional viewpoints from the traditions of the area in which they were born. Of 256 men and 115 women who wrote of the war, more than 200 have grafted personal backgrounds, memories, and traditions onto their works. Such a conclusion is the most pertinent result of my inquiry into the lives of these 371 authors.[9] If they are

7. "The Bonnie Blue Flag," *Sat. Rev. Lit.,* XV (March 6, 1937), 8.
8. DeVoto, "Fiction Fights the Civil War," *Sat. Rev. Lit.,* XVII (Dec. 18, 1937), 4.
9. Adequate biographical data has been found for approximately 70 per cent of the authors represented in the collection. The "lost" authors are concentrated in the period between 1895 and 1910, when historical romances were pouring from every half-trained pen in the land.

romancers, they have developed the oral and written traditions of their communities,[10] and if they engage in military analysis, their work has not infrequently become a vehicle for the justification of their own forebears.[11] Certain of them, those who have been serious students of character, or philosophers seeking the meaning of war, have doubled their burden in an effort both to translate the war into understandable personal terms and, at the same time, to expose the controlling ties which connect their own lives with the crucial events of the conflict. Thus Joseph Stanley Pennell, Kansas scion of a post-war immigrant from North Carolina, possessed of grandfathers and great-uncles who fought with both armies, began his inquiry into his own, as well as his society's origins, with the following prologue:

You awake, [his hero thought], in the vast night of all the years. You awake somewhere in the vast night: Everything is around you, all time forwards and backwards and all space. At night in your bed, you see everything that has been or will be. And you awake at someplace where you never have been, nor ever will be: You awake at Gaines's Mill, lying in the hot, blood-reddened swampweeds with Tom Beckham, or you awake with Robert Lee Harrington, carpenter's bound boy, as he leaves Yadkin County, North Carolina, on his way to make coffins in Abilene, or you awake with Romulus Lycurgus Hanks and General Ulysses S. Grant as they stand in the rain on the night of April 6, 1862 at Pittsburg Landing, Tennessee. Or you awake lying on your own deathbed in a body you do not know. And you cry out: How could I have known? I tell you I didn't know! All right! All right. . . . I go back and look again and heed and look again and heed—[12]

The urge to "go back and look again and heed" is the compulsion which has driven the ablest writers of the war. Among

10. The later romances of George Washington Cable are good examples of this tendency. In *Kincaid's Battery,* and in *The Cavaliers,* Cable adds to his usual New Orleans background elements from his own career with the Fourth Mississippi Cavalry. *DAB,* III, 392-93.

11. Mary Johnston, for instance, took great pains in documenting her defense of General Joseph E. Johnston in *Cease Firing.*

12. Pennell, *The History of Rome Hanks and Kindred Matters,* prologue, n.p. See also *Current Biography,* 1944, pp. 542-43.

the fifteen best novels of the movement listed, pages 12-13, the
observations and lessons of at least thirteen were taken from
close personal traditions.[13] Authors may be removed from
their places of origin at the time of their writings—New York
has had the largest number of residents—but their intellectual

13. The exceptions are Stephen Crane, who apparently had no more
interest in the war than did any youth of the seventies and eighties;
and MacKinlay Kantor, who has no tie known to this writer with the
war years.

On the other hand, James Lane Allen faced the hardships and
bitterness of the war and readjustment during his youth in Kentucky.
George Washington Cable was a soldier of the Confederacy and suffered as a young man the poverty that is the theme of *Dr. Sevier.* John
William De Forest was a veteran of the Union army who translated his
career more promptly than did Cable into a novel. William Faulkner
built the "Sartoris" clan of *The Unvanquished* on the images of his
grandfather and great-grandfather. Ellen Glasgow's dependence on the
lives and opinions of her family is considered at length in the succeeding pages. Caroline Gordon obtained the background for her novel
about planter life in Kentucky from her own family, members of
which, on both sides, have, in her words, "been tobacco planters since
the weed was first cultivated by white men." DuBose Heyward, "quite
hopelessly a southern gentleman," was born to the Charleston inner
circle and descended from the aristocrats about whom he wrote.
Andrew Lytle was bred in Murphreesboro, Tennessee, which is in itself
a career in southern traditions. Ross Lockridge, son of a Hoosier historian of note, spent his childhood in informal preparation for his task
by wandering historical areas of his Indiana community and reciting,
under the direction of his father, speeches in commemoration of events
and people he later introduced into his fiction. Stark Young returned
to his native Mississippi before he wrote his novel—seeking by a pilgrimage through the Natchez memorials to the old South to document
the memories which flowered during the beginnings of his career in
New York as a new critic. Joseph Stanley Pennell re-traveled the
steps of his fathers and re-fought their battles in *Rome Hanks.* These
writers are typical of scores of the "good" novelists in their dependence
on personal background. "J. L. Allen," "Cable," and "De Forest,"
American Authors, 1600-1900, pp. 26-27, 124, 209-10. "Lytle," *Who's
Who in America,* XX, 1587. Beer, *Hanna, Crane, and The Mauve
Decade, passim.* "Faulkner," "Glasgow," "Gordon," "Heyward," "Kantor," and "Young," *Twentieth Century Authors,* pp. 438, 540, 551, 648,
745, 1566. This last volume is a particularly valuable biographical dictionary for use in correlation of the author's personal background with
his published work. Its aim is to present a sketch of each author in his
own words, describing his personal and intellectual background. See
the comment below made by Allen Tate, for instance.

homes appear to have been fixed at birth. Allen Tate spoke for many when he observed:

> As far back as I can remember I was wondering why the people and families I knew—my own family particularly—had got to be what they were, and what their experience had been. This problem, greatly extended, continues to absorb all my study and speculation, and is the substance of my novel, *The Fathers*.[14]

For the representative author, a similar concern with the nature of his birthright is the only personal factor he is likely to hold in common with any large number of his fellow-practitioners of historical fiction. The difficulty of further generalization based on biography is illustrated by Table II, which provides a variety of impressions drawn from study of the birthplaces of 216 representative authors. The table is divided by states, by geographical sub-sections, by the period in which the novels were written, and by note of the sectional viewpoint to which they adhered.[15]

Seven states, 4 northern and 3 southern, each produced more than 10 writers in this group. Leading was New York, with 24, followed by Virginia, 23; Massachusetts, 21; Pennsylvania, 20; Kentucky, 15; Ohio, 13; and South Carolina, 12. Other states within the 5 geographical divisions of the table were represented by fewer than 10 writers, or by none at all. The largest regional group is composed of writers from the Upper South, 66 of the number here considered. In descending order, the Middle States were next, with 51; the New England States, with 40; the Lower Southern States, with 38; and the

14. *Twentieth Century Authors*, p. 1386.
15. Arbitrarily chosen distinctions are necessary in the effort to decide whether a novel is pro-southern or pro-northern. Of a substantial number of the novels there is no question. The theme of Southerners loyal to the union, that of North-South love, and many others, however, raise considerable doubts, particularly when the novelist is a resident of one of the border states. Definitions, for statistical purposes, have been made insofar as possible according to the political and military affiliations of the leading characters. Thus John Fox's Chad in *The Little Shepherd of Kingdom Come* makes of the book which is his vehicle a "pro-northern" statistic; but complications of this sort are not so frequent as to invalidate general tabulation.

Old Northwest, with 36. The contribution of the western states has been negligible.

Within separate periods, the regional groupings appear in a somewhat different ratio. Between 1862 and 1885, the New England states were represented by the greatest number of sons who wrote adult novels, 11 of the group in Table II. The Middle States had 4, and the Old Northwest 2, among the early novelists of the war. The Upper South was represented by 10 writers, and the Lower South by 9—indicating that the border area's predominance in the movement was a later phenomenon.

The ratio which dominates the total regional groupings was fixed between 1885 and 1924, the era of greatest production. New England, with 9 authors, took third place in the North, following the Middle States, with 26; and the Old Northwest, with 16. The Upper South was the birthplace of 32 novelists, compared with 15 for the Lower South.

In recent years, between 1925 and 1948, the Old Northwest, with 18 novelists, led the Middle States, with 10, and New England, with 5. The earlier order remained in the South, the Upper South again leading with 17, as compared with the Lower South's 10.

An over-all view, therefore, established the following trends: (1) New England has dropped from first to last as the birthplace of Civil War novelists. (2) The Old Northwest has emerged as an area increasingly conscious of its part in the war tradition, surpassing even the Middle States, which have maintained a rather constant production. (3) The Upper South has consistently produced more than the Lower South.

Study, however, of the types of novels written by these authors of the Upper South reveals a noteworthy division of sentiment on war loyalties. Of the 66 novelists born in that area, 19 write from a pro-northern point of view. Missouri was dominated by such a trend; 7 of her 9 authors, true to the experience of their fathers, held their fiction firm for the union. Six of 15 Kentuckians took the same attitude. This phenomenon occurred chiefly during the middle period, when

TABLE II*

BIRTHPLACES OF 231 AUTHORS

Birthplace	Authors of Pro-Southern Novels				Authors of Pro-Northern Novels				Juveniles		State Totals		
	1862-84	1885-1924	1925-48	Total	1862-84	1885-1924	1925-48	Total	Pro-South	Pro-North	Pro-South	Pro-North	All
Upper South													
Virginia	6	9	3	18	1	1	0	2	2	1	20	3	23
Maryland	0	3	1	4	0	1	1	2	0	0	4	2	6
Kentucky	1	3	4	8	1	4	0	5	1	1	9	6	15
Missouri	0	1	1	2	0	4	1	5	0	2	2	7	9
Tennessee	0	4	4	8	0	1	0	1	0	0	8	1	9
North Carolina	1	1	2	4	0	0	0	0	0	0	4	0	4
Totals:	8	21	15	44	2	11	2	15	3	4	47	19	66
Lower South													
South Carolina	2	4	4	10	0	0	0	0	1	1	11	1	12
Georgia	2	4	1	7	0	0	0	0	1	0	8	0	8
Florida	0	1	0	1	0	0	0	0	0	0	1	0	1
Alabama	2	1	0	3	0	0	0	0	1	0	4	0	4
Mississippi	1	4	4	9	0	0	0	0	0	0	9	0	9
Louisiana	1	1	1	3	0	0	0	0	0	0	3	0	3
Texas	0	0	0	0	1	0	0	1	0	0	0	1	1
Totals:	8	15	10	33	1	0	0	1	3	1	36	2	38
Middle States													
New York	0	1	2	3	2	12	2	16	4	4	4	20	24
New Jersey	0	0	0	0	1	3	0	4	0	2	0	6	6
Pennsylvania	0	2	1	3	1	7	5	13	2	2	5	15	20
Delaware	0	0	0	0	0	1	0	1	0	0	0	1	1
Totals:	0	3	3	6	4	23	7	34	3	8	9	42	51
Old Northwest													
Ohio	0	0	2	2	1	6	3	10	0	1	2	11	13
Indiana	0	3	1	4	0	1	2	3	1	0	5	3	8
Illinois	0	1	1	2	1	4	2	7	0	0	2	7	9
Michigan	0	0	0	0	0	1	1	2	1	1	1	3	4
Wisconsin	0	0	0	0	0	0	2	2	0	0	0	2	2
Totals:	0	4	4	8	2	12	10	24	2	2	10	26	36
New England													
Maine	0	0	0	0	3	0	1	4	0	1	0	5	5
Massachusetts	0	1	2	3	6	4	3	13	0	5	3	18	21
New Hampshire	0	0	0	0	3	1	0	4	0	2	0	6	6
Vermont	0	0	0	0	0	2	0	2	0	0	0	2	2
Connecticut	0	0	0	0	2	1	0	3	0	2	0	5	5
Rhode Island	0	0	0	0	0	0	0	0	0	1	0	1	1
Totals:	0	1	2	3	11	8	3	21	0	11	3	37	40
Sectional Totals:											105	126	231

*Dates at column heads indicate when these authors published.

14 of the 19 were doing their writing. Such apostasy was not present in the Lower South, where only 2 of the 38 authors listed were pro-Federal.

Like writers of the Lower South, New England authors were resolute in defense of their section's historic position. In the Middle States, however, 9 of 42 authors adopted pro-Confederate views, and 10 of the 36 writers from the Old Northwest took the same stand. In these areas pro-southern writers have appeared more often in the modern period. Indiana, 5 of whose 8 writers expressed southside views, is here an exception; the copperheads of that state did much of their writing in the middle period.

Interpretation of such tendencies as these, based largely on the birthplaces of the authors, has such obvious limitations that further mention of sectional loyalty is reserved for discussion of the themes of all 512 novels. The tabulation of the authors' birthplaces is emphasized because it is one of the few factors which can serve as the basis for biographical comparison. A similar comparison has been made of authors' residences; it reveals few significant shifts. New York, as is natural for a literary capital, gained notably from the other states. California, which is not present in statistics of authors' birthplaces, has had eleven residents. By regions, the Middle States, the Lower South, and the Old Northwest have gained at the expense of the Upper South and New England.

A considerable variety of primary and secondary historical source materials have been employed by the authors considered. Personal memories, of course, played an outstanding part in the early and middle periods of the movement—a study of birth dates, analyzed conservatively, indicates that a third of all the authors could have remembered enough of the war to base writings of subsequent years on unsupported recollections.[16] Of these, at least forty were veterans of the Federal

16. The estimate is conservative because of the reticence of lady novelists about revealing their ages. One-third of the writers located in biographical summaries were born in 1855 or before, but so many of the ladies leave blank their birth dates that the figure would probably be greater were all the statistics in.

and Confederate armies. Battle experience, however, was no guarantee of realistic detail in war novels. For every ex-soldier like John Esten Cooke,[17] whose stories of the Virginia campaigns included accurate memoirs of real battles and leaders, there are two more who follow the pattern of George Cary Eggleston,[18] whose romances are but lightly touched with war realities. Northern veterans tended to remain closer to the homely details of camp life and army politics than did the Confederates. John William De Forest is the notable representative of these reporters,[19] but there were many competent observers with eyes for authentic detail. Not the least of these were James Kendall Hosmer,[20] Joseph Kirkland,[21] George W.

17. Cooke, prominent Virginian and author of ante-bellum days, served on the staff of General Jeb Stuart, and after the latter's death, was with General Lee until Appomattox. This Confederate captain had an uncle, Philip St. George Cooke, who became a major general with the Federal army. In *Surry of Eagle's Nest*, and in its sequel, *Hilt to Hilt*, he frequently interrupts the narrative flow for anecdotes documented as "true." *Mohun* is memorable for its description of Richmond's last days. *American Authors, 1600-1900*, pp. 172-73.

18. Brother of Edward Eggleston (author of *The Hoosier Schoolmaster*), he was a prolific romancer who became a successful journalist in New York. His Confederate service burdened his several books with no very harsh memories of war's realities. Typical is *Dorothy South*. *DAB*, VI, 54.

19. A Connecticut volunteer, he served as a captain in the southwestern campaigns of the Federal army, in the closing days of the war in Virginia, and in the Freedmen's Bureau in South Carolina until 1868. Both fictional and factual reports of his adventures have excited renewed attention in recent years. His war novel, *Miss Ravenel's Conversion from Secession to Loyalty*, was republished in 1939; and his *A Volunteer's Adventures*, praised by one writer as "vivid, accurate, perceptive factual reporting," was issued for the first time in 1946. See the latest reissue of his writings: *John William De Forest* (Croushore and Potter, eds.), p. v.

20. *The Thinking Bayonet*. Hosmer's career included service as a Unitarian minister, as a volunteer in Massachusetts troops, as a professor of English at various universities, and finally as librarian in Minneapolis. See also his *The Appeal to Arms, 1861-1863*. *DAB*, IX, 244.

21. *The Captain of Company K.* Kirkland, who rose from private to major during his service with McClellan and Fitz-John Porter, was a midwestern realist regarded as precursor to Hamlin Garland. *DAB*, X, 431-32.

Nichols,[22] and Wilbur F. Hinman.[23] Among the stories for a juvenile audience appear the works of General Oliver O. Howard, who made his own career the model for a novel,[24] and Warren Lee Goss, who attempted to indoctrinate yet another generation with the horrors of Andersonville Prison.[25] Civilians of the war years constitute too large a group for any effective generalization. Among their writings can be found such largely autobiographical memoirs as William Mumford Baker's *Inside;*[26] effective social and economic criticism, like the works of Henry Morford;[27] the partisan morality tales of

22. *The Sanctuary.* Nichols, who served on the personal staff of General William T. Sherman in 1864, wrote this novel in an effort to duplicate the success of his factual *The Story of the Great March,* which sold 60,000 copies. The novel was not much noticed, however. *DAB,* XIII, 494.

23. *Corporal Si Klegg and His "Pard."* This Ohio veteran's characters and style were revived in two later novels by John McElroy, who became Senior Vice-Commander-in-Chief of the Grand Army of the Republic in 1901. See *Si, "Shorty" and the Boys on the March to the Sea* and *Si Klegg, His Transformation from a Raw Recruit to a Veteran. Who Was Who,* p. 810.

24. Howard was an 1854 graduate of West Point who transferred to the troops of his home state, Maine, at the opening of the war. His rise to major general was rapid, and his bravery—which cost him an arm at Fair Oaks—was unquestioned, though he was accused of bungling at both Chancellorsville and Gettysburg. He was appointed Commissioner of the Bureau of Refugees, Freedmen, and Abandoned Lands in 1865, a post he held until 1874, and during the same period was founder and president of Howard University. His novel is *Henry in the War. DAB,* IX, 279.

25. Author of a number of juvenile books which emphasized prison experiences, Goss was president and historian, in 1890, of the National Union of Ex-Prisoners of War. His bitter *The Soldier's Story of His Captivity at Andersonville, Belle Isle and Other Rebel Prisons* was quoted extensively by the House Committee of 1869 which recorded testimony of thousands of ex-prisoners in southern camps. Hesseltine, *Civil War Prisons,* pp. 252, 265. *Who Was Who,* p. 472.

26. A Presbyterian preacher, Baker presented a partisan account of the trials suffered by southern unionists in the course of the war. *DAB,* I, 527.

27. Morford was a War Democrat who was acutely conscious of the corruption which went hand in hand with the good works of certain northern patriots. His best book is *In the Days of Shoddy. DAB,* XIII, 162-63.

Louisa May Alcott[28] and Augusta Jane Evans Wilson;[29] and the loving recollections of Thomas Nelson Page.[30] Participation in the events of the war era, in other words, provided no distinguishing characteristics for works so informed; the accounts of individual observers must be considered one by one for effective evaluation.

Personal experiences have survived, of course, in the facts and influences which control the novels of authors born since the war ended. Author after author has given testimony to the importance of family traditions as the basis for his interest in the war, if not as the substance of the incidents he relives. The Civil War was so much a part of conversation in Margaret Mitchell's family that she was reported to have been horrified, at the age of ten, to discover that the Confederacy had been defeated.[31] Yet she was born in 1900, when old soldier talk in the cities and hamlets of the land was subsiding somewhat and was no longer a compelling guide for the imaginations of the young.

Some understanding of separate elements in the influence of public and private memories on children born after the war may be drawn from two case histories. Stephen Crane, born in

28. Notable among abolitionist reformers, she is one among many writers whose novels were bathed in pious sentimentality and northern partisanship. Her *Work* shared characteristics typical in novels by Henry Ward Beecher, Lydia Maria Francis Child, Mrs. Sarah Towne Smith Martyn, and Anna Elizabeth Dickinson. For the efforts of this group toward abolition, temperance, women's suffrage, and piety in general, see *DAB*, I, 141-42; II, 129-35; IV, 67-68; XII, 352; and *Who Was Who*, p. 322.

29. She was outstanding among southern ladies who were, to the South, what the writers mentioned in the preceding note were to the North. Without zeal for social reform, their reliance was on religion, sentimental sacrifice, and Confederate partisanship. See *Macaria* and pp. 46-47 in this work for their attitudes and performance.

30. Page was a notable ambassador of good will between the sections, as a result of his gentle romances of southern virtues. Widely read, his stories largely skip the war, the outcome of which he approved, in favor of ante-bellum days or post-war problems. A good example of his work is *Meh Lady*. See Buck, *The Road to Reunion, 1865-1900*, pp. 203-8.

31. *Twentieth Century Authors*, p. 968.

1871, and Ellen Glasgow, born in 1874, wrote the outstanding novels of the middle period in war fiction. Study of the channels through which war lore flowed into their books reveals the nature of the novelist's "research" process—and suggests, at the same time, the separate methods and attitudes which regularly distinguish contributors of war fiction in the North from those in the South.

Crane, son of a Methodist minister in Newark, New Jersey, had an elder brother who was an expert in the strategy of Gettysburg and Chancellorsville, and another brother made him annual gifts of the "Frank" series of war juveniles written by Charles E. Fosdick. On rainy days the lad would hang over *Harper's* illustrated history of the rebellion, and when bored with this he would pour "all the buttons from his mother's store into battalions and regiments that marched and countermarched about his knees in endless conflict, incomprehensible to the family." When he was eleven, he explained to a horrified aunt who found him digging a playmate from the sand of a nearby beach that "Johnny was a corpse foolishly planted by the burial squad while he still had a canteen full of whisky on him and that Stephen was his provident comrade retrieving supplies." The lad had encountered early the innumerable realists who "sat on fences and the steps of stores in the sprawled depth of the nation and made a topic of war when political campaigns and labor held no thrill. . . ."[32]

In college Crane was exposed to the reminiscences of a teacher who had served as chaplain with a brigade which had been cut off and decimated at Antietam—a tale which featured the bravery of a color sergeant who was hit five times, and who died with a cry for his comrades to take on the colors from his hands. Elements of this story, introduced into *The Red Badge of Courage,* were to confuse scholars who could relate rather neatly the scene and action of the book to the Battle of Chancellorsville, as reported in *Century's* "Battles and Leaders of the Civil War."[33]

32. Beer, *Hanna, Crane, and The Mauve Decade,* pp. 235-43.
33. Berryman, *Stephen Crane,* pp. 18, 78.

Crane was twenty-two when he borrowed back volumes containing *Century*'s account of the conflict, the reading of which constituted his formal preparation for his famous novel. "I wonder that some of those fellows don't tell how they *felt* in those scraps," he complained to a friend. "They spout of what they *did,* but they're as emotionless as rocks."[34] He revealed what they "felt" in *The Red Badge of Courage.* The first version of the book was completed in the spring of 1893, within a few weeks of its conception. Revisions were made during the year, and in February, 1894, Crane sold the book to a syndicate for $100. The book was thus quickly conceived, briskly executed, and the author was done with the topic. His mind turned to other wars and other struggles; he was a professional literary man, not a regional apologist.

Ellen Glasgow, like Crane, was descended from signers of the Declaration of Independence, but since she was a Virginian, she kept in closer touch with her ancestors. She lived in Richmond "in a century-old grey stone house . . . covered with ivy and wisteria, its garden concealed by box and magnolia and by a high iron fence." She was thoroughly conscious of "belonging" to her home. "We live," she said, "where we are born." The primer from which she learned her alphabet was a volume by Sir Walter Scott.[35] Against this genteel background, however, she early directed a "slowly kindling fire of revolt," a mood stimulated in no small part by the Confederate romances she received each Christmas from maiden aunts. "I could not believe that war was like that," she said.

I had never been young enough to believe it. I could not believe that the late invasion had been a romantic conflict between handsome soldiers in blue uniform and Southern ladies in crinolines. Although I was not born until the middle of the eighteen-seventies, I could well remember the hungry "eighties"; and I could remember, too, that when I wanted a doll with "real hair," I was told I could not have it because we had "lost everything in the war." A war in which one had lost everything, even the right to own a doll with real hair, was not precisely my idea of a romance. All I

34. *Ibid.,* p. 66.
35. *Twentieth Century Authors,* p. 540.

knew of the Civil War was what I heard from my mother, supported by a chanting chorus of male and female voices. There was, in particular, a grand-aunt of lugubrious bearing, as unlike the Southern belle in fiction as one could imagine; and I never think of her without recalling a speckled engraving of Hecuba lamenting over the ruins of Troy.[36]

Miss Glasgow's reaction to the "formal, the false, the affected, the sentimental, and the pretentious, in Southern writing" was the production of a six-volume fictional social history of Virginia after 1850. She labored to construct her work with infinite care. Before writing *The Battle-Ground,* she visited every scene in her story. While she wrote, she kept with her complete files, 1860-1865, of *The Richmond Enquirer, The Richmond Examiner,* and *The New York Herald.* To these sources she added available diaries and letters. Her chief dependence, however, was on incidents reported by actual participants. "Always I was collecting impressions," she said, "rather than facts. . . ." Characters of the story were composite assemblies molded after her mother, relatives, and living men and women they described to her. All the while, she sought to reveal the "rich and deep material *under* the transparent legends of the South." She worked with the zeal of a true believer to outline a society worth her respect and affection; and she exposed with critical disdain legends of an "aristocracy" which she regarded as "shallow-rooted, at best, since, for all its charm and its good will, the way of living depended, not upon its own creative strength, but upon the enforced servitude of an alien race."[37]

The approaches of Ellen Glasgow and Stephen Crane to the war experience and war materials are the common avenues of Southerners and of Northerners, not only of their own periods, but of subsequent ones as well. To expand traditions inherited from the war, each consulted written records in a quest for some degree of authenticity. The critical attitudes brought by

36. Glasgow, *A Certain Measure,* pp. 11-12. This work is a book of prefaces, written many years after the novel in question, which describes her attitude and motives at the time of the writing.
37. *Ibid.,* pp. 3-20.

each to his chosen problems were not often shared by their contemporaries, but the sectional distinction between their methods was typical. Miss Glasgow's technique was one of submersion in her materials, whereas Crane reached for severely defined segments of the war experience and worked without the compulsion to adore, as well as to describe, his scenes and people. Northerners have in general been inclined to set closer limits for their work than have Southerners, and have written with a degree of detachment uncommon to the South. The best of them have exploited the war tradition but have escaped its domination. Southerners, whether they have written in romantic vain, in irony, or in partisan hate, have shown little desire for such escape. The war has been their apology and their defense, and they have treasured their version of the war record as the final and authentic flash of a legend to which time has not always been kind.

The growing chain of years between the sixties and the present has so thinned the public consciousness of war issues that casually assimilated oral traditions no longer give adequate support to Civil War novelists. Recent works have depended more and more on the records and physical survivals which are the historian's chief resource. The formal bibliographies occasionally attached to novels appear to bear little relationship to the quantity of recorded fact or the original research they incorporate. A considerable reputation for painstaking historical method sometimes may be dissolved, moreover, by close examination of the result; Joseph Hergesheimer, for instance, has lately been revealed as one more romancer who felt free to make off with the phrases of dry-as-dust investigators without bothering to make his own synthesis.[38] Ever since Shakespeare looted the pages of Plutarch, popular writers have displayed no considerable devotion to such scholarly amenities as the quotation mark. A larger obligation to professional historians is evident in the general interpretations of such works as *Raintree County,* by Ross Lockridge, Jr., or *The Tide of*

---

38. Fain, "Hergesheimer's Use of Historical Sources," *Jour. So. Hist.,* XVIII (Nov., 1952), 497-504.

Time, by Edgar Lee Masters, but in these the authors give as much as they take. Their preparation did not differ either from that of the historian; each work followed long and painstaking investigations in both primary and secondary records of Indiana and Illinois.[39] Occasionally the sources of general views are revealed; a biographical sketch of Clifford Dowdey, for instance, mentions the fact that *Bugles Blow No More* was begun while he was a reporter for the Richmond *News Leader* and that editor Douglas Southall Freeman helped to guide both his research and writing.[40] Andrew Lytle, in the preface to his brilliant reconstruction of middle-class life in ante-bellum Alabama, credited historian Frank Owsley with telling him the story which is the basis for his narrative.[41] Lytle, Dowdey, and Masters, furthermore, are among the twenty-three novelists who have also written formal history and biography.[42]

A more startling influence than attention to scholarly method appears among certain recent Southerners who have accepted in varying degrees the habits of rural life, if not the formal principles of the Agrarian philosophy. Three of the

39. Lockridge had assisted his father in historical research on Indiana subjects and had lived in an atmosphere of almost professional antiquarianism. See footnote 13, p. 25. Masters turned from formal history to the novel in his studies of the war. His *Lincoln the Man* was a savage assault on the character and motives of the wartime president.

40. "Dowdey," *Twentieth Century Authors,* p. 395.

41. *The Long Night,* preface, n.p. Frank Owsley is distinguished for studies of the yeoman classes to which Lytle turned in his work. Frank L. and Harriet C. Owsley, "The Economic Bases of Society in the Late Ante-Bellum South," *Jour. So. Hist.,* VI (Feb., 1940), 24-45.

42. The twenty-three are: Holmes Alexander, Thomas Alexander Boyd, Clark E. Carr, Charles Carleton Coffin, Clifford Dowdey, Warren Lee Goss, Joseph Hergesheimer, James Kendall Hosmer, Gerald W. Johnson, Andrew Lytle, Lucy Foster Madison, Edgar Lee Masters, John McElroy, Meade Minnigerode, Thomas Nelson Page, Louis Beauregard Pendleton, Walter Adolphe Roberts, Edwards Robins, Philip Van Doren Stern, William O. Stoddard, Allen Tate, Everett Titsworth Tomlinson, and Henry Tyrrell. The discipline of formal history apparently influenced the novels written by nineteen of this group, who in their fiction attempted to remain close to the fact and the spirit of their time. The four whose work seems unaffected by historical discipline are Charles Carleton Coffin, Lucy Foster Madison, Walter Adolphe Roberts, and Henry Tyrrell.

contributors to *I'll Take My Stand* [43] have written Civil War novels, but many more of the outstanding novelists here considered are agrarians with a lower case "a." William Faulkner divides his time between Oxford, which is scarcely metropolitan, and a thirty-five acre farm in the Mississippi hills, has done "his own brewing," and once reported reservation of "his afternoons for fishing and hunting." [44] Roark Bradford, who claimed his New Orleans home as "the earliest apartment house in the United States," kept in touch with the rural Negro society of his novels by frequent retreat to his Little Bee Bend Plantation, near Shreveport. [45] James Boyd, a resident of Southern Pines, North Carolina, built his home as a replica of William Byrd's Westover; among the enthusiastic fox-hunters with whom he lived, he was master of the hounds; and at least once he was called on to preach a Negro funeral. [46] Caroline Gordon and Allen Tate, as husband and wife, maintained a century-old home on the Cumberland River, near Clarksville, Tennessee. Lafayette slept there. [47] And in the distance, Stark Young, continental traveler and new critic, sighed, from New York, at his separation from pastoral traditions and rural southern delights. [48] The vitality of Agrarianism as a guide to responsible citizenship is somewhat wasted of late, but followers of the faith may take comfort in the fact that their philosophy has proved to be an excellent discipline for the historical novelist. There is a high degree of correlation between authors who have consciously chosen to live by the social and intellectual patterns of another day, and novels that recapture, with astonishing fidelity, the tempo of life in the Old South.

Every reference to use of sources by the historical novelist must remain inconclusive; the account of Stephen Crane's

43. By Twelve Southerners. The three Civil War novelists who contributed essays to this indictment of modern industrial living are Andrew Lytle, Allen Tate, and Stark Young.
44. *Twentieth Century Authors*, p. 438.
45. *Ibid.*, p. 177.
46. *Ibid.*, p. 172.
47. *Ibid.*, pp. 551, 1385-86.
48. *Ibid.*, p. 1566.

preparation is sufficient demonstration that the quality of the research for a novel provides no proper measure of successful artistry. Critical distrust of the form springs in part from realization that recorded fact may be used to conceal the absence of creative talent—and such a sword cuts both ways, for able dreamers have found themselves imprisoned by the record they sought to vivify. One is continually surprised, with Hillaire Belloc, at "how little [scholarship] is sufficient for the man who has the right kind of genius, and how much remains quite insufficient for the man who has it not." [49]

One final generalization should be made about authors of Civil War novels: the writing of such works is a labor that might be visited on anybody. Among the twenty-three politicians who have succumbed, there have been an unsuccessful presidential candidate,[50] a governor of Wisconsin,[51] four congressmen,[52] and two diplomats.[53] A mayor of Sioux City,

49. "The Character of an Historical Novelist," *London Mercury*, IX (November, 1923), 41.

50. Thomas Edward Watson, author of *Bethany*, was the presidential candidate of decayed Populism in 1904 and 1908, congressman from Georgia, 1891-1893, and United States senator, 1921-1922. This fiery agrarian rebel was a prolific writer in many fields and the novel mentioned above is a very respectable inquiry into middle-class manners of the Old South. Woodward, *Tom Watson, passim.*

51. G. W. Peck, author of *How Private George W. Peck Put Down the Rebellion,* was mayor of Milwaukee in 1890-1891 and governor of Wisconsin, 1891-1895. He is better known as the creator of "Peck's Bad Boy." *Who Was Who,* p. 952.

52. Three served at critical times during or close to the war. Jeremiah Clemens, author of *Tobias Wilson,* represented Alabama in the United States Senate from 1849 to 1855, was a signer of the state's secession ordinance, but a deserter from the South during the war. *DAB,* IV, 191-92. Benjamin Wood, brother of New York's Mayor Fernando Wood, was a Democrat in the National House of Representatives, 1861-1865, and 1881-1883. His novel, *Fort Lafayette,* exhibited a Democratic sympathy for the South, but is a remarkably balanced treatment of all sides. *Biog. Dict. Am. Cong.,* p. 1724. John Beatty, author of *McLean,* was a Republican presidential elector in 1860 and 1868, and an Ohio congressman, 1869-1870. *Who Was Who,* p. 75. Watson, referred to in footnote 50, served in both the United States House and Senate.

53. Norval Richardson, author of *The Heart of Hope,* was a career diplomat whose service carried him to Havana, Copenhagen, Chile, Lisbon, and Tokyo. *Who Was Who,* p. 1031. Thomas Nelson Page,

Iowa, enlivened his declining years with such an effort.[54] Two judges,[55] a utilities commissioner of Massachusetts,[56] the first woman member of the United States Civil Service Commission,[57] and a private secretary to President Lincoln[58] joined the list. State legislators,[59] an executive director of the Republican National Committee,[60] and a chaplain of the United States Senate[61] should be noted. Of three local postmasters, one, William Faulkner, was fired for inattention to duty.[62] One of the most prolific romancers of the entire group was a United States officer in each of the nation's wars, 1861-1920,[63] and another was chief of artillery for the Guatemalan and

---

whose works have been noted earlier, was Ambassador Extraordinary and Plenipotentiary to Italy during the years of World War I. *Who Was Who*, p. 928.

54. Herbert Quick, author of *Vandermark's Folly*, was mayor of Sioux City, Iowa, 1898-1900, after early service as associate editor of *LaFollette's Weekly*, Madison, Wisconsin. *Who Was Who*, p. 1004.

55. George Ticknor Curtis, author of *John Charaxes*, in 1852 returned a slave to a southern claimant while he was serving as a United States commissioner under the Act of 1850. *DAB*, IV, 613-14. Albion Winegar Tourgée, author of several novels dealing largely with Reconstruction in North Carolina, from a Radical point of view, was outstanding among the carpetbaggers in high positions during this era. *DAB*, XVIII, 603-5.

56. John T. Wheelwright, author of *War Children. Who Was Who*, pp. 1329-30.

57. Mrs. Helen Hamilton Chenoweth Gardener, author of *An Unofficial Patriot*, was appointed to this post in 1920. *Who Was Who*, p. 439.

58. William O. Stoddard, author of *Long Bridge Boys* and *The Battle of New York*, was an Illinois newspaperman who served as assistant private secretary to President Lincoln. *DAB*, XVIII, 60.

59. These include Holmes Alexander, Thomas Dixon, Jr., and Winston Churchill.

60. Clarence Budington Kelland.

61. James J. Kane.

62. Clark E. Carr, Henry Morford, and William Faulkner, the last of whom was dismissed from the Oxford, Mississippi, post office for the above named offense. *Twentieth Century Authors*, p. 438.

63. The seven Civil War novels written by this author, first signed "Captain," and then "General," Charles King, indicate the author's rise through the service. A veteran of every United States war from 1861 to 1920, King died a major general. *Who's Who Among North American Authors*, IV, 578-79.

Peruvian armies.[64] Six college presidents[65] have not regarded
the subject as beneath their dignity, nor indeed, have the
bankers,[66] accountants, and the numerous preachers in the
group. One may speculate about the urge which directed a
professor of chemistry[67] to the task, but certainly he would
not have felt out of place with the neurologist[68] and the gyne-
cologist[69] in whose company he found himself. Poets and
editors are commonplace contributors to the movement, as are
the lawyers, teachers, and reporters whose names swell the
total number. The writing of Civil War novels is protected by
no closed shop for professional novelists; amateurs, gifted and
otherwise, have had a basic part in molding fiction's account
of the war.[70]

64. George Forrester Williams, author of *Bullet and Shell,* was the
only Civil War novelist born on the Rock of Gibraltar. His Latin-
American duty was in 1868. *Who Was Who,* p. 1352.

65. The six are, with their colleges and novels: Oliver Otis Howard,
Howard University, Washington, D. C., *Henry in the War;* Thornwell
Jacobs, Oglethorpe University, Georgia, *Red Lanterns on St. Michael's;*
George Ward Nichols, Cincinnati College of Music, *The Sanctuary;*
William Henry Peck, Masonic Female College, Georgia, *The McDon-
alds;* and George Nauman Shuster, Hunter College, New York, *Look
Away!*

66. Gouverneur Morris and William Sage.

67. Wyman, *After Many Years.*

68. Silas Weir Mitchell, author of a number of historical novels set
at various periods, wrote around the turn of the century. A successful
doctor, he sought the advice of Dr. Oliver Wendell Holmes on the
maintenance of a dual career, and on such authority became firmly
established in the medical profession before he repeated his success in
the field of fiction. *Who Was Who,* p. 351.

69. Gilliam, *Dick Devereux.*

70. No general similarities were evident in the approaches of novels
written within the various professions listed, except for the fact that
politicians tend to emphasize favorite interpretations of the events they
describe and fill their books with quotations from actual statesmen.

At this point in my survey of biographical data, I was somewhat at
a loss as to what further use might be made of various facts from the
authors' lives. I realize the danger of becoming like the collector of
curiosities once discovered by *The New Yorker.* The prize item in her
houseful of useless possessions was a box labeled "pieces of string too
small to use." I have hundreds of cards in the same category.

III

The Mass Product

A certain ubiquitous straw man has commanded excessive
attention in generalizations about the dominant themes of Civil
War novels. The prevailing critical view of the war literature
appears to stem from a celebrated comment by Albion W.
Tourgée, to the effect that the South, vanquished in reality,
had snatched victory from the best-seller lists. "Not only is
the epoch of the War the favorite field of American Fiction
today," said Tourgée in 1888, "but the Confederate soldier is
the popular hero. Our literature has become not only Southern
in type but distinctly Confederate in sympathy."[71] Scholars
have repeatedly endorsed the famous carpetbagger's observations, and his view has been accepted as "definitive" since Paul
H. Buck completed a careful survey of the literary heritage of
the war in his study of sectional reconciliation. Basing his con-
jectures on magazine literature and plays during the 1880's,
Buck asserted in 1937 that "For better or worse, Page, Harris,
Allen, and their associates of the South, with the aid of Northern editors, critics, magazines, publishing houses, and theaters
had driven completely from the Northern mind the unfriendly
picture of the South implanted there in the days of strife."[72]

Now if the northern mind were ever so completely captured,
it was not held for very long. The southern victory Professor
Buck perceived on the stage and in periodical literature ended
no more than a skirmish in a war which continues to this day.
The general strategy of this conflict must be sought in novels,
for the war has ceased to be important in magazine fiction,
and has been almost forgotten by the stage. Analysis of the
themes in all the novels, moreover, reveals that the war literature, like the war itself, is composed of many things—of sec-

71. "The South as a Field for Fiction," *Forum*, VI (1888), 405.
72. *The Road to Reunion*, p. 235.

tional hate as well as reconciliation amenities, of bloody reality as well as romance. Radically opposed philosophies and opinions are still nurtured in hearty and separate traditions. Neither the North nor the South, as we shall see, has monopolized fictional battlegrounds—for its authors, its ideas, or its history. Had unanimous acceptance of any point of view been permanently reached, then the intellectual conflict maintained in good war novels would have long since been resolved. The Civil War would not exist, as it does today, as an institution of American fiction.

A substantial record may be found, of course, to illustrate the stereotyped pattern I reject as less than representative. Romancers by the score have persistently reported the sections to have been so respectful of mutually held virtues that a reader is sometimes baffled that such courteous opponents should have lowered themselves to the graceless clamor of a battlefield. A great many novels published around the century's turn began with the assumption that in the Civil War there was glory enough for all and that each side had a full measure of justice and honor with its flag. Even before this period, the reconciliation theme had proved useful to authors who wanted to be read. The first concessions leading to a return of tolerance appear to have been made by Southerners who hoped to sell books in the North. By their admission that the South was *properly* restored to the old union, they qualified for entry into the hostile Federal market, and once there, sought to subvert Yankee righteousness with a sympathetic report of the southern cause.[73] Rather than exercises in logic, their arguments lay in the simple technique of making repeated assurances that the South *believed* it was fighting for justice. "History," said Mary Tucker Magill, ". . . may bring in a verdict of guilty against [the South] . . . but if ever there was pure patriotism, an earnest, honest conviction of right, it nerved the arms and inspired the hearts of the people of the South. . . ."[74] The righteousness of the southern cause was

73. *Ibid.*, pp. 207-8.
74. *Women*, p. x.

somehow proved by account of the energy with which it was pursued. ("What pen could properly tell the story of those four years; what fittingly record the glory of that struggle, hopeless from the beginning, yet ever appearing to pluck success from the very abyss of impossibility. . . .") [75] Nationalistic Northerners also had a stake in the perpetuation of the tradition of southern valor. They revered the basic and commonly-held "Americanism" of the re-united sections. Pride in the whole union would be tarnished by eleven states in perpetual disgrace; so the passage of years permitted generous distribution of the honors that came with reputation for heroism and courage. A nationalistic spirit asserted the unity and the similarities of the sections, rather than their divisions. In this vein, Joseph A. Altsheler noted in 1900 that the "merciless drum rolling out its ironical chuckle" gathered to the separate standards "Northern and Southern countrymen . . . alike" in their devotions and pleasures. [76] The issues?—"One side was as honest and patriotic as the other—the North loyal to the Union, the Southerners to their several States." [77] This interpretation of the war was a best-seller view at the turn of the century; genteel broadmindedness before the torment of brothers divided served as standard palliative for lingering bitterness. A million readers were charmed into sympathy with the conclusions of Fox's *The Little Shepherd of Kingdom Come*—"That every man, on both sides, was right—who did his duty." [78]

With so sympathetic a foundation, the myth of a war ruled by ante-bellum courtesies rather than military necessity can be more easily understood. Novels written in such a spirit avoided violence to the feelings of either North or South, and within the limitations fixed by their atmosphere of mutual tolerance, they explored with realistic understanding the manners and opinions of the war period. The extent of the limitation fixed

75. Page, *Red Rock*, p. 49.
76. *In Circling Camps*, pp. 62-63.
77. J. W. Eggleston, *Tuckahoe*, p. 146.
78. P. 400. For statistics on this novel's popularity, see Hackett, *Fifty Years of Best Sellers*, p. 104.

by this method varies with the user; in extreme cases tolerance is reduced to absurdity. Troopers of the sixties there may have been who shared the sentiments of Irvin S. Cobb's Confederate soldier: "Hasn't a free-born white man got a right to be wrong—if he thinks he's right?. . . . It's the brave man who takes sides when taking sides may be dangerous."[79] It is more difficult, however, to accept a succeeding scene in the same novel, when Kentucky companies slated for opposing service pause for the Confederate captain's words of courteous farewell to the Union contingent: "So, gentlemen, we have stopped today to bid you farewell and to wish for each one of you good luck and a safe return even though we do not wish your cause good luck. We claim there's neither treason nor disloyalty there. We are hoping that for your part you feel the same toward us. . . ." Through such sentiments as these we arrive at the scene of that frequently described war which was conducted with the formality of a duel, within the blood lines of gigantic families. Union officers in this war could count on being captured by their cousins, and at twilight on the battle's day sip wine in paneled libraries, comforted by gracious hospitality: "You are always welcome, Hubert, no matter the color of yo' regimentals."[80]

Used with proper restraint, the reconciliation theme is a door through which readers of succeeding generations may enter on the war scene without serious readjustment. The softening of sectional recrimination into sentimental ceremony is so basic a distortion, however, that many of the best novelists have avoided it altogether. They have realized the degree to which the folklore of gallant battle may cripple serious effort to select and reassemble the passions and opinions which led to war in 1861. The reconciliation idea, at any rate, is neither the most frequent nor the most important theme of Civil War novels. Critical emphasis on this thread of fictional history has too long obscured more important aspects of the war literature.

Few precise findings, I should hasten to say, reward syste-

79. *Red Likker*, pp. 31, 35.
80. Van Wyck Mason, *Hang My Wreath*, p. 55.

matic effort to isolate any "dominant" themes or to categorize authors according to their interpretations of the war experience. Novelists do not confine themselves to scholarly patterns; a majority of them, in fact, plunge lightheartedly into the whole stew of tradition and reality which bubbles through their undisciplined romances. Separating them according to type reveals clusters of novels, rather than clearly defined schools of history or fiction. So complicated is their intermixture of various plot devices and stock characters that statistical assignment of a book to this or that thematic category produces false or unreliable conclusions. Concern with slavery and Negroes, for instance, runs through a great many of the books here surveyed, but this concern is a major theme in relatively few books. Scores of works, on the other hand, may be clearly identified with the "divided kinsmen" theme, but within this heading there is tremendous variation, depending on the authors' acceptance or rejection of the reconciliation mood. I have shuffled and redealt my deck of "theme" cards many times, and the resulting hands in this historical game are rarely the same. Certain clusters of books, certain general concerns, appear with enough regularity, however, to illustrate major trends in the war literature, even though caution curbs temptation to list such ideas in order of prominence or to cite the number of books dominated by these selected themes.

The earliest general conventions governing production of the novels grew from sentimental reactions to war of professional and amateur lady writers. These ladies fixed the pattern of tales in the 1860's and early 1870's with their admiration for Christian sacrifice and their uncritical and violently partisan pride in sectional virtues. The cliff-hanging renunciation scenes between the hero and heroine of *Macaria*;[81] the marital woes of *Bertha the Beauty*,[82] who had to lay away a villainous Yankee husband before seeking happiness with a noble South-

---

81. By Augusta Jane Evans Wilson. Mrs. Wilson was no amateur, of course; her novels were widely read both before and after the war by a generation which, to the modern reader, had incomprehensible tastes.
82. By Sarah J. C. Whittlesey.

erner; and the gusty Confederate rhetoric of Sally Rochester Ford[83] were typical features of novels written by a whole corps of southern ladies.[84] In the North, Mrs. Sarah Towne Smith Martyn, a disputatious lady, if her secession from the Moral Reform Society of New York may be considered evidence, proved in pious fashion the divine purpose of the undivided union.[85] Louisa May Alcott, in *Work: A Story of Experience,* illustrated the ennobling aspects of patriotic death and celebrated the virtues of the good, gray ladies who were exalted by their hospital association with expiring soldiers. Women writers of both sides were full of righteousness about their sections' efforts, though the Northerners had the specific goal of abolition of Negro slavery as a proof of high purpose.

Appearance of the Negro in early northern fiction was only the beginning of a continuing concern with his life, service, and hopes. Lydia Maria Francis Child, veteran abolitionist, found rich husbands for the quadroon heroines who were objects, as were all alien peoples, of her respect.[86] Anna Elizabeth Dickinson, whose *What Answer?* was popular as campaign literature for Grant in 1868, also shed her tears over the plight of the quadroon girls, though her heroine—after a later pattern—died unwed across the body of her northern lover. The lady sentimentalists had no exclusive rights to popular abolition themes, of course. Some of the most powerful partisan novels of the early period, like Epes Sargent's *Peculiar: A Tale of the*

83. *Raids and Romance of Morgan and His Men.* Mrs. Ford was a preacher's wife who refugeed to Mobile from her Memphis home during the war. Raymond, *Southern Writers,* VI, 182.

84. Other southern ladies of this ilk, with their works, include Sallie F. Chapin, *Fitz-Hugh St. Clair;* Mary Ann Cruse, *Cameron Hall;* Mary Tucker Magill, *Women;* and Mrs. Lorenzo Dow Whitson, *Gilbert St. Maurice.*

85. *Our Village in War-Time. DAB,* XII, 352.

86. *A Romance of the Republic.* This Massachusetts reformer was a prominent pamphleteer in the abolition crusade and edited the *National Anti-Slavery Standard,* New York weekly, from 1841 to 1849. Her correspondence with the governor of Virginia seeking an interview with condemned John Brown was widely publicized. She turned toward spiritualism in her later years, after exhibiting Radical impatience with the policies of Lincoln. *DAB,* IV, 67-68.

Great Transition, and John Townsend Trowbridge's *Cudjo's Cave,* followed the fortunes of noble Negroes. Within a generation, however, the noble child of nature was replaced by the southern concept of the former slave—loyal during the war to his masters; shrewd, with the wisdom of a contented and rooted peasant; and carefree, happily confident in his security under the plantation system.[87] This is the Negro of Thomas Nelson Page,[88] Joel Chandler Harris,[89] and Joseph William Eggleston.[90] A creation of the middle period in the novels here considered, he was a stereotype who remained prominent in the southern novel. Northerners tended to forget the Negro after the early period; he virtually disappeared from post-abolition fiction. Southerners, who ignored him early and glorified him in their writings of the century's turn, have in modern times, like Northerners, tended to avoid him. The plantation stereotype is present in books like that of Stark Young, of course, but the prominence given servants in *So Red the Rose* is rare. Abolitionism in the novel is not entirely dead; Philip Van Doren Stern relied on the best scholarship for the creation of his abolition hero in 1942;[91] and L. P. Wyman kept alive the old concern with the plight of the quadroon woman. Even this modern professor of chemistry, however, bowed to convention in his decision to forestall racial intermarriage with death.[92] Roark Bradford's *Kingdom Coming* is unique in its effort to present, within the limitations of slave knowledge and experience, the plantation laborer's version of the war.[93] In general, however, the story of the Negro has been told from the point of view of the white South.

This point of view is by no stretch of the imagination "Con-

87. An excellent investigation of the Negro's place in the plantation legend is to be found in Gaines, *The Southern Plantation, passim.*
88. See, for instance, *Meh Lady.*
89. *On the Plantation.*
90. *Tuckahoe.*
91. *The Drums of Morning.*
92. *After Many Years.*
93. The most brilliant modern effort to recapture slave hopes during the war is Faulkner's symbolic study in *The Unvanquished,* pp. 87-122 and *passim.*

federate in sympathy" after the fashion of Albion Tourgée's lament. An extended digression on the changing role of the Negro in war fiction may serve here to illuminate the inadequacy of positive and simplified judgments on the general character of literary interpretations of the war. In the first place, it should be noted that novelists, like historians, have failed conspicuously in their occasional efforts to breathe life into the story of emancipation. This failure, in both history and fiction, does not appear to be unconscious; white authors have not tried very hard to understand individual slave characters or to wake in readers any real sense of identification with them. The novelists have stood apart and have shaped the Negro men and women they describe to symbolize their own philosophies of race relations. The Negro of the Civil War novel is, on the whole, a personification of each writer's conception of what he ought to have been.

Inadequate characterization of slaves is in part a mechanical fault; the Negro is rarely a central figure in Civil War novels—he only hovers near the white heroes and heroines to whom space and interest is given. As a minor character, he has remained a type, while an occasional white character, described at greater length, has emerged a whole man. The "types" have sometimes become engaging caricatures, but they rarely escape from the twilight world of abstraction. The standard type, moreover, varies little with the sectional viewpoint used to describe him. Outstanding Negroes of war fiction are memorable for noble simplicity, rather than for complex human characteristics. Abolitionist and Confederate were from the start in incongruous agreement in their essential views; each has given testimonials to slave character that would extend the wingspan of an angel. Some of the essentials of this agreement may be illustrated by comparison of representative views from the North and the South.

The abolitionist was first on the ground with a standard version of Negro nobility. John Townsend Trowbridge, in *Cudjo's Cave,* was typical. The two Negroes who were the leading characters of his work were in startling contrast to one another—Pomp was the educated, sensitive rebel against the South's customs, a man whose proud spirit had survived degrading indignity; while Cudjo was a brutalized, cunning savage, a normal product of the lash. Pomp was "upwards of six feet in height, magnificently proportioned, straight as a pillar, and black as ebony . . . dignified, erect, of noble features." Cudjo was "ugly, deformed, with immensely long arms, short bow legs resembling a parenthesis, a body like a frog's, and the countenance of an ape." The two made common cause in their hatred of slavery and in their determination to avoid recapture by the masters from whom they had escaped. Their home was in a maze of caverns in the Tennessee mountains—an admirable base for their operations in defense of downtrodden fellows, their missions of assistance to deserving union men. The cave was a dank and lonely refuge, but infinitely preferable to the hardships from which they had fled. "Dreadful?" replied Pomp to a question about his depressing home. "There are worse places, my friend, than this. Is it gloomy? The house of bondage is gloomier. Is it damp? It is not with the cruel sweat and blood of the slave's brow and back. Is it cold? The hearts of our tyrants are colder." Cudjo's reaction against slavery was not quite so spiritual; his back was corrugated with scars from the lash. "Not much skin dar, hey? Rough streaks along dar, hey? Needn't pull you hand away dat fashion, and shet yer eyes, and look so white! It's all ober now. What if you'd seen dat back when 'twas fust cut up? or de mornin' arter?" Why had he been punished? "De oberseer didn't hap'm to like me; dat's what me don. But he did hap'm to like my gal; dat's what more me don!" Cudjo and Pomp struck manful blows against the Slave Power as soon as the war was under way. The former achieved his revenge in death, when he dragged the overseer who had punished him down to a common grave in a subterranean river. Pomp trembled on the brink of murder for revenge, but was saved from this sin by the pleas of a noble southern girl; his character untarnished, he survived his private war to serve as a scout with the union army, renowned for his "intrepidity, intelligence, and wonderful celerity of movement."

The abolitionist version of Negro character, in other words, was a lament against slavery, rather than a presentation of Negro men and women. Cudjo and Pomp were stereotyped symbols, smaller not larger than life. The report of their adventures, further, employs none of the eloquence typical of southern efforts to demonstrate through similar symbols the contentment of slaves with their ante-bellum lot. Innumerable stories of Negro courage and devotion run through southern novels at the turn of the century; one long example may illustrate the type. Molly Elliott Seawell's Peter, in the following vignette, was a body servant who followed his master to the death:

"Twas las' Sunday mornin'," Peter continued, gasping for breath between his sentences, "in de big battle wid de Yankees. De shot went right thru' Marse Richard's heart. He was a-leadin' he battery on an' cheerin' he men an' de big gun was a-bellowin' an' de balls was flyin' fast. De ho'ses to de guns dey ra'r an' pitch, an' Marse Richard he speak kin' o' coaxin' to 'em an' brought 'em down, an' dey went off at a hard gallop, de artillerymen arter 'em, yellin'. Marse Richard was gallopin' ahead, de Yankees was comin' out of de woods into an open fiel' where we could see de ridges blue wid 'em, thousands on 'em, an' dey had a heap o' cannon a-spittin' shells an' grapeshot. De guns was a-thunderin' an' de bullets was a-flyin' wus an' wus an' de yearth a-shakin' wid all dem ho'ses an' gun carriages poundin' over it. I was runnin' 'long arter de long gray line, an' kep' my eye fixed on Marse Richard, jes' like old Missis tole me. He tun' roun' in he saddle, an' takin' off he cap he wave it jes' de same as a little boy an' hollered, 'Come on boys! Marse Robert say we got to git dem guns,' an' while he was lookin' back an' smilin', his ho'se went down. It warn't no time to stop for nuttin', an' de artillery went a-gallopin'. When I got up to where Marse Richard was, de ho'se had done riz up, an' Marse Richard lay on he side, wid he arm under he haid, jes' de same as when Mammy Tulip put him to sleep when he wuz a little boy in de trundle-baid. I done saw enough daid soldiers for to know that Marse Richard was gone. He drawed he breff once or twice an' open he eyes and look at me an' say, 'Pete,' an' den he breff stopped."

Peter paused, his brawny frame trembling. Not a sound was

uttered; only Mrs. Tremaine's glance wandered from Peter, with tears streaming down his face, around the group, as if she were in some painful dream.

Colonel Tremaine's face was set like iron as he said in a strange voice, "Go on, boy."

Peter sighed heavily and leaned against the great brick pillar of the porch nearest him. He had scarcely slept or eaten since that terrible hour, five days before. But he spoke again after a minute:

"Dey warn't no doctor about, nor no nuttin', jes' cavalry, infantry, an' artillery a-chargin', de guns a-boomin', an' de soldiers fallin' over an' hollerin' sometimes when de bullets struck 'em an' de shells cut 'em all to pieces. I tek Marse Richard's sash from roun' he waist, an' wrop it roun' he chist, so as to soak up de blood. De ho'se stan' stock-still, an' I lay Marse Richard 'cross de saddle, an' tie him on wid de surcingle, an' lead de ho'se offen de fiel'. I warn' skeered, dough de bullets was a-flyin', an' I warn't thinkin' 'bout Marse Richard. I was thinkin' 'bout ole Marse an' Missis. I come 'long 'bout four miles to a tavern, an' dey laid Marse Richard out on a baid upsty'ars, an' I foun' a carpenter to mek him a coffin. When de orficers foun' Marse Richard dat night, I had done wash him an' dress him an' put him in de coffin. Didn' nobody tech him, 'scusing 'twas me. I lay he so'de an' de hat wid de feather in it an' he epaulets inside de coffin, an' de cloak over it, an' den I wrop' de coffin up in he blanket. I had some gold in a belt roun' my waist, dat Marse Richard tole me fur to keep, case he was wounded or kilt, fur to bring him back to Harrowby, an' I hired dis heah ho'se an' cyart, an' druv it every step of de way myself. I got 'way from de tavern jes' as quick as I could, fur I didn't want nobody fur to be axin' questions. I knowed what ole Marse an' ole Missis want me to do, an' I gwine do it. When people on de main road ax me what I got in de cyart, I tole 'em 'twas my little Marse dat was kilt, an' I was tekin' him home to ole Marse an' old Missis. Den I whip up de ho'se an' nobody didn't try fur to stop me. An' I done brought him home, Missis, jes' like you tole me."[94]

Similar stories could be quoted from scores of books; but the one long example above is sufficient to indicate the general character of the South's loyal servant. He was a Negro of mature years who did not flinch from unusual responsibility, acted with initiative, exhibited personal courage regardless of danger (where his own white folks were concerned), and yet

94. Seawell, *The Victory*, pp. 350-52.

maintained his accustomed humility. The scene, the incident, the result changes, but the theme of humble loyalty is a constantly repeated theme.[95] The Negro in these stories never forgot his "place," a fact that guaranteed him southern praise. A good enough symbol for the South's good and faithful servant is Thomas Nelson Page's Uncle Billy. When "Meh Lady" married her northern lover after the war, and their son came along in due time, he was named Billy. When the old Negro was questioned about the source of the boy's name, he scoffed. " 'Go 'way, Marster,' he said deprecatingly, 'who gwine name gent'man after a ole nigger?' "[96]

Modifications of these initial slave portraits were begun, of course, almost as soon as the types were institutionalized in war fiction. The idealized Negro, whether of abolitionist or Confederate origin, was simply too good to be true; fiction, as it has become more realistic, has gradually extended such characters to life size. Alteration of the romantic legends of Negro nobility, curiously, has been left to southern craftsmen; the North has shown little interest in continued interpretation of slave life.

The basic shift in the southern approach has come from the growing realization that the slave had a stake in the war which was not related to protection of the person and property of his master. Novelists have attempted to give reality to Negro character by describing a hope of freedom which glimmered in the most primitive of slave hearts. This hope has almost invariably been interpreted as tragedy—as hope, unrealized, and to most of these authors, unrealizable. Nevertheless, even the Negroes of the plantation described above by Molly Elliott

95. The body servant who accompanied his master to battle, who brought his body home from the war, can be documented, of course, in the records of actual cases, but the emphasis on this service, and on other evidences of the Negro's unwavering devotion to master and mistress somewhat distorts the views of such writers as Bell Wiley, whose studies of the slave during the war proved the existence of black heroes, but by no means indicated that they were representative of any substantial number of their fellows. Wiley, *Southern Negroes, 1861-1865*, pp. 134-45.

96. Page, *Meh Lady*, p. 70.

Seawell made sure that the "Federals know all they want to
know" about movements of the Confederates around Harrowby. A Tremaine son might visit Harrowby without fear
of betrayal, but the slaves were quick to pass on casual information which might hasten the southern defeat. More recent
novelists have tried to describe the almost hysterical effects of
the rumors on which Negroes built their dream of the New
Jerusalem. In William Faulkner's *The Unvanquished,* the
tension of their longing grew unbearable; the approach of
invading armies sent them in a great surge on the public high-
ways, clogging the wake of the soldiers, shouting the glories
of the Jordan ahead. But freedom remained a hollow word.
They discovered, in Roark Bradford's words, that "White
folks is about de same, anywhar you take, f'm what I hyars."
Freedom? "Dey wouldn't put up with hit." They had feared
all the while that this would be the end of their desires. "I
don't know," one black driver had said, even before he quite
believed in the reality of Yankee armies. "Some say one thing
and some say de yuther. Aunt Free say even did you make
Up Nawth and git free, hit ain't nothin' to hit. She free as a
bird herse'f, and she slave like de rest. She say, even back in
Af'ica, hit all go 'long 'bout de same."[97] Emancipation, often
admitted to be a good idea, is never explicitly condemned,
but freedom is assumed to have been from the start a false
hope.

The effort to comprehend the Negro's point of view, in
other words, was no less a defense of ante-bellum institutions
than the older idea of Negro contentment with slave life. The
defensive attitude appears to run more and more strongly
through a number of recent southern novels much concerned
with slavery. In some cases, defense has given way to a savage
and masochistic obsession with guilt—such words are not too
strong for Allen Tate's *The Fathers.* Tate's book, or T. S.
Stribling's *The Forge,* to use another example, provide powerful confirmation for W. J. Cash's view of the South as a "society beset by the specters of defeat, of shame, of guilt."[98] At

97. Bradford, *Kingdom Coming,* pp. 186-87.
98. *The Mind of the South,* p. 61.

the core of the violent climax to each of these works is the fact of miscegenation. Stribling even details a rape scene, in which the most successful of the Vaiden boys forces his mulatto sister.[99] Old man Jimmie Vaiden at the moment of his death symbolized Stribling's conception of southern degeneracy. He was alone with Gracie, the mulatto girl, when the stroke that killed him came. He called for Marcia, who had eloped when he refused consent to her marriage.

"Lef' me—went away an' lef' me. I wanted to die in my daughter's arms."

"Oh! Oh! Ol' Pap—you are, ol' Pap!" sobbed the woman, holding him up and looking into his ashen face.

"What do you—mean?" He gasped.

"My mammy—old Hannah, you remember—the woman you owned in South Carolina—she told Aunt Creasy I was your daughter."

The old man made a great exertion, put up a hand and pushed away the face of the woman who held him.

"You—nigger," he panted, "lay me down—lay me back down—in the dirt—"

Complete revulsion against the southern tradition, however, only proves more completely the conclusion with which these comments on fiction's slave were introduced; it is white society, white viewpoints, which writing about the Negro has clarified. The Civil War novels have failed to enter slave minds or revivify slave ambitions; Negro characters have remained, for the most part, lacking necessary elements of unique individuality. Imaginative art has done little to supplement the historian's factual record of what remains the least-known phase of Civil War life.

Slaves have been accorded a smaller and smaller place in the twentieth century's novels of the war. The greatest concern with Negro life was expressed in early northern novels of the war; after that, the story of the southern servant was reduced to sub-plots and stage-dressings in novels about white men and women.

Another early obsession with northern writers, also abandoned in modern times, was the story of the persecuted union-

99. *The Forge*, pp. 159-61, 524-25.

ists of the South. With writers like James M. Hiatt, who published *The Test of Loyalty* in 1864, this theme was a part of the North's propaganda; his work was in equal parts attack on Indiana Democrats whose antagonism to the war effort lowered morale in the armed forces and description of the plight of persecuted followers of "Parson" William G. Brownlow in Tennessee. For a time after the war, the southern unionists themselves emerged to tell their story—William Mumford Baker recorded the derision and personal dangers borne by a loyal minister of the cloth;[100] Jeremiah Clemens celebrated the heroism of North Alabama union irregulars;[101] and A. O. Wheeler extracted cloak and dagger romances from the wartime experiences of southern loyalists.[102] Use of the theme persisted—was even intensified—during the novel's middle period. It was a significant route by which northern writers could arrive at the romantic materials of the southern tradition without tarring their work with the taint of rebellion. Edward Payson Roe employed this device in *"Miss Lou,"*[103] as "Marion Harland" had done earlier in *Sunnybank*.[104] Southerners paid little attention to their dissenters, although Thomas Cooper De Leon's *John Holden*, published in 1893, was a thoughtful effort to trace the career of an Alabama mountain man, unionist, and later scallawag.[105] The modern Civil War novel has largely abandoned the theme—so much so that *Tap Roots*, by James

---

100. *Inside: A Chronicle of Secession.* See note 26, p. 32.

101. *Tobias Wilson.* See note 52, p. 39.

102. *Eye-Witness.*

103. A fabulously successful romancer of the eighties, Roe, a minister, had turned to fiction after successful exploitation of the Chicago fire in 1873 proved his ability. His novels tended to extreme partisanship (he was an abolitionist), but his strong dependence on conversion of his characters to testifying Christianity tempered much of his bitterness. In tone, his works belong to the earlier school of expressive sentimentality. *DAB*, XVI, 84-85.

104. Mrs. Terhune, who wrote under this name, was a Virginia novelist who had gone with her husband to New Jersey in 1859. She successfully combined union sentiments with a loving view of the virtues of the Old South. *Who Was Who*, p. 521.

105. Editor of the Mobile *Register* from 1877 to 1914, De Leon was a veteran of four years Confederate service. *DAB*, V, 224.

Street, was heralded by its publishers as an innovation in Civil War fiction, and its author was somewhat shrill in his proofs that the unionists he depicted had basis in fact.[106]

The middle period's grand device for healing wounds between the sections, providing southern markets for northern writers, and northern markets for southern ones, was reunion by marriage. The hero was usually a man in blue, and hoop-skirted belles were passionately devoted to the grey. Neither the war nor reconstruction produced problems which could not be solved, according to these novels, by an adequately consummated marriage.[107] Novelists early and late, good and bad, have resorted to the theme of North–South love in scores of novels; the device is by my count the most frequently used theme of the Civil War novel. John William De Forest and Thomas Nelson Page used it in the novels already referred to, and they were neither first nor last in the practice. General Charles King relied on it often in his seven novels of the war;[108] the *Bear Wallow Belles* of C. R. Wilson smoothed the hurt of Kentucky's division with it; and a host of ex-Confederate sympathizers gave similar testimony to the virility of the northern male.[109] The theme was a tailored device by which lovers might be kept apart for the requisite three hundred pages and then triumphantly united as a breathing monument to the reunion. Requited love, uncomplicated by sectional separation, was also a frequent enough theme, but it never attained the appeal of divided lovers.[110]

106. See the dust jacket for assertions about his "unique" theme. A recent northern version of the southern unionist theme is Lancaster's *No Bugles Tonight*.

107. Sectional intermarriage, of course, was a phase of the reality as well as the romance of the war, though not to the degree the mass of these novels indicate. See Simkins and Patton, *The Women of the Confederacy*, pp. 55-56, 58-64, and Buck, *The Road to Reunion*, pp. 215-16.

108. See, for example, *Between the Lines* and *A Broken Sword*.

109. Among them are G. C. Eggleston, *The Warrens of Virginia;* C. C. Harrison, *The Carlyles;* Kennedy, *Cicely;* Parrish, *Love Under Fire;* Richardson, *The Heart of Hope;* and countless others.

110. In connection with love themes, it should be noted that the Civil War novel has not joined the main stream of historical fiction in service to the contemporary American obsession with bare bosoms.

Closely associated with the theme of North-South love is the application of a similar romantic view to more general war issues. In this costume war when young lovers were not keeping trysts in no-man's land, they were involving themselves as daring spies, brave ladies, loathsome villains, and foursquare heroes in remarkably improbable situations, for the performance of incredible deeds. Their brass buttons and shoulder straps were mounted on costumes, not uniforms; and smoke or blood rarely stained them. Such appropriation of the war scene for fanciful romance appeared very early; James Dabney McCabe in 1863 placed his southern hero in a secret passageway outside Lincoln's office and made him an eyewitness, not only to the union's most secret plans, but also to the subservience of a drunken president to a degenerate Seward.[111] Partisanship was largely removed from such writing before it reached its peak, however; writers like Cyrus Townsend Brady were able to locate heroes first on one side, and then the other,

---

Civil War novels, even recent ones, would come close, on the whole, to satisfying the late Gaithings Committee. One rises, in fact, from reading great numbers of war love stories with the wish that authors had paid more attention to sex—or even, if necessary, to secondary sex characteristics. Wartime couples are presented as philosophic, Christian, self-sacrificial, tender, impetuous, and heroic, but rarely passionate. Lust, with a capital "L," was darkly noted by abolition sympathizers with quadroon girls of the South, but the first romantically naked lady of the Civil War novel appeared in 1911, in the Reverend Mr. Brady's *As the Sparks Fly Upward.* She paid the wages of sin, however, by throwing herself off a cliff. Earlier there had appeared a shockingly casual account of wife-swapping in G. W. Hosmer's *As We Went Marching On;* and in Yopp's *A Dual Role,* a male hero disguised as a woman spent the night in a room with the girl he later married, but for all the author tells us, they slept with their clothes on. Modern employment of sex varies, of course, with the intent of the user. The naturalistic presentation of Kantor, in *Long Remember,* has proper psychological motivations and is an integral part of his theme. Sexual promiscuity among aristocratic southern women is made a symbol of southern decadence, a temptation to northern innocence, in Stern's *The Drums of Morning* and Lockridge's *Raintree County.* In contrast might be noted the alacrity with which Morna Dabney, heroine of Street's *Tap Roots,* added to the course of physical therapy which cured her polio a deep-woods bedding with the novel's hero.

111. *The Aid-de-Camp.*

in the string of romances issuing from their pens.[112] There was great variety in books of this sort, ranging from the harmless and reasonably accurate story-telling of Joel Chandler Harris, in *The Shadow Between His Shoulder-Blades*, to the bawdy prostitution of war themes by James M. Cain in *Past All Dishonor*.

Serious use of military campaigns themselves has been a prominent feature of many novels. The best of these, like Mary Johnston's *The Long Roll* and *Cease Firing*, thoroughly review the strategy of generals and the details of military life. Johnston's work, like that of Clifford Dowdey in *Bugles Blow No More*, was notable for its accuracy, though both writers suffer from their effort to include too much of the war—annals burden them down and destroy the reality of the characters on whom they place their primary emphasis. An interesting phase of this theme is the distinct difference between northern and southern novels that attempt ambitious military sagas. At the North, after the pattern set by Wilbur F. Hinman[113] and others, concern is more likely to be with private soldiers and personal experiences, than with the generals and top-level strategy common to southern novels. Bernard DeVoto has suggested that the South has had to mobilize all the high brass at its command to win the victory denied by reality to the Lost Cause;[114] but the explanation more probably lies with the persistent orientation of southern writers toward upper class symbols. In any case, concern with the military side of the war has produced countless efforts to make vivid and real the actual fighting and has left such memorable achievements as MacKinlay Kantor's Gettysburg[115] and Andrew Lytle's Shiloh.[116] Southern writers are more likely than northern ones to concentrate on military history; their authentic heroes are surrounded

112. For another achievement of Brady, naval officer, minister, and writer, see footnote 110. See also *DAB*, II, 582-83.

113. *Corporal Si Klegg and His "Pard."* See note 23, p. 31.

114. "Fiction Fights the Civil War," *Sat. Rev. Lit.*, XVII (Dec. 18, 1937), 4.

115. *Long Remember, passim.*

116. *The Long Night*, pp. 193-307.

with ready-made legend which invites the story-teller and finds ready acceptance among readers. The mass of campaign stories was written during the middle period, but Southerners have continued the theme as a frequent feature of their modern writing.

The striking development of the novel's middle period was a greatly increased effort by able southern writers to render intelligible, by definition and by use of skillfully selected detail, their conception of the hopes and ideals of the whole society destroyed by the war. Paul H. Buck, in mapping the road to reunion, has emphasized the influence of this theme in the hands of George Washington Cable, Joel Chandler Harris, Thomas Nelson Page, and Mary Noailles Murfree, who discovered, during the eighties, that "a culture which in its life was anathema to the North could in its death be honored. . . . Without offense to any living interest they could at last tell what they deemed to be the truth about the land they loved."[117] Southerners from Augusta Jane Evans Wilson[118] to Stark Young[119] have nurtured carefully the traditions enshrined by these writers and have repeatedly sought the spirit which breathed through the achievements of the great foursome. The concern of critics and historians with the stereotypes fathered by this school, however, has obscured a similar movement which is a marked characteristic of the modern northern novel about the war. Such writers as Edgar Lee Masters, Ross Lockridge, Jr., MacKinlay Kantor, and Joseph Hergesheimer[120] have exhibited an equal concern with northern society on the eve of war—but the spread northward of the southern penchant for regional interpretation has not been accompanied by the passionate loyalties which have bound Southerners to all-

117. *The Road to Reunion,* pp. 203-8.

118. Mrs. Wilson's contribution came too early, of course, for the simplification of southern society into the aristocrat, loyal slave, and poor white divisions developed by later defenders of the section. *Macaria* is a poor boy–rich girl story, but its excessive southern patriotism is distinctly a part of the later tradition.

119. *So Red the Rose.*

120. The novels of Masters, Lockridge, and Kantor have already been referred to. Hergesheimer was author of *The Limestone Tree.*

out defense of their section's life. The cause of these North-erners is not a lost one, and they bring a contemporary sense of social responsibility to their realistic investigations of what was both good and bad in the northern crusade. Often their heroes, like those of the South, tend to be swept aside by the unleashed might of industrial empire; but their tragedy is un-relieved by the consolation of defeat at the hands of an invad-ing enemy, for they are victims of their own achievements. To Masters and Lockridge, the war is an unending battle in which the conflict of the sixties was only a phase; in their realistic definition of its issues they reject the stereotyped symbols of slave driver or puritan as satisfactory villains for either section. They have created heroes unsupported by blind confidence in amorphous sectional ideals, heroes who battle directly with the greed perceived but vaguely by the southern writers who had seen Mammon as the distant enemy. The success of these northern writers has given new dimension to the novel of so-ciety during the war.[121]

Subordinate themes in the novels of society have in certain cases been presented with such frequency that they deserve independent consideration. The story of kinsmen and neigh-bors divided is one such major plot device. Northern writers have emphasized it more often than Southerners, though some of the best of the latter have based their stories on it. Further, its locale in the southern border states, and the pres-ence of two sides to the various questions argued, makes division into the North-South category somewhat unreal. Early writers were not much concerned with this element of the war; their enthusiasm for a single cause left them with little sympathy for the families and areas whose loyalties were

121. The above paragraph leaves the implication that this phase of northern writing is purely modern, which is not entirely correct. North-erners like Beecher in *Norwood* celebrated the virtues of northern civil life from the very beginning; and Morford, frequently referred to, probed often to the heart of tinsel patriots whose motives were less than worthy. A good middle-period novel of a soldier's disillusion with slackers and profiteers on the home front was Kirkland's *The Captain of Company K.*

complicated by doubts and indecision. In the middle period, however, writers like John Fox,[122] Molly Elliott Seawell,[123] Paul Laurence Dunbar,[124] and James Lane Allen,[125] filled this gap with genuine artistry. In the modern period, Allen Tate has made such division the basis of a psychological horror story,[126] and Holmes Alexander has struck off into virtually unworked territory with his story of the division of Virginia into two states.[127] Missouri, surprisingly, has been the locale of more of these stories of division than have Kentucky, Virginia, or Maryland, the other leaders.

A similar theme pursued almost exclusively by northern writers is the story of the Copperhead opponents to the northern war effort. A constant element in northern novels of society, the Copperheads emerged in the middle period as an important device in the section's notable tendency to self-criticism. Indiana and Illinois most frequently were the scenes of such investigation, although New York City's draft riots and the state's reluctant support of war necessities drew a number of writers. Harold Frederic's *The Copperhead,* a notable study of upstate New York, was issued in 1893, and an able modern writer, Constance Robertson, has succeeded with similar materials.[128] Indiana scenes have been less skillfully presented in recent novels by Laura Long[129] and Leone Lowden.[130]

Emphatic attention should be given to one final departure from orthodox concepts in novels of civil life. An important group of southern writers has abandoned many time-tried

122. *The Little Shepherd of Kingdom Come.*
123. *The Victory.*
124. *The Fanatics.* Dunbar was a Negro novelist, the son of Kentucky slaves, who achieved his reputation as a poet. His story of war divisions in an Indiana town is distinguished in no way, except by literary superiority, from stories by white novelists on the same theme.
125. *The Sword of Youth.*
126. *The Fathers.*
127. *American Nabob.*
128. *The Unterrified.*
129. *Without Valor.*
130. *Proving Ground.*

symbols of aristocratic life in an effort to render a true account-
ing of agrarian existence in the old South and the Confederacy. The southern home described by Tom Watson

> did not, in the least, resemble a Grecian Temple, which had been
> sent into exile, and which was striving, unsuccessfully, to look at
> ease among corncribs, cow-pens, horse-stables, pig-styes, chicken-
> houses, negro cabins, and worm-fenced cotton fields. It did not
> perch upon the top of the highest hill for miles around and brow-
> beat the whole community with its arrogant self-assertion.[131]

In kindred vein, Ellen Glasgow wrote that one of her basic
purposes was to dramatize the tragedy of "a Southerner who
had never owned a slave, and rarely seen one, offering his life
in defense, not only of an abstract right, which meant nothing to him, but also of institutions which bore more hardly
upon the illiterate white man than they bore upon the black
man in chattel slavery."[132] The story of the South's middle
and lower classes, rare when Watson and Glasgow wrote,
has become an outstanding feature of modern Civil War
novels about the South. James Boyd, in 1927,[133] William
Faulkner[134] and Andrew Lytle[135] in the mid-thirties, as well
as other less able writers[136] have become interested in the
middle-class farmers, rather than the planters, of the region
they portrayed. In their emphasis on these neglected classes,
the novelists anticipated similar trends in the historical literature of the past decade.[137] Abandonment of the more florid

131. Watson, *Bethany*, p. 8.
132. *A Certain Measure*, p. 22. This reference is to the mountaineer
character, "Pinetop," in *The Battle-Ground*.
133. *Marching On.*
134. *The Unvanquished.*
135. *The Long Night.*
136. See, for instance, Bristow, *The Handsome Road,* and Kroll, *The
Keepers of the House.*
137. Frank L. and Harriet C. Owsley concluded, in 1940, that even
among the slaveholders of the black belt, the majority were "farmers
rather than planters, who owned a few slaves and worked in the field
with them." Professor Owsley's own studies, and those of his students,
have developed this interpretation in a number of monographs and
articles which emphasize the importance of yeoman classes in southern
life. Their concept is not new, of course; they tend, rather, to document

elements of the plantation legend has not made objective realists of these writers; their tendency has been to surround their
southern yeoman with a new idealism. They come to their
work with the opinion of Tom Watson, that the homestead
of the Old South was "a little kingdom, a complete social and
industrial organism, almost wholly sufficient unto itself, asking less of the outer world than it gave. How sound, sane,
healthy it appears, even now, when compared to certain
phases of certain other systems."[138] Within the limits of similar agrarian preconceptions, modern southern writers have
eliminated much that was hackneyed, sentimental, and untrue
from traditions of the South's effort, and have established a
new foundation for more accurately informed dreams of ante-
bellum life.

Most novels of the Civil War cluster about the various plot
devices suggested in the foregoing pages. These divisions
according to plot are nowhere precise, but the ten basic themes
identified embrace most of the books that have been written
about the war. Tables based on these categorical distinctions
would reveal the considerable dependence of the novelists on
certain catch-all ideas—particularly those here labeled "North-
South love," "campaign history," and "costume war." Tables
would obscure such impressive essays in social history as those
grouped under "studies of civil ideals" or "the southern middle
classes." They would eliminate from the count subordinate
themes which have been pursued with some consistency—
the early excrescences of "sentimental patriotism," the struggle
with "Negro life," the stories of "southern unionism," "divided

<hr />

ideas frequently expressed by earlier historians of the South. John
Spencer Bassett, for instance, in 1899 described the farmer, as opposed
to the planter, as the backbone of southern society. The facts for such
a view seem implicit in findings like those of U. B. Phillips, who
pointed to the fact that six of the eight million white Southerners "were
out of proprietary touch with the four million slaves." Owsley, "The
Economic Basis of Society in the Late Ante-Bellum South," *Jour. So.
Hist.*, VI (1940), 39. See also B. H. Clark, *The Tennessee Yeoman;*
Weaver, *Mississippi Farmers;* Bassett, *Slavery in the State of North
Carolina*, pp. 47-48; Phillips, *Life and Labor in the Old South*, p. 339.
138. Watson, *Bethany*, p. 12.

kinsmen," and "northern Copperheads." These thematic variations have been itemized at some length to reveal the dangers of generalization about war fiction from knowledge of a single group of authors, from study of a single period of fictional production, or out of fascination with the impact of a few best sellers.

The problem of the important, widely-circulated book must be considered, of course, in an effort to weigh the influence of various fictional views of the war. Among the over-all best sellers of American fiction, only four novels about the Civil War appear—a fact which should aid in returning to proper proportion the largely quantitative aspects of the foregoing analysis.[139] The most successful of these, *Gone with the Wind,* has recently, with a sort of poetic justice, surpassed in popularity *Uncle Tom's Cabin,* "its nearest rival for topmost position in all the history of American readership." Of the other three, one, *The Red Badge of Courage,* had little connection with the partisan passions common to the others; and two, Winston Churchill's *The Crisis* and John Fox's *The Little Shepherd of Kingdom Come,* though firmly national in their sympathies, were full of loving respect for the vanquished enemy.[140] High on the list, but falling slightly short of the circulation necessary for inclusion among the all-time best sellers, are three polemic novels of early Northerners—James R. Gilmore's *Among the Pines,* John T. Trowbridge's *Cudjo's*

139. There is only one work which establishes adequate bases for comparison of best-seller statistics—Mott, *Golden Multitudes*. Mott's investigation of extravagant claims made by authors and publishers appears thorough, and his decision that, to be a best seller, a book should circulate to a total number equal to 1 per cent of the national population in the year of its issue, seems reasonable. Less reliable is Hackett, *Fifty Years of Best Sellers,* which is based on the figures in various trade magazines and book reviews—sources which were themselves, on occasion, based on unscientific sampling techniques. For estimates of the popularity of books before 1895, she resorts to little more than guess-work—as illustrated by her inclusion of a work by Mary Jane Hawes Holmes on her list, because it was reported to be very popular by the Boston Public Library.

140. Mott, *Golden Multitudes,* pp. 258, 312-14. Total sales of *Gone with the Wind* have reached three million in the United States, and one and one-half million abroad.

Cave, and Albion W. Tourgée's *A Fool's Errand.*[141] Notable favorites in their day were Hervey Allen's *Action at Aquila,* George Washington Cable's *Dr. Sevier,* Mary Jane Holmes' *Rose Mather: A Tale,* Mary Johnston's *The Long Roll,* Thomas Nelson Page's *Red Rock: A Chronicle of Reconstruction* and *Gordon Keith,* and Stark Young's *So Red the Rose.*[142] Among these fourteen leading sellers, six were written from the Confederate point of view, and eight from the Federal. Four of the northern group were written in the early period; three in the middle, and one in the modern. Four of the southern ones appeared in the middle period, and two were offered recently.

Juvenile novels have not been considered in the separation of novels into themes; their division would properly rest on the ages of the heroes they present. Boys over twelve were old enough, in these books, to go out and save the union or rescue the Confederacy; but under that age they had to work at home for their sectional ideals. In quantity, the juveniles were overwhelmingly northern in their sympathies—89 of the 113 included in this survey were so oriented. With one notable exception, the outstanding authors of boys' series have passed the South by. Six writers alone wrote 54 of the 113 juveniles here considered, and of these, 46 of the 54 were pro-northern in sympathy.[143] The ablest writer of the group, however, divided his sympathies equally. Joseph Alexander Altsheler, a Kentucky-born New York newspaperman, alternated

141. *Ibid.,* pp. 321-23. Mott's list of "better sellers" is made up of novels high on the list which did not attain the requisite sales for inclusion among the "all-time" best sellers.

142. The book trade, according to Hackett, *Fifty Years of Best Sellers,* p. 104, regarded these works among the ten leading sellers of the years in which they were published.

143. William T. Adams ("Oliver Optic") was the most prolific writer of the group, contributing eighteen pro-northern juveniles to the total. His ideal, according to the preface of *Brave Old Salt,* p. 6, was to "present a lofty ideal to the young man of today—one who will be true to God, true to himself, and true to his country, in whatever sphere his lot may be cast, whether on the forecastle or the quarterdeck; as a private or an officer, in the great army which must ever battle with life's trials and temptations till the crown immortal be

between northern and southern themes in the eight novels of the Civil War he published between 1914 and 1916.[144] He went to great pains in seeking accuracy for his novels and claimed historian Francis Parkman as his inspiration.[145] While his influence probably was not so great as that of "Oliver Optic" (William T. Adams), whose endless chain of war juveniles appeared from 1863 to 1897, he has attained a lasting popularity. In 1918, by vote of public libraries, he was chosen

---

won." His early works, bitterly pro-northern, gave way to more generous Federalism in later series. In *Taken by the Enemy*, pp. 6-7, he denies any "desire or intention to rekindle the fires of sectional animosity. . . ." See *DAB*, I, 102-3. Next to Adams in quantity of production was Byron Archibald Dunn, Republican politician and veteran, who published eleven pro-northern and one pro-southern juvenile. *Who's Who in America*, XII, 981. Charles Fosdick, ("H. C. Castlemon"), who served on Federal gunboats during the war, wrote five novels from a union point of view, and three from a southern. In his southern series, however, the hero concludes in the third volume that the South's cause is not just and retires from the fighting. See *Sailor Jack the Trader*. See also *DAB*, VI, 539. Warren Lee Goss and Everett Titsworth Tomlinson each published four novels, entirely northern. Joseph Alexander Altsheler's eight novels are listed below.

144. His eight books were: *The Guns of Bull Run, The Scouts of Stonewall, The Sword of Antietam, The Guns of Shiloh, The Star of Gettysburg, The Rock of Chickamauga, The Shades of the Wilderness,* and *The Tree of Appomattox.* Earlier in the century, he also published three adult novels on war themes.

145. "Altsheler," *DAB*, I, 233. The scope of his war juveniles is indicated by his own list of the leaders and battles treated in the eight volumes, which he listed in the preface to *The Tree of Appomattox,* pp. viii-ix. The leaders included Abraham Lincoln, Jefferson Davis, Ulysses S. Grant, Robert E. Lee, Thomas J. Jackson, Philip H. Sheridan, George H. Thomas, Albert Sydney Johnston, A. P. Hill, W. S. Hancock, George B. McClellan, Ambrose E. Burnside, Turner Ashby, J. E. B. Stuart, Joseph Hooker, Richard S. Ewell, Jubal Early, William S. Rosecrans, Simon Bolivar Buckner, Leonidas Polk, Braxton Bragg, Nathan Bedford Forrest, John Morgan, George J. Meade, Don Carlos Buell, William T. Sherman, James Longstreet, P. G. T. Beauregard, William L. Yancey, and James A. Garfield.

Battles included Bull Run, Kernstown, Cross Keys, Winchester, Port Republic, The Seven Days, Mill Spring, Fort Donaldson, Shiloh, Perrysville, Stone River, The Second Manassas, Antietam, Fredericksburg, Chancellorsville, Gettysburg, Champion Hill, Vicksburg, Chickamauga, Missionary Ridge, The Wilderness, Spottsylvania, Cold Harbor, Fisher's Hill, Cedar Creek, and Appomattox.

"the most popular boys' writer in America."[146] His works are still recommended reading in the nation's public schools. In general, however, the quality of juvenile works was as varied as that of the collection at large; their passions and attitudes differed in the same general proportions as did adult novels written during the same eras.

Introduction to Civil War novels, juvenile division, completes my descriptive catalogue of authors and themes. Quantitative analysis is not offered as a substitute for critical examination of the novelist as historian, but the foregoing summaries may document my reservations about the confident opinions with which this chapter was introduced.

Certainly any generalizations based on casual reading of the war literature must be qualified almost to extinction if they are to be made at all. As for the question of who won the literary war, North or South, we must answer that the issue is still joined. It will remain joined so long as Southerners hold to their southernism and Northerners treasure their achievement. Clearly Albion W. Tourgée, ex-carpetbagger, abandoned the field too soon when he declared that "today" (1888), the Confederate point of view had prevailed. If the period from 1885 through 1888 may be accepted as a reasonable time period for his "today," this notion would be undermined by the fact that during this interval seventeen pro-northern novels and seven pro-southern ones were published. Within the northern group, only one had as its outstanding character a Confederate—a gloomy lady who put a hex on the northern hero.[147] Five others, it is true, pursued the reconciliation theme, but with union heroes. Ten were simply war stories from the union's point of view, in which the South was the enemy, and no more. The seven southern novels included George Washington Cable's *Dr. Sevier,* in which the union cause was declared just,[148] and Thomas Nelson Page's famous juvenile,

146. *Twentieth Century Authors,* p. 20.
147. J. J. Kane, *Ilian.*
148. P. 377. This novel may have won Northerners to more sympathy with southern life, but in the South it confirmed opinion that Cable had become a scallawag writer, untrue to his native region. *DAB,* III, 392-93.

Two Little Confederates. More famous at that time were
S. Weir Mitchell's realistic study of cowardice behind the
northern lines, *In War Times;* and three of the northern
romances (one based on North-South love) published by
abolitionist Edward P. Roe, whose works all expressed the
"middle-class Northern view of the war as a Heaven-directed
blessing in disguise whose problems all yield to love and business enterprise. . . ."[149]

However much the time period may be expanded, no definitive measure of victory or defeat for Blue or Grey may be
deduced from Civil War fiction. By quantitative measure,
pro-northern works are more numerous; and in juvenile literature this majority is overwhelming. Among best sellers, however, 3 of the 4 top novels are full of loving respect for the
old South,[150] and the fourth has no stake in partisan issues.[151]
Among "better sellers" 7 pro-northern works appear, as compared with 4 pro-southern. The 45 novels of the movement
which meet reasonable critical standards, listed on pages 12-13,
present a more adequate source for conclusions. Of these, 27
were southern, and 18 northern. Thirteen of the southern
group were distinctly outside traditional concepts, however,
while only 5 of the 18 northern ones were based on reconciliation principles. The opposed philosophies of the war have
been sufficiently profound to command continuing partisanship.

Now speculation based on limited periods of this conflict
can be very fruitful, as Paul Buck has demonstrated, but
enthusiasm for the contribution of the reconciliation literature of the 1880's to sectional reunion is obviously no adequate substitute for general judgment of war literature. Perhaps southern writers did learn that unless their literature
"became sufficiently American in tone to appeal to Northern

149. R. W. Smith, "The Civil War and Its Aftermath in American
Fiction," p. 32.
150. Mitchell, *Gone with the Wind,* is thoroughly romantic in its
view of the old South, of course; and Fox, *The Little Shepherd of
Kingdom Come,* and Churchill, *The Crisis,* despite warmly national
sympathies, were in the same vein.
151. Crane, *The Red Badge of Courage,* could be a story of any
side in any war anywhere.

readers there would be no Southern literature";[152] but it seems more important that they learned how to write. Politics did not replace artistry as a route to literary preferment. The bloody shirt seems to have intimidated very few southern novelists, and them in only minor fashion. Reconciliation of the sections did not prevent subsequent popular success by such unreconstructed rebels as Mary Johnston, Stark Young, or Margaret Mitchell. The achievements of these latter writers were not dependent, either, on the suffocation of northern principles in the cloying fragrance of magnolia blossoms. Even during the middle period of the Civil War novel, only half the better books written by Southerners were devoted to traditional themes; and during the same period northern writers kept fresh their faith in the justice of the North's cause. The mellow ghost of Thomas Nelson Page, it appears, has more often haunted critics and historians of the movement than the authors who inherited his sources.

My insistence on this point has become contentious, I realize, but extravagant emphasis on the continued presence of partisan feeling in the novels seems merited in the light of such preconceptions as that, for instance, which led a recent observer to remark that William Faulkner, in *The Unvanquished,* was "as conventional in his prejudices as any old-fashioned romancer."[153] Such reactions to most novels about the war have become almost instinctive, it is true, among observers who have some acquaintance with the mass of novels which aspire to no higher level than costume romance; but jaded critical appetites should appreciate artistic vitality—and historical reality—when such qualities separate so excellent a study as Faulkner's from the pot-boiled copy-work so frequently encountered. Costume romances have introduced basic distortions to fictional interpretation of war traditions, but concern with the nature of the error is no proper substitute for recognition of war memories which preserve honest, authentic, and vivid moments of the era. Further, such a concern dis-

152. Buck, *The Road to Reunion,* p. 199.
153. Simkins, *The South Old and New,* p. 348.

tracts attention from essential questions: What unsatisfied desire attracts so many authors and so many readers to this constant sifting of the war experience? What version of the American past is offered for the satisfaction of that desire? What lessons has the historian failed to provide, that the service of the novelist finds such eager acceptance? The questions are pretentious; but answers are worth seeking, even if in the end they prove less than profound.

3

FICTION AND HISTORY

I
The Novelist as Historian

THE NOVEL, according to the *Encyclopedia Britannica,* "is the name given in literature to a sustained story which is not historically true, but might very easily be so." Within the context of this cautious observation lie the governing rules for the next step in my analysis—a study of the qualities which make some novels "historically true," and of the reputability of the Civil War novelist as historian. The criteria for evaluating fictionalized history are of course quite separate from those that are applied for the measure of monographs. In clothing the skeleton of historical fact with the flesh of human purpose, a successful artist must cross beyond the limits of documentary sources and draw from the primary sources of imagination the selective litter of unique detail that alone warms fiction with the breath of reality. As the novelist abandons the security of the accidentally preserved records on which the historian depends, he gambles on the total impression which results from his manipulation of recorded fact. Informed, as we have seen, by public impressions, oral traditions, and anecdotal scraps of evidence, he "proves" his case with public acceptance of his hypothesis. The validity of his account is measured by the extent of the conviction he builds in the reader's mind; for this conviction constitutes the "truth" as he understands it. He thus serves as a sort of tribal recorder rather

72

than scientific scholar; his satisfaction of the public appetite for romantic explanations of national crises gives him more the role of soothsayer than savant.

The susceptibility of this process to error is obvious. When imagination is given precedence over documented fact, when entertainment is demanded before accuracy, the quest of the novelist for the sense of history may often be misdirected. But fear of the dangers implicit in the method should not lead to prejudgment of the product. The historical novelist, by choosing to live with these dangers, wins freedom from the rigid restraints put by sources on the intuition of the professional historian. Our task here is to examine the use to which the freedom has been put.

The creative writer enjoys a second basic freedom equally alien to formal historical standards. He is consciously a partisan, with no interest in concealment by some scholarly apparatus of the preconceptions which filter past the caution of the most scientific of historians. No complacent satisfaction with "objective" analysis may be permitted to cool his report of the unfamiliar rage to which he introduces his reader. His first task is to keep alive the passionate feeling from which the historian attempts to escape; fictional history, if it succeeds, must be a primary account of some aspect of the bitter divisions of the sixties. In the conflict which is at the root of any story, the reader must be provided with a point of view, if he is to participate vicariously in the events described.[1] Ideally, this would be the view of a partisan contemporary with the setting of the story, though it is more likely to be the philosophic attitude of

1. The degree of the distinction between the method of the historian and novelist should not be magnified at this point. Responsible historians increasingly feel obligated to choose, argue, and conclude—even at some expense to the "scientific" research methods to which they can always retreat. The outstanding scholarly critic of the substitution of "annals" for history was Charles A. Beard, who taught many of his fellows to seek paths through their materials, even at the risk of error. ". . . conceivably," Beard said, "it might be better to be wrecked on an express train bound to a destination than to moulder in a freight car sidetracked in a well-fenced lumber yard." *The Rise of American Civilization*, I, xiv-xv.

the author about his period, fastened on a hero who may or may not be typical of his time. In either case, partisanship holds no danger for the novelist, who seeks the dramatic unity of positive views, undiluted by objective detachment.

The partisan position selected has mixed uses. The historian, for instance, reads in it the novelist's interpretation of the era described. The author, on the other hand, is likely to think first of the fact that he is seeking the attention and sympathy of a casual reader from an alien generation. His point of view must effect a reconciliation between the realities of the period under study with surviving popular traditions and convictions about it. There must be familiar corners on the strange scene, points of entry through which the reader may slip without conscious abandonment of his own opinions. Only gradually can he be lulled to a state of receptivity in which the past is seen rather than explained, the novelist's opinions felt rather than learned.

The average novelist seeks to serve both truth and the market by rather self-conscious adoption of a familiar rationalization. He proceeds from the assumption that there are basic qualities in men which are held in common through the ages and seeks to hold his story within the boundaries of a spiritual community that keeps its identity through both geography and time. According to this standard, "If you model the man in the street of pre-Christian Rome after the man in the street of Twentieth Century New York, you will be nearer to that vanished actuality than if you construct him from documentary erudition, because every man belongs more to humanity than he does to a period."[2] It is this assumption that gives the author courage to reunite the fragments of forgotten days and that wins among readers a sufficient identification with issues of other years to bring them comfortably into their presence. Such a view of history is not exclusive with the novelist, of course. Carl Becker emphasized the control of the "specious present" over the historian's interpretations and noted the degree to which the "form and significance of remembered

2. Colton, "Gospel of Likemindedness," *Sat. Rev. Lit.,* IV (June 9, 1928), 942.

events . . . will vary with the time and place of the observer."[3]
We seek in the past our own image and find most congenial
those philosophies which satisfy our current view of what is
logical and proper. As our ideas change, so must our history
and fiction, for otherwise we would be swiftly alienated from
our origins.

Historical novelists seem, on the whole, to be quite conscious
of the threat to the accuracy of their work posed by the addition of too much of the present. It is hardly more than a
truism to note that "Historical fiction, like history, is more
likely to register an exact truth about the writer's present than
the exact truth of the past."[4] Fewer critics have noted the
greater burden that too much history puts on a novel. Saintsbury observed a half century ago that the "commonest and
most obvious form" of error lay in "decanting too much of
your history bodily into your novel."[5] The virtue of fiction's
report lies in its revelation of large events through a record of
small, intimate details. Historical generalizations often sound
hollow in the mouths of amateurs; the successful novelist cuts
his canvas to the size of his talent and knowledge.

Other varieties of misrepresentation to which the historical
novel is subject might be listed indefinitely; for accuracy proceeds, in the end, from artistry and gifted intuition rarely
encountered in any field. The most cursory reading of any
quantity of costume romances reveals frequent violation of
Paul Leicester Ford's advice, that "events and characters must
be typical, not exceptional," to convey the tone of another generation.[6] Capture of readers by appeal to the dramatic and
unusual in the affairs of the past has been so common that the
average rental-store reader may never discover that life went
on, in other years, in a reasonably matter-of-fact way. Distortion by concentration on heroes greater than life is more common than misuse of verifiable fact. A novelist who introduces

3. *Everyman His Own Historian*, pp. 251-52.
4. Canby, "What Is Truth?" *Sat. Rev. Lit.*, IV (Dec. 31, 1927), 481.
5. *Essays in English Literature*, pp. 323-24.
6. "The American Historical Novelist," *Atlantic*, LXXX (Dec., 1897),
724.

public occurrences into his work quickly learns caution in the use of such material; for the illusion of reality is shattered completely by recognizable inaccuracy. This is no major hurdle, because the author of a successful historical novel rarely burdens his work with too much from the record; and when he employs it, fact is the bare frame which ordinary caution will build truly.

The whole problem of factual accuracy as a basis for judgment is altered when the novel, rather than the monograph is being considered. The fact that Evelyn Scott, for instance, introduced barbed wire to a Virginia farm before such fencing was invented[7] in no way invalidated her sensitive portrayal of northern and southern society under the pressure of war. A reader finishes her novel with the conviction that this is the way war must have seemed to its participants; it is overpowering in its total effect. James Street, on the other hand, remained quite within his prerogatives when he adopted as the basis for *Tap Roots* the exploded legend of the secession of Jones County, Mississippi, from the Confederacy;[8] but his story of southern unionism is without value because he appears to have

---

7. *The Wave,* p. 402. The development of barbed wire is described by Webb, *The Great Plains.*

8. The alleged secession of Jones County, in southern Mississippi, from both the state and the Confederacy is a legend which has been inflated by certain writers until the "Republic of Jones" was reported to have a president, cabinet, two-house congress, and an army. See the *Literary Digest,* LXIII (Dec. 27, 1919), 56. Street, in *Tap Roots,* foreword, did not pretend that his story followed established facts—"I have taken many liberties," he said. "I had to. . . ." In fitting the story of southern unionism to his version of the Jones County saga, he followed the "rule" which historical novelists rarely abide by; instead of concentrating on a period and incident where the facts have been clearly established, he wrote about an area of unsettled fact and provided a thesis which known facts do not completely prove or disprove. Historians agree that a company of unionist Southerners, commanded by Newton Knight, made their base in Jones County during the war but conclude that these irregulars, despite their effort to make contact with union forces, were not distinguished from other disloyalist groups of the Confederacy. See Goode Montgomery, "Alleged Secession of Jones County," *Pub. Miss. Hist. Soc.,* VII (1904), 13-22; and Tatum, *Disloyalty in the Confederacy,* pp. 97-99.

taken his notions of character from Hollywood, rather than from life.

Historian and novelist share one elusive problem—the degree to which each must cater to reader prejudices, must measure the popular temper before they frame unfamiliar interpretations of a period about which prevailing opinions are held strongly. Initially, the novelist appears to bear the greater burden here; he can never escape his primary obligation to entertain. He seeks a wider audience than the historian, whose opinions and observations are expressed to a public presumed to be smaller and more highly educated. Proof of a fact sometimes brings a measure of security to the historian, but the novelist must make his fact palatable. Some such observations follow plausibly enough on theoretical analysis of the effects of reader censorship; but in actuality reader dogmatism seems more prevalent in the scholar's audience than among the rental library patrons. Only in the period immediately following the war was there notable evidence, in fiction, of the mincing caution about new ideas so familiar to readers of scholarly reviews. Southern novelists, for a brief season, consciously trimmed their views in their effort to escape the confining fog of loyalist suspicion which hampered their efforts to enter the northern market.

Consider, for instance, the response of Sidney Lanier, in 1867, to a warning from his father that assignment of war guilt to the North might be unwise. He cut from the text of *Tiger-Lilies* his reference to the "calculating vindictiveness of Messrs. T. Stevens and C. Sumner" but let stand the southern portion of the blame. ". . . if there was guilt in any," he said, "there was guilt in nigh all of us, between Maryland and Mexico."[9] Lanier was moved by no changing views before such editing; he bowed to the necessity of appeasing the victorious opponent. Some novelists carefully underlined such recognition of the market realities. Mary Tucker Magill prefaced in 1871 her tale of the war in Virginia with the guarantee

9. Greever and Abernethy, eds., *Sidney Lanier, Tiger-Lilies and Southern Prose,* V, xxxv, 97.

that "She has attempted no political view of the subject; she has never once attacked the actions of the Government. . . ."[10] Few Southerners, perhaps, felt driven to such extremes, but then few of their novels won more than a very limited hearing. Nor did war issues alone provide the only dangerous ground on which the novelist had to move cautiously. John William De Forest was long an unread author, because his realistic comments on the weapons and tactics of women proved too strong a dose for his squeamish contemporaries.[11] Not being read is certainly the worst thing that can happen to a novelist, but this fate, for at least the past two generations, cannot be attributed to reader censorship of historical fiction. A remarkably tolerant audience will generally approve the work of an author amenable to the discipline suggested in the preceding pages.

This discipline invites the novelist to make what he will of the historical problem he defines—or leaves him free, at least, to search honestly for the meaning of events along the unmarked boundaries between the known and the unknowable. It is his privilege and obligation to "answer" larger problems than the scholar may safely pose; if bold, he seeks to define the content of hope, the anatomy of torment, the nature of man. He rarely exercises these privileges, to be sure; most historical novelists are more cautious than bold. They are generally satisfied to conform to the revealed legend of their section; and only a few enrich our knowledge of the past with artistic rephrasing of public memories.

My concern in the following pages is with the cautious many, rather than with the bold. Admiration for the few has so regularly confused attempts to comprehend the whole literature of the war that, in this section of my study, I have tried to come to grips with the whole pedestrian bulk of my sub-literary source material. Mass measures of literature invariably

10. *Women*, p. x.
11. Spiller, Thorp, Johnson, and Canby, eds., *Literary History of the United States*, II, 882-85. The novel in question is De Forest, *Miss Ravenel's Conversion from Secession to Loyalty.*

have a clumsy look, of course, and those taken by historians usually demonstrate them to be more competent at cataloguing literature than at summarizing its content. Still, I think that in the novelist's answer to a historian's question we can come closest to finding a common denominator which will illustrate the contributions of novelists in general, as opposed to artists in particular, to our knowledge of the past. By reserving notable achievements for later analysis, I hope to avoid the critical confusion which comes with representing the best novels as samples of the whole literature.

My cross section of all the Civil War novels is based on fiction's report of a controversial moment in history about which historians are disagreed. My selected issue is the endlessly debated problem of why the Civil War was fought. If in the average run of novels about the war there are maintained tenable hypotheses for answers to such an issue, then the novelist wins the right to judgment by standards usually reserved for more formal scholarship. A report of the causes of the war, according to fiction, provides a means for sketching in the variety of historical viewpoints found in fiction, and indicates, at the same time, the novelist's method in handling conventional historical material.

I chose the origins of the conflict for my test theme because I found no other subject through which the whole literature could be surveyed. The author of the most ephemeral romance must take a stand on the meaning of secession and war, even if his work is only remotely concerned with grave national problems. Very few of the novels here considered are so localized and personalized that the sources of sectional division are completely ignored. Tales of high courage, scenes of tender renunciation, or reports of noble sacrifice demand purpose and principle if the illusions of fiction are to be warmed by the breath of reality. Historical interpretations may not be explicitly stated, but they must at least be implied in any convincing account of life during the Civil War. Heroes cannot prove themselves against unnamed villains, nor can brave defenders of the right mount their ramparts without due cause.

No very decisive chronology asserts itself in the following summary of the theories by which fiction has explained the coming of the war. Every major theme developed to reveal why the war came was at least indicated in the forty-odd novels which were written before the last shot was fired—[12] as the generations passed only the degree of emphasis on various factors changed. The notable distinction between the "modern" Civil War novel and work cut to a nineteenth-century pattern appears to be a result of changing literary standards, rather than of changing historical views. For many years after the war the burden of history proved almost too much for novelists who wrote of the conflict. Authors seemed dominated by the impulse to make clear their interpretation of the war, and only after identifying their own position did they attend seriously their normal task of story telling. They loaded their books with elaborate sets of historical generalizations, theories of human behavior, explanations of forces—abstractions which tagged along near the fictional narrative but often had little to do with its completion. This urge to interpret led to bad novels and bad history; and until the demands of art were reasserted over the impulse to partisanship, historical fiction lacked life, focus, and unity. In more recent Civil War novels historical generalizations may be implied, but they are revealed as essential elements in the personalities of the heroes and villains described. "New" views of the war, therefore, represent analysis which can be completed with a report of individual behavior and opinion. The current versions of war causes in fiction seem to be the result of a tighter and better disciplined literary form, of a more sophisticated grasp of human behavior, rather than the result of changing views of the conflict.

This contrast in purposes—between the novelist operating as frustrated historian and the story teller satisfied with the nat-

12. The same observation may be made about formal histories of the war. For a summary of the views and methods of historians dealing with the causes of the war, see Beale, "What Historians Have Said about the Causes of the Civil War," *Theory and Practice of Historical Study.*

ural limits of his trade—is the basis for the division in the following analysis of fiction's report of war causes. In the first section I have tried to demonstrate the difficulties facing the novelist who embraced the historian's orthodoxies and forced into fictional patterns study of the war as the fruit of evil conspiracies, as the result of conflicting constitutional theories, or as the inevitable collision between freedom and slavery. I have then attempted to illustrate performance according to more recent standards, by which novelists have tended to restrict their interpretations to individual particulars, have sought to illuminate cultures through complete understanding of persons within them, and have emphasized their explorations in irrational as well as rational patterns of ante-bellum behavior.

II
History Frustrates the Novelist

Let me say at the outset that neither North nor South produced during the war any "standard" version of war causes: the contradictions and doubts expressed even in the novels of the early sixties surprise a reader accustomed to the totality of twentieth-century war. Majority views, of course, were expressed by abolitionists or by southern ladies whose blind faith in the righteousness of their respective causes led to bitter documents in sectional hatred. Yet there remains a surprising element of sectional self-criticism, an occasional effort at impartial commentary which transcended the shallow limits of official propaganda. As I have already pointed out, almost any interpretation one is inclined to label "new" is likely to have been worked in novels contemporary with the war—a fact which not only builds respect for the reporters involved but which also discourages any confident presentation of chronological schemes or ideological patterns.

According to the authors of the 1860's, the Civil War, like most wars the world has known, was fought *against* an immediate threat—against a conspiracy to divide and destroy the union, a plot to set slaves over their masters, or calculated destruction of republican and constitutional government. Primary emphasis was placed on fear of the enemy's purpose rather than explanation of the friend's ambition. The northern view of such imminent disaster was stated in elaborate indictments of a southern conspiracy that had matured through generations. James Roberts Gilmore, Yankee businessman and contributor to the New York *Tribune,* relied on his background as a cotton broker to acquaint him with the plot for "Southern Empire."[13] In 1835, he said, the Knights of the Golden Circle had been organized by John C. Calhoun and William L. Porcher, with their "sole object the dissolution of the Union and the establishment of a Southern Empire...."[14] *Among the Pines* was more travelogue than novel, and its realistic details reinforced its assertion that it was "by means of ... [the Knights'] secret but powerful machinery that the Southern States were plunged into revolution, in defiance of the will of a majority of their voting population." Gilmore described plans for a southern union with Cuba and Mexico which would establish, even without the adherence of the border states, a nation with a population of twenty million: "We are founding, sir, an empire that will be able to defy all Europe—one grander than the world has seen since the age of Pericles."

Gilmore, subsequently prominent as one of the union's peace messengers to Jefferson Davis in 1864, was careful in this novel of 1862 to deny that Lincoln or his cabinet were abolitionists; in their administration, he said, the South would have found protection for southern property. He shared this view with a number of northern novelists, who, avoiding abolitionist

13. *DAB,* VII, 309-10. Gilmore subsequently played an interesting role as a behind-the-scenes representative for anti-Lincoln forces, before his conversion to admiration for the President after a visit with the latter in 1864. He was then active during the exchange of peace feelers that year with Jefferson Davis.

14. Gilmore, *Among the Pines.*

extremes, based the North's case on the union versus treason and conspiracy. Abolitionist writers, on the other hand, were able to state the conspiracy case in even stronger terms, for the "Southern Empire" became the "Slave Power," ruled by "men in favor of lynching, torturing, murdering those opposed to their institution." To Epes Sargent, Boston editor, abolitionist, spiritualist, "Slavery is the cause of war and must end."[15] Slavery had plunged the nation into the Mexican adventure, "for the lords of the lash well knew that to circumscribe their system was to doom it, and that without ever new fields for extension it could not live and prosper." The southern states had continued along the route of conspiracy and treason to raise an army for seizure of the border states and Washington. Loyal Southerners were unable to offer effective opposition to the movement, for "the whole code and temper of the South reply to you, that men *may* not differ, and *shall* not differ, on the subject of slavery."

More moderate Northerners stressed the simpler idea of giving protection against treason to a union which had produced "the best system of government known to the history of the world. . . ." Patriotic citizens could have no choice but to spring to defense of the glorious flag, "insulted and disgraced" by "red-handed traitors." Henry Morford, who wrote these words in *The Days of Shoddy,* was a Democrat who saw elements other than patriotism in his own side's effort, however. Selfless loyalty was supported by northern greed in its opposition to southern treason. The villain of his work was a merchant whose concern with secession and war was waked by his early fears that southern debts to northern businessmen might be repudiated, and maintained by his subsequent discovery that war meant profit and power to the shrewd entrepreneur.

The element of self-criticism in northern description of the war effort, which was in Morford's case expression of a Democratic point of view, was on occasion carried to the extent of

15. *Peculiar.* "Peculiar," the slave hero of this novel, bears the surname, "Institution."

complete detachment, to attempt to present an impartial review of the laudable ends sought by both armies. In 1862, Benjamin Wood, brother of New York's Mayor Fernando Wood and Democratic Representative to the United States Congress, made in *Fort Lafayette* a remarkable effort to give the arguments of all parties to the conflict. His hero was a loyalist who denied the right of secession as one "which is utterly inconsistent with any legislative power. We either have a government or we have not. If we have one, it must possess within itself the power to sustain itself." Affection for the union, "our pride and the world's wonder," was offered as the primary motive behind the North's decision for war. Other union views, however, were also suggested. "A tall, thin gentleman, with a white cravat and a bilious complexion," spoke for the glorious opportunity to "win God's smile by setting a brand in the hand of the bondman to scourge his master. . . . Assuredly unless we arouse the slave to seize the torch and the dagger, and avenge the wrongs of his race, Providence will frown upon our efforts, and our arms will not prevail." To such ideas, sharp opposition was expressed by an officer of the army, who declared that "The people will not arm if abolition is to be the watchword." Protection of southern institutions, the military man declared, had to be guaranteed. The patriot, soldier, and abolitionist all reject the concepts of the man of wealth, a "stout gentleman" who saw in the maintenance of the union "security . . . for property." "It is money, sir, money," he said, "that settles every question of the present day, and our money will bring these beggarly rebels to their senses."

Southerners were represented in this argument by a Virginia belle whose concern lay in protection of her slaves from the "world's cold charity," and who defended them against "Northern fanaticism as firmly as I would guard my children from the interference of a stranger, were I a mother." She saw "the spirit of abolition sitting in the executive chair" and predicted that soldier and demagogue would destroy northern liberty if they succeeded in subjugating the South by arming the slaves. The warmth of her argument was supported by the logic of another Virginian, who pointed to the impossibility of controlling six million citizens with bayonets. He stated a faith in the right of local self-government and declared that "the General Government was never a sovereignty, and came into existence only by the consent of each and every individual State." The right of coercion was specifically denied.

Insofar as the author presents a point of view in *Fort Lafayette*—if his views can be singled out from the various arguments he presented—it appeared in the comments of his detached observer, an Englishman who had traveled through both North and South. The observer declared:

I like your country; I like your people. I have observed foibles in the North and in the South, but there is an undercurrent of strong feeling and good sense which I have noted and admired. I think your quarrel is one of foibles—one conceived in the spirit of exaltation. I believed the professed mutual hatred of the sections to be superficial, and that could be cancelled. It is fostered by the bitterness of fanatics, assisted by a very natural disinclination on the part of the masses to yield a disputed point. If hostilities should cease to-morrow, you would be better friends than ever.[16]

Devotees of the Confederacy were not so generous in recognizing potentiality for virtue in the opposing side. In their catalogue of southern rights, there was no room for compromise, no suggestion that reasonable alternatives to secession had existed. "Political bondage—worse than Russian serfdom —or armed resistance; no other alternative, turn it which way you will; and the Southern people are not of stuff to deliberate as to choice in such an issue. God is witness that we have earnestly endeavored to avert hostilities—that the blood of this war rests upon the government at Washington; our hands are stainless." Thus Augusta Jane Evans Wilson saw the war crisis, and her rigid views were shared by other ladies on whom was placed the burden of defense of the South in fiction.[17]

16. Wood, *Fort Lafayette*, pp. 114-15.
17. *Macaria*, p. 340. More than half the pro-southern novels of the war era which are in the Wilmer Collection were written by women. In contrast, the lady novelists produced only 25 per cent of the North's wartime fiction.

"The sole enthusiasm of my life," said the author of *Macaria,* "was born, lived, and perished in the eventful four years of the Confederacy."[18] According to her view, the union was destroyed with Lincoln's election in 1860, when "Abolitionism, so long adroitly cloaked, was triumphantly clad in robes of state—shameless now, and hideous, and while the North looked upon the loathsome face of its political Mokanna, the South prepared for resistance." The course for this resistance had been clearly labeled by the "sleepless watchmen on the tower of Southern Rights—faithful guardians like William L. Yancey, who had stood for years in advance of public opinion, lifting their warning voices far above the howling waves of popular faction and party strife, pointing to the only path to safety. . . ." Southerners claimed confirmation of the soundness of their policies after the rapid destruction of constitutional forms and traditional liberties by the new administration. "Liberty fled from her polluted fane, and sought shelter and shrine on the banner of the Confederacy, in the dauntless, devoted hearts of its unconquerable patriots." A serene future lay before the South (*Macaria* was published in 1864), which held promise of enjoyment of life as a homogeneous people, "with no antagonistic systems of labor, necessitating conflicting interests." Gone forever was the virulent seed of New England Puritanism, which "springs up pertinaciously where even a shred is permitted."

The overpowering rhetoric of Mrs. Wilson was a major gun in the batteries of southern propaganda. The effect of *Macaria* on the morale of the invading unionists was reported to have been so great that certain Federal officers ordered it burned.[19] Civilians in the North, better hardened, perhaps, than the military to such prolix sentimentality, suffered the work to be published in New York the same year it appeared in Richmond.

Another lady novelist sought more subtle purposes than abolition alone in the aggressive policies of the North. Slavery

18. *DAB,* VI, 195-96.
19. *Ibid.*

was only a pretext for northern opposition to southern rights, said Mary Ann Cruse. Without slavery, the North would have found other rights to curtail: "This will be no war, on the part of the South, in defense of negro slavery; as well say that the Revolution was a war for the tea overturned in Boston harbor."[20] Secession was entered upon only after "wonderful forbearance," when repeated compromise on sectional issues had shown the North to be conciliatory only to a more convenient season for the reduction of southern rights. "Up to a certain point forbearance is a virtue, and that point the South has already reached. Tame submission to oppression and wrong is cowardice; it is what she has never done and will never do."

The exact ambition of the scheming North is nowhere defined; Mrs. Cruse merely spoke with grave alarm of the "jealousies of governments and the machinations of politicians." She took reluctant notice of the cost which the Confederacy would have to pay for its birth; "the best blood of the land" would be the price for the defeat of the "refuse population of European cities" constituting the northern armies. "It will be in this respect . . . a most unequal contest."

Suggestion of divided opinion in the respectable South was rarely present in novels by southern patriots. An occasional southern unionist wrote novels about the war, but the only outlet for such writing was in the northern publishing houses, if the surviving books give accurate testimony. It was in the post-war period that such writings were popular; I have found only one which was published before the end of 1865. In *Tobias Wilson, A Tale of the Great Rebellion,* Jeremiah Clemens, former United States senator and major general in the service of the "Republic of Alabama," expressed the unionist view after his departure to Federal territory.[21] Despite his own

20. Cruse, *Cameron Hall,* p. 81. The manuscript for this novel, according to the author, a Virginia-born schoolteacher of Huntsville, Alabama, was prepared during the war and left unchanged when it was later published.

21. *DAB,* IV, 191-92. Clemens was a member of a well-to-do Alabama family. His career included service as a Federal district attorney, as a commissioned officer in the Mexican War, as senator (1849) from

signature on Alabama's ordinance of secession, he saw in the movement for division a violation by wily politicians of the southern majority will. He denied that there was danger to the South in the conditions of 1861 and declared that "There has never been a time when our peculiar institution was hedged round with so many defenses as it now is. . . ."

Clemens' conclusions differ from the dominant note of the other opinions reviewed only in the quality of his emotions. Novelists who wrote while the war was raging believed that their trials were the result of schemes of ambitious and unworthy men. Northerners found the arrogant planter-politician the villain, while Southerners feared the destruction of their rights and their society by the aggressive hypocrisy of a Puritan North. The southern apportionment of blame was very definite, and southern opinions were less divided than northern ones on the sources of the crisis. Submerged themes in these early novels, however, were the roots of arguments which matured through succeeding years. One by one, subordinate factors have been examined elaborately, inflated, and given a prominent place in the novel's continuing reflection on the war's causes. Authors have sought to prove the validity of the constitutional theories that divided the sections; to indicate the economic bases of patriotism; and to suggest how the northern and southern cultures were separated by their way of living, by artificially contrived misinformation about each other, by biological differences, and by irrational emotions. In adjusting their arguments to the post-war realities, Southerners had the greater concessions to make, for their war literature had not been tempered by the degree of introspection and self-criticism which had been a part of the North's writing. The South had not been inclined, under the pressure of military invasion, to lift the "intellectual blockade"[22] it had maintained in ante-

---

Alabama, and as a member in the Alabama Secession Convention. Despite his opposition to the secession ordinance, he signed and became a major general in the Alabama militia. His unionist tendencies led to unpopularity, however, and he went North in 1862 where he was active as a pamphleteer against the course of his native state.

22. Eaton, *Freedom of Thought in the Old South,* pp. 331-32.

bellum times against public expression of doubt about the
justice of its beliefs and institutions. Southerners, moreover,
were not an introspective people given to analysis of their fail-
ings, despite their possession of some disastrously effective
logicians.[23] They were not accustomed to wrestling with their
souls. Also, they did not enter the war with an organized political party out of office, ready to capitalize on administration
mistakes in the hope of taking power. The North was simply
under less pressure than the South and did not reach its peak
of unanimity until it was flushed with the righteousness of
victory. Victory, of course, settled much argument—particularly
on the problem of slavery—and subsequent northern novels
were for a time more decisive in their explanation of the war
crisis.

Northern authors, once the war was over, could continue
their dependence on reports of treacherous conspiracies and
fanatic southern plots. Southerners, on the other hand, had to
abandon some of their wartime themes; their changed attitude
toward a dead Lincoln, and their necessary adaptation to the
war's results, put a damper on their castigations of secret
cabals and monstrous ambitions. Irreconcilable Southerners
turned toward analysis of the "insidious sophistries" of such
men as Daniel Webster and devoted themselves to demonstra-
tions of error in northern constitutional theory.[24] Northerners
remained comfortable in the notion that victory had confirmed
their more extreme views of the war years; in 1868, Henry
Ward Beecher[25] observed that thoughtful southern politicians
had entered the decade "fully determined at all hazards to
separate from the North. It was not a sudden freak but a matured purpose." Concessions and compromises by the North
were hopeless from the start, for such efforts were attempts to
"prescribe for the wrong disease. The South had no grievances

23. Cash, *The Mind of the South,* pp. 94-99.
24. Floyd, *Thorns in the Flesh,* published as a refutation of Tourgée's *A Fool's Errand.*
25. *Norwood,* pp. 382-83. Note the similarity of this point of view
with that expressed by Von Holst, *The Constitutional and Political
History of the United States,* VII, 458.

whatever . . . it *had* ambitions, and was determined to realize them."

Sweeping generalizations about a whole region rising in secret conspiracy against the union or against southern institutions tended to be reduced, soon after the war, to specific identification of the conspirators and plots involved. The conspiracy theme in fiction survived past the turn of the century as a major explanation for the coming of the war, but it shrank to size rather more quickly than did scholarly presentations of the same hypothesis. As the years passed, the charity of William Mumford Baker, a persecuted unionist preacher of Texas, became more and more typical of the northern attitude toward the disunion movement. Baker was satisfied in 1866 to lay the secession plot at the door of a "minority," and devoted his novel, *Inside,* to analysis of the techniques by which unscrupulous editors and preachers manipulated public opinion. As noted an abolitionist as Lydia Maria Child restricted her 1867 report of the conspiracy to mild comments on the "heartless gambling" of politicians.[26]

The southern plot as seen through northern eyes gradually shrank to the incidents of the closing days of President James Buchanan's administration, when the lack of decisive action against disunionism lent credence to reports of official sympathy with the southern cause. The novelists have not joined certain recent historians in sympathetic reinterpretation of President Buchanan's course during the last months of his administration. They have ignored monographic notice of the "principles" involved in his adherence to the idea of compromise, his respect for "Congressional representation of public opinion," his belief in the right of minority groups to protection, and most of all, his horror at the use of "bloodshed as cement for the union."[27] In fiction Buchanan has been some-

26. *A Romance of the Republic,* p. 403.
27. Klingberg, "James Buchanan and the Crisis of the Union," *Jour. So. Hist.,* IX (Nov., 1943), 474. Auchampaugh, in *James Buchanan and His Cabinet on the Eve of Secession* and in numerous articles, was the historian longest active in pleas for a "generous judgment" of Buchanan.

what contemptuously low-rated for his "weak indecision"—a
view which involves acceptance of the hypothetical conclusion
that "action" of some sort might have prevented disunion and
war. Novelists have in particular concentrated on the "equivo-
cal role" played by Secretary of War John B. Floyd in selling
arms to the South.[28] This is their "concrete evidence" of treason
in high places. Edward P. Roe concluded that "all talk of compromise on the part of the Southern leaders was deceptive—
that they were relentlessly pursuing the course marked out
from the first, hoping, undoubtedly, that the government would
be paralyzed by their allies at the North, and that their purposes would be effected by negotiation and Foreign intervention. . . ."[29] Southerners believed, however, that official circles
of the period were pregnant with "delusive art" and that the
Confederate Commissioners were detained "until certain war-
like preparations were secretly made" before rejection of southern plans for peaceful division. Under these circumstances, the
relief of Fort Sumter was "a defiance and provocative of
war. . . ."[30]

Novelists of both the North and the South concentrated more
and more on the importance of individuals rather than parties
and combinations in their examination of the plots of 1861.
Recognition of political opportunism as a greater factor than
conscious intrigue was the result of this changing view. The
"blundering generation" recently indicted by historian James
G. Randall appeared regularly in these accounts.[31] War as the
result of the failure of statesmanship, rather than the success of
conspiracy, became a standard interpretation of late nineteenth-

28. R. F. Nichols, *The Disruption of American Democracy*, p. 426.
Nichols concluded that "either . . . [Floyd] had a careless faith in the
failure of secession, or he was helping possible enemies of his country."
Auchampaugh exonerated him almost completely, however, and concluded that the Secretary of War was no more than the "scapegoat of
Northern public opinion." Auchampaugh, *Buchanan and His Cabinet*,
p. 89.
29. *His Sombre Rivals*, p. 188.
30. Russell, *Roebuck*, p. 57.
31. "The Blundering Generation," *Miss. Val. Hist. Rev.*, XXVII
(June, 1940), 3-28.

century writers. In all the South on the eve of war, wrote Virginius Dabney in 1886, "there was not to be found one solitary statesman; nor one throughout the length and breadth of the North."

For years before we came to blows the animosity between North and South had been deepening, reaching at last this point, that he who would catch the ear of either side could do so only by fierce denunciation of the other; he that would have it thought that he loved *us* had only to show that he hated *you*. Men of moderation found no hearers. The voices of the calm and clear-headed sank into silence; and Wigfall and Toombs, and Sumner and Phillips walked up and down the land.

Yes, no doubt we had thousands of statesmen who knew better. But who knew *them?* And so Seward kept piping of peace in ninety days, and Yancey—Polyphemus of politicians—was willing to drink all the blood that would be shed. A Yankee wouldn't fight, said the one. The slave-drivers, perhaps, would, said the other; but they were, after all, a mere handful; and the poor white trash would be as flocks of sheep.[32]

The plots of leaders, earlier regarded as refined evidence of Machiavellian skill, were thus replaced more and more frequently by studies of the popular influence of extremist politicians. "It's a funny thing to me," observed Joseph A. Altsheler in 1900, "that the people of this country, who do most things so well, and are so keen, should allow themselves to be led off by any man with the gift of gab that comes along."[33] The conclusion of more recent writers seems to be that of John Erskine, who attributed to Ralph Waldo Emerson reflections on the political incapacity of the American people: "The question of slavery will not down," this fictional Emerson said, "and we lack the political wisdom to grapple with it. Strange that our fathers did not bring from England the political talent."[34]

In considering the failure of political leaders, however, the novelists are agreed only on the fact that they did fail; in specific assignment of praise and blame, the writers have stated widely divergent views. President Lincoln, for instance, was

32. Dabney, *The Story of Don Miff,* pp. 440-41.
33. *In Circling Camps,* p. 21.
34. Erskine, *The Start of the Road,* p. 233.

accused by J. V. Ryals of critical irresponsibility because of his failure to commit himself earlier on the right of the federal government to coerce a state.[35] In similar vein, Tom Watson noted that "had Mr. Lincoln lifted a finger in favor" of such a proposal as extension of the Missouri Compromise line, the war might have been averted.[36] On the other hand, Thomas Dixon, most professional of Southerners, saw the President as God's chosen instrument for the salvation of the nation. "No such responsibility was ever before laid on the shoulders of one man. In all the history of the world he has no precedent, no guide—"[37] Orthodox worshippers at the Lincoln shrine have exempted their hero from the criticisms which they have applied to lesser figures and have elevated the war-time president to a level quite removed from the worldly plane on which ordinary politicians operated. Lincoln's decisions and reflections have been presented as prophetic visions, informed by sure knowledge of ultimate consequences. Typical is Honoré Willsie Morrow's portrayal of his decision to relieve Fort Sumter—to her a step taken as a knowing invocation of war, a war consciously begun for freedom's purpose.[38] Less prominent leaders were not often treated with much respect. Stephen A. Douglas and Franklin Pierce were characterized by Winston Churchill as "playing at bowls on the United States of America; while Kansas was furnishing excitement free of charge to any citizens who loved sport. . . ."[39] Men like Douglas, Churchill said, were

35. *Yankee Doodle Dixie*, p. 354.
36. *Bethany*, p. 108.
37. *The Southerner*, p. 105.
38. *Forever Free.* On such a debated issue as Lincoln's purpose in sending a relief expedition to Fort Sumter, the novelist is thus privileged to write without burdening decisive opinion with the doubts and the qualifications which a cautious historian must feel. Charles W. Ramsdell, however, largely agreed with Morrow's view of the Sumter relief as a conscious maneuver which forced the South to fire the war's first shot. James G. Randall also reports the significant evidence in the Orville H. Browning diary which confirms this thesis, but concludes that Lincoln simply took the course which "offered the nearest approach to the preservation of the *status quo* which was possible." Ramsdell, "Lincoln and Fort Sumter," *Jour. So. Hist.*, III (Aug., 1937), 259-88. Randall, *The Civil War and Reconstruction*, p. 238.
39. *The Crisis*, p. 13.

"capable of sacrifice to their country"; but "personal ambition is, nevertheless, the mainspring of their actions." The crisis in Kansas he attributed to the necessity which the Little Giant felt for remaining in the public eye. The passing of "that race of supermen"—Clay, Calhoun, Webster, and their contemporaries—was evidence to the Thomas Dixon of 1921, however, that the voice of the mob had replaced responsible leadership by 1861. A United States which "had been shaped from its birth through the heart and brain of its leaders" had given way to "the process of leveling."[40] Men like Douglas, constructive statesmen in Dixon's eye, were helpless before the popular tendency "to degrade power, to scatter talent, to pull down our leaders to the level of the mob, in the name of democracy."[41]

Similar interpretation of the mass pressures within the sections which exploded into war have virtually eliminated efforts to fix responsibility for the conflict on single individuals. Artistic problems, too, have made historical novelists very cautious in mingling prominent historical characters with the creatures of fiction. Among their countless efforts to introduce in intimate fashion the public men of 1861, they failed regularly in their effort to present a completely realized personality. The contradictions inherent in human behavior violate art's demand that action and reaction proceed from logical motives. The recorded facts of biography pose too many insoluble questions for the novelist to answer in his effort to tell why men act as they do. Since history limits fiction's right to mold historical character to fit the artist's conception of the past, successful twentieth-century Civil War novels have depended largely on imaginative persons entirely subservient to the author.

40. Dixon, *The Man in Gray,* p. 8.
41. *Ibid.,* pp. 8, 26. To Dixon, Douglas' stature grew from innate personal superiority, rather than from the principles which the Little Giant espoused. Dixon contradicts Churchill's view of the Illinois leader as no more than an opportunistic politician, but he fails to reach the modern view of the man most notable for national vision, when sectional leadership was in the ascendency. For a sympathetic account of Douglas, see Milton, *The Eve of Conflict.* A good brief reinterpretation of Douglas is offered by Randall, *The Civil War and Reconstruction,* pp. 128-35 and *passim.*

Whatever the reason, interpretation of the coming of the war through analysis of the actions of leading statesmen is a phenomenon of the nineteenth- rather than twentieth-century fiction. There are still occasional attempts to utilize dramatic careers as the subject of fiction, but the resulting novels have not overcome the difficulties noted above. Reference to specific schemers who designed the war has been subordinated to less tangible factors; writers have turned to reflection on the insignificance of puny men, pitted against vast social forces—a trend which has eliminated from many novels any effort to fix personal blame at all.

Declining emphasis on theories of conspiracy left many southern novelists of the late nineteenth and early twentieth century dependent on the South's second major rationalization for her conduct in 1861. In the measured logic by which the doctrine of state rights was inflated from a means to an end among constitutional theorists of the South, the pro-Confederate novelists found principles to which the most high-minded hero could be devoted. Defense of slavery, as we will see, embarrassed them; the passage of time let them look back to see that the most radical of Republicans might have acted from honest motives; but these intellectual concessions to the northern victory only inspired a more fervent devotion to theories of state sovereignty. For years after the war, novelists were so well versed in the intricacies of state rights doctrine that they reduced it to a sort of mumbling creed, an undertone accompanying most accounts of southern patriotism. They treated state rights argument as a structure of such transparent simplicity, such self-evident authenticity, that its conclusions could be chanted as first principles for all logical thought about the war. Like Jefferson Davis, "Constitutionalist," they wrote to prove that the "Southern states had rightfully the power to withdraw from a union into which they had, as sovereign communities, voluntarily entered; that the denial of that right was a violation of the letter and spirit of the compact between the states; and that the war waged by the federal government against the seceding states was in disregard of the limitations of the Constitution, and destructive of the principles of the

Declaration of Independence."[42] Mrs. Sallie F. Chapin found the relation of a state to the nation as clear as that of a family to a church congregation. "Joining the church does not interfere with our family relations. Our minister takes care of the religious interests of his people; but you would not permit him to manage your family affairs, or correct your children,—these are your reserved rights; and his are so distinct, it seems impossible to clash."[43]

Simple analogies did not satisfy more vehement advocates of the state sovereignty principle. J. V. Ryals weighted his *Yankee Doodle Dixie* with a heavy burden of political commentary which reviewed events since 1800, when popular endorsement of the authors of the Virginia and Kentucky Resolves fixed on American politics the principles that were "strictly adhered to by the dominant parties clear down to the election of Mr. Lincoln in 1860."[44] The Missouri Compromise was "beyond a shadow of a doubt" unconstitutional, because of the violence it did to rights guaranteed in the compact to the person and property of citizens in the states. Northern statutes in "clear contravention" of established southern rights were borne with wonderful patience by the South, before the final legal remedy was sought. Further, "The doctrine that any State might secede in case of a plain and palpable violation of the Federal Constitution had been admitted by every statesman of any distinction from the foundation of the government to the election of Lincoln."

Southerners were moved by no "sordid fear of losing their slaves," said Mrs. Flora McDonald Williams. Secession pro-

42. Jefferson Davis, *The Rise and Fall of the Confederate Government*, I, vii.

43. Chapin, *Fitz-Hugh St. Clair,* p. 55.

44. Ryals prefaced his work with a standard promise to readers: "I have tried to give a clear, concise, and accurate statement of the facts and circumstances which culminated in the war between the States, because I believe a full knowledge of all the facts, and a clear understanding of the feelings and opinions to which they give rise, is the only ground upon which the North and the South can meet in friendly greetings, and the only means that can be employed that will destroy sectional prejudices and sectional animosities."

ceeded from "the firm conviction that sacred rights had been assailed" and the "South rose as a man to defend them . . . in a manner which she interpreted to be lawful and a just one."[45] Inordinate stress on the idea of "firm conviction" was the central idea in the fictional account of the southern rights movement. Any southern motive could be purified through a convincing demonstration of "honest" conviction. Readers with either northern or southern sympathies were invited to stand reverently before a spectacle which might include sectional suicide, but which was thus all the more proof of the moral stature attained by a South willing to sacrifice all for "principle."

A peculiar phenomenon of the novels emphasizing this argument was their concentration on the action of Virginia in 1861 —a phase in the chronology of Civil War novels which coincided with refinement of the state rights motif. "Virginia neither desired nor countenanced Secession. The hot-headed impulsiveness of South Carolina was not reflected by the great calm state which had given Washington to the land and was soon to give Lee as evidence of the quality of her manhood."[46] Lincoln's call to arms, however, put the issues so clearly that "There was only one course [Virginia] could pursue." Such exposition of the southern argument in terms of Virginia's action involved more than sturdy maintenance of the state sovereignty concept. Description of the reluctance with which the Old Dominion departed was in a negative sense praise for the glory of the old union. The state's decision, cast in sorrow rather than in triumph, was convincing proof of the South's devotion to principle, even at great cost. Guilt there might have been in such a course, but it was a guilt possessed of its own absolution. Devotion to principle is a virtue honored by all men, and neither disagreement with nor defeat of its premises can tarnish its bright purpose. Sure defeat might be a predictable consequence of Virginia's support of the Confederacy; nevertheless, the young Southerner cries, "That's why

45. Williams, *Who's the Patriot?* p. 37.
46. Brady, *The Patriots,* p. 23.

I'm going to fight for them. . . . They stand for a principle—their equal rights under the Republic their fathers created. They haven't paused to figure success or failure."[47]

The pre-eminent symbol of Virginia's reaction to the crisis was the person and decision of Robert E. Lee, whose "feelings did not make him hesitate a moment as to his course. . . . Virginia called him, the land of his fathers, the land of his wife, the land of his children, the land of his friends—his home. Whatever happened he was hers. . . . He was a Virginian first, a citizen of the United States second."[48] Lee knew that "There is no such thing as citizenship of the Nation. . . . We are as yet a Union of Sovereign States."[49] And in the end, the career of the "Man in Gray" was a monument to principle—principle identified by Thomas Dixon as "reverence for law." To Lee and to the other fictional statesmen presented by the novelists, all of whom were men who had given fullest proof of their loyalty to the union, the breaking point in the crisis came with the call for volunteers. "The Virginians believed firmly and without doubt or question in the right of any state to withdraw from the Union at will." They regarded the coercion of a seceding state "as iniquity, a crime, a proceeding unspeakably wrongful and subversive of liberty."[50] In the simplest definition, by history or by logic, right of secession was self-evident. "That word [secession] . . . means . . . that Virginia leaves of her free will a Union that she entered of her free will. The terms of that Union have been broken; she cannot, within it, preserve her integrity, her dignity, and her liberty. Therefore she uses the right which she reserved—the right of self-preservation. Unterrified she entered the Union, unterrified she leaves it."[51]

Novelists of the two generations succeeding the war proved fit successors to the generations of logicians, politicians, preachers, teachers, and editors who had drummed the ideas of state

47. Dixon, *The Southerner,* p. 152.
48. Brady, *The Patriots,* preface, n.p.
49. Dixon, *The Man in Gray,* pp. 345, 414.
50. G. C. Eggleston, *Dorothy South,* p. 384.
51. Johnston, *The Long Roll,* p. 37.

sovereignty into the American mind. In romance, adventure, and veiled polemic the whole paraphernalia of the argument was maintained, documented, and grafted in its complete outlines to the literary traditions left by the crisis years. In the expression of this theme, authors very frequently laid aside imagined characters to surround the principle with the authority of their living personalities as students, historians, and memorialists.

Writers sympathetic to northern principles have avoided any comparable effort to expound the legal views of Story, Webster, Seward, or Lincoln. They have registered their disagreement with the southern conclusions, but have spent little time developing their own ideas in fact and argument. They have tended to admit, with the Southerners, that the "seeds of the great rebellion were really sown in the convention which framed our constitution."[52] The "pernicious and dangerous doctrines" of the South have been regularly denounced and condemned, but by refutation categorical, not logical. The North's humanitarian purpose, and its intuitive outrage at the spectacle of a violated union, have been its preferred weapons against the ponderous machinery of southern constitutional debate.[53] Northerners have reacted in some indignation against what they regard as the South's higgling affection for irrelevant argument. "I defy anyone to point out an instance where they have been deprived of their rights," says the northern church-

52. Musick, *Union,* p. v. Musick carefully maintains in this work the following plan of composition: "Throughout the series I have adhered to the original plan of making fiction subordinate to history, even at the expense of unity." Unity paid very heavily, for great chunks of factual review, unrelated to plot and action, interrupt this last volume in a series of historical novels which ranged in time back to the voyages of Columbus.

53. Novelists are not the only northern writers who have confused emotional pleading and categorical judgments with reasoned refutation of southern constitutional argument. John W. Burgess, for instance, saw in northern victory "the plan of universal history." He found arguments for the right of secession, "from every point of view, a mere juggling with words." Lincoln's views, said Burgess, in 1901, "are today unquestioned by any true jurist or political scientist." Burgess, *The Civil War and the Constitution,* pp. 24, 76, 135.

man sketched by Edgar Lee Masters. "We are willing that they should have their slavery, bad as it is, and all rights properly belonging to them. But no, they must have all, or destroy all."[54]

Southern novelists of recent years have reduced their emphasis on the state rights theme, not because they have changed their minds about their argument, but because rising literary standards have tended to eliminate the artistic monstrosity of a political pamphlet embedded in fiction. The season for leisurely digression into abstract argument is past; recent novelists are careful not to abuse the tolerance of their readers by setting out constitutional argument which does not rise logically from their selected themes.

Also, modern southern writers do not appear to be nearly so self-conscious as were their nineteenth-century forebears on the issue of slavery. The earlier group turned to constitutional debate, in considerable part, so that they could avoid the embarrassment of defending the institution. If Southerners admitted the war was fought to free slaves, then the conflict was put in terms which left their cause unpalatable to the post-war reader; they insisted, therefore, that slavery was only a pretext for the northern assault on republican institutions. They hurried to declare themselves enemies of slavery—so bitter a Rebel as N. J. Floyd, for instance, defined slavery in 1884 as "A thorn, grown into the very flesh and blood of the country and of society."[55] Similarly J. V. Ryals contributed a hero who, on the eve of the conflict, was "no advocate of slavery" and who looked forward to the day "which should behold with safety to the mingling races, the black man disenthralled and regenerated by the genius of universal emancipation. . . ."[56]

Northerners, untroubled by the necessity of changing their ground in this argument, depended heavily on their version of the war as an anti-slavery crusade. The problem was simple: ". . . when the touchstone of human reason was applied to the fabric of chattel slavery—property in human beings—it fell."

54. Masters, *The Tide of Time*, pp. 178-79.
55. *Thorns in the Flesh*, frontispiece.
56. *Yankee Doodle Dixie*, p. 52.

The mind could not accept "the abomination of the human-brute."[57] "Slavery . . . had long been doomed, like other relics of barbarism, by the spirit of the age," and its elimination was sure, with or without war, by the "irresistible force of the world's opinion. . . ."[58] Southerners, by the time a generation lay between their writing and the war, took little exception to such views. Joseph William Eggleston concluded that "Sane men everywhere saw that the institution could not long endure even if left alone. . . ."[59] Thomas Nelson Page declared that the South, in holding to slavery, was attempting to stay "the power of universal progress."[60]

Slavery, in other words, was doomed, irrespective of the fact that war had ended it. Northern and southern writers were in agreement on this point—though writers at the North empha-sized their partnership with "the God of nations . . ." who "had decreed that slavery, the gangrene in the body politic, must be cut out. . . ."[61] In coming to a similar view, novelists of the South abandoned much of the logic by which their fathers had justified the institution. Ante-bellum spokesmen for the South had seen that if slavery were wrong, no expedient reasons for its preservation would justify it; their argument had been firmly grounded on the physical, spiritual, and social justice of slavery. Subsequent modification of this argument by post-war Southerners required complicated explanations of the sources and growth of slavery. Admitting the evils of a bad system, southern novelists fashioned a back-handed defense from the fact that "blame" for its existence belonged to the North as well as the South and from evidence of a prior concern in the South about the moral issues involved.

According to their report, abolition came to New England only "when the market price of slaves fell to sixpence a pound in the open Boston markets. . . ."[62] Before the spirit of profes-

57. Tourgée, *Toinette*, p. 252.
58. E. P. Roe, *His Sombre Rivals*, p. 186.
59. *Tuckahoe*, p. 146.
60. *Red Rock*, p. 41.
61. E. P. Roe, *His Sombre Rivals*, p. 186.
62. Fox, *The Little Shepherd of Kingdom Come*, p. 218.

sional freedom was abroad in the North, however, many Southerners were freeing their slaves, at considerable personal cost. But Puritan New England, "with that conscience that is a national calamity," was unable to tolerate the wise and cautious plans which were maturing in the South for emancipation and colonization of the slaves. Mary Johnston wrote of Virginians who in 1861 were still struggling for a reasonable approach to the venture of African settlement, hoping against hope that extremists would allow time for a peaceful solution.[63] Robert E. Lee, according to Thomas Dixon, concluded that the "school" of slavery had to close, the Negro race having completed its lessons in agriculture, religion, and the rudiments of civilized life.[64] Robert Toombs, said Tom Watson, saw the futility, however, of hoping for patience at the North while the South settled its problems. "They envy us our wealth and growing power; they will never forgive us that we made a success out of negro slavery where they tried it and failed; they sold us pretty near all the niggers we've got, and now that the slave-trade is at an end and no more money can be made out of us, they clamor for emancipation."[65] The resulting harsh feelings brought the southern reaction which moved in a direction opposite to the emancipation spirit. "The South knows that slavery is wrong even when she says it's not; but

63. *The Long Roll,* p. 13.
64. *The Man in Gray,* p. 75.
65. Watson, *Bethany,* p. 40. Watson's view of envy as being part of the North's reaction against the South is supported by the recent studies by Avery Craven of abnormal abolitionist psychology. According to Craven, the dislocations suffered by the New England farmer led him to "envy and even hatred" of the merchant and industrialist classes who were rising from the ruins of the older economy; and in the Northwest consciousness of the widening gulf between privilege and poverty came with the rise in land prices because of speculative activities. The demand for an English market for wheat, similar to that which existed for cotton, was a first principle of the Liberty party, which also attacked slave-holder opposition to the "sound" commercial policies of the Northeast. As the abolition crusade became more widespread, its effect was to make the slave-holding aristocrat do "scapegoat service for all aristocrats and all sinners. To him were transferred the resentments and fears born out of local conditions." Craven, *The Coming of the Civil War,* pp. 131, 141, 150.

she's been abused so much about it, and charged with so many things that she hasn't done by the Northern people—some of whom are still living on the inherited profits of the slave trade, and whose consciences have spoken late—that she's put her back up, and she says: 'All right; I've got slavery, and I'm going to keep it; what are you going to do about it?' "[66]

It was this latter spirit that northern writers emphasized. Instead of a tendency toward emancipation, they saw in the South an effort by the Slave Power "to hide its deformity with the veil of faith, and take refuge with religion in the sanctuary of simple belief."[67] Even within the churches, Bible chapter and verse were cited so skillfully that abolitionists were forced to resort to "higher law" doctrine to maintain their position.[68] Instead of evidence that slavery was declining toward a moderate end, the North saw it as an increasingly aggressive, brutal system, gravely threatening the bases of free society. Northerners had seen the Senate of the United States yielding to "the lash and spur of the imperial-minded Calhoun." They had discovered in fugitive slave laws that every free man was required to become "the agent of the slavery propagandists, in its support and protection. . . ." The Kansas–Nebraska Act "was equally distasteful, as it thrust slavery, even by fraud and violence, into territory which had been until that day consecrated to freedom."[69] Slavery was the "black, piratical power" that had poisoned the nation from the start, "beating it back from its goal, despoiling it of its priceless heritage. . . ."

The North thus professed to believe that Southerners were primarily *"slave drivers*. . . . That they knew nothing but force, that their whole political system is nothing but the incarnation and the apotheosis of force. . . ."[70] Greater problems in the maintenance of liberty were involved than merely the confinement or expansion of slavery. The Buchanan administration, smiling on the descent of the Supreme Court to pro-slave

66. Altsheler, *In Circling Camps*, p. 22.
67. Tourgée, *Toinette*, p. 253.
68. Le Cato, *Tom Burton*, p. 20.
69. Tourgée, *Toinette*, pp. 250-51.
70. Upton Sinclair, *Manassas*, pp. 263, 267.

propaganda, packing the cabinet against the majority will, plotting against liberty in the territories, was "rapidly demoralizing a free people. . . ."[71] And the very institution demanded that action be taken to prevent "our great, good Republic" from being "turned into a polluted factory of monstrosities with the shape of men and the souls of worms. We can't let the South turn the Land of Liberty into a breeding-pen for slaves!" The first sentence of the Declaration of Independence had become a "ghastly joke . . . a signboard over a shop for making slaves."[72] Then, of course, there was Eliza, crossing the ice. Northern hearts warmed to the "poor, long-sufferin' creeters," suffered with "children as dear as ourn tore from their mothers; and old folks kep slavin' eighty long, hard years with no pay, no help, no pity, when they git past work. . . ."[73]

This was slavery, as the North's writers remembered it; and the slave master, arrogant, despising the liberty cherished at the North, looked with contempt, they thought, on the ideal of freedom and equality. Consider James K. Hosmer's conception of the views of Claiborne, the southern aristocrat, caricatured in *The Thinking Bayonet*:

These Northern men,—workmen, and proud of being workmen,— why are they workmen but for this? Norman conquerers eight centuries ago, subdued them, and made them serfs. Mere hunters and fighters they were: but these Normans put them to the soil, and to the arts; made them labor until they got the habit of labor. I am of this Norman stock, and would do here, in this new world, and with this other race, what was done in the old by my ancestors. I do not set these negroes down as mere brutes. The stock is as good, perhaps, as were those Saxon boors whom William and his followers put underfoot. They are indolent barbarians; that is all. I shall do them a service by holding them under my mastery. Under this mastery, they will, in time, learn to work, become industrious, and reach the level of these Northern people, who were once as low down as they. I belong to these Normans,—tamers we are! We have tamed these Saxon boors; we will tame these negroes, and some day tame still other races.[74]

71. Churchill, *The Crisis*, pp. 75-80.
72. Hughes, *The Whirlwind*, pp. 141-42.
73. Alcott, *Work*, p. 371.
74. Hosmer, *The Thinking Bayonet*, pp. 94-95.

Writers sympathetic with the South did not deny all the features in such portraits of southern pride, power, and purpose. Their task was to show these qualities in a different light and to illustrate the fact that they existed apart from slavery, were born in noble southern blood. They had to repudiate slavery, while they condemned abolitionism—a nice distinction, often sought but not always achieved. Ex-Confederates were not particularly anxious, of course, to bow to the northern demand that the South see "she was in the wrong . . . and it was best that they should suffer defeat."[75] Southerners revered the Declaration of Independence, too, but "its glory may be due rather to the sword of Washington than to the philosophy of Jefferson."[76] Negroes were properly "hewers of wood and drawers of water. The Lord had made them so, and the Bible said it was right. . . . Slaves were sleek, well-fed, well-housed, loved, and trusted, rightly inferior and happy. . . ."[77] Maintenance of the Negro in his subordinate status was vital to the well-being of the republic; otherwise citizens with "the Magna Charta and the Declaration of Independence behind" them, having established a government of which "the basis of stability is the self-control of the individual," would be swamped by "niggers, sir, that have lived like wild beasts in the depths of the jungle since the days of Ham. . . ."[78] The Negro was a greater threat to southern society than the slave. His ability to live cheaply would degrade the free white farmer. It had been the slave who had forced the South to make demands for entry into the territories; slave labor had wasted the land of the great plantations. "It destroyed the small farms and drove out the individual land owners. It destroyed respect for trades and crafts. It strangled the development of industrial art."[79] Southerners "knew" the Negro, knew him as "wonderfully and fearfully made, of materials partly good and partly bad."[80] Out of this knowledge, the South made her stand, not

75. Musick, *Union,* p. xi.
76. Russell, *Roebuck,* p. 130.
77. Fox, *The Little Shepherd of Kingdom Come,* pp. 239-40.
78. Churchill, *The Crisis,* p. 80.
79. Dixon, *The Man in Gray,* pp. 59, 74.
80. Watson, *Bethany,* p. 14.

for slavery, but for "The Racial Supremacy of the White Man.
. . . The South chose death before racial treason."[81]

However conscious they were of the fact that slavery was a
declining institution, Southerners still could not contemplate
with equanimity methods of abolition which would "ruin millions" of citizens. "The welfare of the whole South, as matters
now stand, sir, depends upon slavery." Wherever righteousness
might lie, the fact was that slaves, in tradition and law, were
property; and "conservative people . . . respect property the
world over. . . . If men are deprived by violence of one kind
of property which they hold under law, all other kinds of property will be endangered."[82] The abolitionist fury had already
set trembling the foundations of American society by its denunciation of the constitution as "a covenant with death and an
agreement with hell." Abolition had raised the sectional
Republican party, "that party which tolled the bells, and fired
the minute guns, and draped its churches in black, and all-
hailed as saint and martyr the instigator of a bloody and servile
insurrection in a sister State, the felon and murderer, John
Brown!"[83] Personal liberty laws had been adopted to deprive
the South of her right to the recapture of fugitive slaves; and a
constitution already tattered had been further torn by denial
of "the fundamental principle of equality in the common territory. . . ." The South believed too that the union and the
constitution were in danger—but in danger from men of the
North, who had elected to office "avowed enemies to the Constitution . . . men who had declared over and over again that
there was a 'higher law' than the Constitution, men who
declared that the Union must be dissolved if slavery could be
got rid of in no other way. . . ."[84]

In the contest of invective, the South has acquired a traditional advantage in the two words which most commonly
were used to designate the extremists of either side. Characterization of the zealots was typically expressed by John Fox,

81. Dixon, *The Man in Gray,* p. 414.
82. Churchill, *The Crisis,* pp. 75-80, 55.
83. Johnston, *The Long Roll,* pp. 7-8.
84. Watson, *Bethany,* p. 218.

by a reference to "The fanatics of Boston, the hot-heads of South Carolina. . . ."[85] At the North, the fanatic; at the South, a hot-head—the difference here is basic to fiction's approach to extremists of both sections. Not always consciously intended, this distinction in nouns has been made by authors of each generation, who in thinking back to the beginnings of the war have, whatever their stated position, thus indicated a distaste for the radical reformer and a sympathy with conservative defense of the *status quo*. With or without the advantage in labels, however, southern novelists have held their own in the denunciatory arts. The "miserable fanatics"[86] were like a "little fice dog . . . yelping at the heels of the South for more than two generations," which finally succeeded in "getting up a fight between the usually good-natured mastiff, the North, and the plucky little spitz, the South. . . ."[87] To Southerners, the abolitionists were also Puritans ("Puritan fanatic" is almost a preferred form for reference to the anti-slave Northerner), and as such were by nature a drearily righteous people.

. . . it is not only the right . . . [the Puritan gentleman declared vehemently], but the duty of a highly civilized and God-fearing people, like ourselves, to correct error and punish wrong and crime wherever found! . . . I pity the poor, God-condemned creatures, whose social crimes are such that they cannot make their religion their politics and their politics their religion. I am happy to say that our Puritan stock has always been able to do so.[88]

In thus reporting the contempt and fear that lay between the sections, the novelists have realized that such conditions might not necessarily have led to war. Extremely bitter feeling was illustrated in these reports of the passions preceding the war; the next step in the logic of the argument that slavery brought the war lay in the measure of the extent to which the abolition spirit represented majority opinion in the North. Post-bellum writers have not carried their disavowal of the slave system to the point of approval for the abolitionist method of ending

85. *The Little Shepherd of Kingdom Come,* p. 218.
86. Chapin, *Fitz-Hugh St. Clair,* p. 60.
87. Floyd, *Thorns in the Flesh,* pp. 97-98.
88. *Ibid.,* p. 56.

it; their beliefs were in "eventual freedom" for the slave, rather than in sudden, ruthless destruction. By showing that Lincoln's election was a forecast of aggressive action against slavery within the states, southern writers have justified their adoption of radical policies designed to preserve their right to act cautiously.

Few novelists have stated a definite opinion on the real danger to the South of Lincoln's election. As a whole, fiction has inclined to the view of Arthur C. Cole, that Lincoln was a moderate whose election, in itself, posed no direct threat to slavery in the South.[89] Even southern writers have avoided the extreme position of J. G. deR. Hamilton, who has insisted that the president-elect was "all broke out" with abolitionism, with new spots appearing all the time.[90] The novelists, with a few exceptions, have ignored the facts cited recently by James G. Randall, that if southern congressmen had not withdrawn from the Thirty-seventh Congress, the Republicans would have been a minority in both houses.[91] Fiction's treatment of this issue remains quite vague. Early northern writers found that the idea of a "wicked and *causeless* rebellion" was a "boon to 'loyal editors' "[92] and asserted that the legal rights of the South were safe from Lincoln's intervention; but at the same time they insisted that an early end to slavery was guaranteed by his success at the polls. "The Avowed Abolitionists," said Albion W. Tourgée, "were comparatively few," yet "at the same time, there was a latent animosity toward the institution which existed all over the free States, and embraced, probably, three-fourths of their voting strength." Politicians who denied that the government could interfere with the peculiar institution within the states were rewarded with the "sorrowful

89. "Lincoln's Election an Immediate Menace to Slavery in the States?" *Am. Hist. Rev.,* XXXVI (July, 1931), 740-67.

90. "Lincoln's Election an Immediate Menace to Slavery in the States?" *Am. Hist. Rev.,* XXXVII (July, 1932), 703.

91. *The Civil War and Reconstruction,* pp. 227-32. Randall summarizes also the celebrated debate of Professors Cole and Hamilton, which was a feature of the 1930 meeting of the Mississippi Valley Historical Association in Chattanooga, Tennessee.

92. Dabney, *The Story of Don Miff,* p. 35.

assent" of the northern electorate. But Southerners sensed the subconscious will of the North more accurately than did the Northerners. "The South was not deceived. Their politicians read the mystic symbols, which the hands of groping millions thus unconsciously had traced, with surer ken than their brethren of the North."[93] Similarly, Edward P. Roe argued that men "deemed the worst fanatics in the land were merely exponents of a public opinion that was rising like an irresistible tide from causes beyond human control;" but at the same time Roe presents a hero who is incensed "beyond measure that the South could be made to believe that the North would break through or infringe upon the constitutional safeguards thrown around the institution."[94]

There are, of course, exceptions to contradictory coupling of the North's stated purpose with its unconscious will. Virginius Dabney endowed the abolitionists with "the courage of their convictions" and saw them as men who would have resolved the problem by letting the " 'erring sisters depart in peace' so as to rid the Union of the blot of African servitude. . . ."[95] Thomas Dixon believed that secession would never have come "if reason had ruled," for the "new administration could have done nothing with the Congress chosen."[96] More typical, however, were the Southerners who believed that Lincoln was honest in his promise to preserve southern rights but who saw at the same time that he "is not a man to condone what he thinks wrong. If he is elected, it means the end of slavery."[97] Thus writers of both the North and the South, despite careful effort to feature the essential moderation of the new administration's view of slavery, have as a whole agreed that "somehow Lincoln and slavery and the ultimate question of Union or North and South were irrevocably bound together in some obscure but inevitable destiny."[98]

93. Tourgée, *Toinette,* pp. 249-53.
94. E. P. Roe, *His Sombre Rivals,* pp. 168-69.
95. *The Story of Don Miff,* pp. 35-36.
96. *The Man in Gray,* p. 323.
97. Page, *Red Rock,* pp. 11-12.
98. Harold Sinclair, *The Years of Growth,* p. 9.

The meaning of this "inevitable destiny," the problem of whether it would have been satisfied without war as an essential component, has remained curiously vague in the writings of the novelists. General conviction that slavery was fated to destruction has been confused with the question of whether the will of God might have been realized without use of His terrible swift sword. There is a progression in the opinions of the novelists which tends to begin with definite opinion, and lead gradually to the statement of a profound enigma. In 1868, Henry Ward Beecher viewed the war as the inevitable result of radically opposing aims. "For thirty years, it is now apparent . . . the two great halves of this nation were deepening into radically antagonistic convictions—not about politics, in its common sense, but upon the question of humanity which underlies and finally controls states, churches, philosophy, and religion itself."[99] By 1883, however, Edward P. Roe, convinced that slavery had been doomed, was conscious of the fact that Lincoln and his party might not have harmed slavery—but he still thought talk of peace was idle because "all talk of compromise on the part of the Southern leaders was deceptive. . . ."[100] At the turn of the century, however, Joseph A. Altsheler presented a narrator who said "if you could find a wide plain, lead all the thirty million people of the United States into it, introduce 'em to each other, and let 'em see what they really are, the whole trouble—slavery, State rights, and everything else—would be finished in ten minutes."[101] In the wake of World War I, Thomas Dixon saw the civil conflict as "the most utterly senseless and unnecessary struggle in the history of our race."[102] Novelists arrived at a clear expression of this view before it became the wide-noted thesis of certain recent historians. George Fort Milton's idea of a "needless war," avoidable,[103] and Avery Craven's report of the gradual sacri-

---

99. Beecher, *Norwood,* p. 405.
100. *His Sombre Rivals,* pp. 186-88.
101. *In Circling Camps,* p. 22.
102. *The Man in Gray,* p. 352.
103. *The Eve of Conflict,* p. 2.

fice of reason and moderation to emotional fantasies,[104] came more than a decade later. Fiction continued to refer to "fate" in describing the war's coming, but such a writer as Edgar Lee Masters, for instance, balanced his sympathetic conviction that "men are in the hands of a Power that is making history" with denunciation of William H. Seward's idea of "irrepressible conflict."[105] Novelists seem satisfied in recent times to avoid the positive conclusions they imply; they stand with Harold Sinclair, who reduced the problem in 1940 to an "obscure but inevitable destiny."[106]

Firm interpretations may be found, of course, to prove the belief of some novelists in the position recently taken by Arthur C. Cole, that opposed northern and southern societies moved to an irrepressible conflict.[107] Such a view was expressed by Joseph William Eggleston, who wrote in 1903 that "Secession and war were the necessary result of differences so wide."[108] John Fox presented authorities who argued that the "struggle was written in the Constitution."[109] Upton Sinclair, while tender in years but already stern in judgment, cited as the clearest vision the intuition of Seward: "It is an irrepressible conflict between opposing and enduring forces."[110] Such views are outside the usual interpretations of twentieth-century Civil War novels. Serious effort to analyze the connection between abolition and war has posed an unresolved dilemma: abolition, inevitable; but war, somehow, avoidable.

Emphasis in the novels on the distinction between the problem of abolition on the one hand, and the coming of the war on the other, has reduced the importance of slavery as a primary cause of conflict. The issue remains basic in these fictional studies of historical causation, but only as a contributing factor to more elaborate explanations than those generated by

104. *The Coming of the Civil War*, pp. 15-16.
105. *The Tide of Time*, p. 181.
106. *The Years of Growth*, p. 9.
107. *The Irrepressible Conflict*, pp. 406-7.
108. *Tuckahoe*, p. 147.
109. *The Little Shepherd of Kingdom Come*, p. 219.
110. *Manassas*, p. 273.

review of the slave problem alone. A summary of the slavery issue in fiction's interpretation of the coming of the war becomes, therefore, a report of a loose cycle of opinion. In early novels, during and immediately after the war, slavery was the outward sign, the pretext, which brought the sections into collision for the satisfaction of malign ambitions, or in defense of their deep-seated constitutional principles. Changing views of these underlying causes left the "pretext" standing alone, as the independent and important cause of war. Southerners, although they repudiated slavery, excoriated abolition and concluded that fanatic purpose put such unbearable pressure on the South that secession and war resulted. Northerners held more simply to a belief that the nation, unable to exist half-slave and half-free, drifted to violent resolution of the issue. Early in the twentieth century, however, novelists began to return slavery to its role as a "factor," a "pretext": the institution was once more treated as an integral part of a more general economic or cultural conflict.

I should emphasize the fact that of all the explanations for the war, the Negro in bondage is the one which the novelists are least likely to ignore. They have maintained the issue of slavery in a more central position than have the historians, whose concern with the problem follows a somewhat similar cycle. Fiction has rarely subordinated the moral issue to the background position it occupies in the writings of some economic or constitutional historians;[111] slavery remains, for fiction, a constant and important factor. The issue, moreover, demonstrates the force with which fiction can document historical movements suited to presentation in the novel form.

111. Novelists have avoided the de-emphasis on slavery which may be found in the writings of the Beards, for instance. They remain closer, on the whole, to views such as those of Herman E. Von Holst, in the late nineteenth century, or to more recent opinions like those of Dwight L. Dumond, who saw the war as a basic conflict between the anti-slave reform movement and the South's militant defense of its peculiar institution. See Beard, *The Rise of American Civilization,* I, 628 ff.; Von Holst, *The Constitutional and Political History of the United States,* VII, 459; Dumond, *Anti-Slavery Origins of the Civil War in the United States,* p. 121.

With analysis of slavery, novelists of the late nineteenth century demonstrated the capacity of historical novels to carry their fictional and their factual burdens in the same compartment—an achievement which marks the beginning approaches of Civil War novelists to maturity. From the local particulars of the slave economy, novelists could draw, without distortion or interruption of their narrative, impressions that had continental significance. History and fiction, well-met here, were to maintain their union in the development of other themes that demonstrated even more clearly the harmony of their purpose.

III
Personal Details and Public Events

Realization that detailed analysis of local institutions and local passions might serve as a reasonable explanation for the war's coming is the key to successful Civil War novels of the twentieth century. When novelists began to concentrate on small cultural units and brief moments of human behavior—when they sought to account for general movements through the illumination of particular facts—the level of their historical performances rose sharply. The shift from studies of conspiracy or state rights to studies of individual responses to slavery showed the way to this advance; the problem of the modern novelist has been to extend the number of themes which permit generalization to be implied when individual conduct is explicitly described.

The search has not been without its false starts. An early and continuing effort in the modern Civil War novel has been the impulse to work the fruitful vein of economic interpretation so important to modern historical analysis of the war's meaning. Economic interpretations, however, have proved to be no less a burden for the novelist than the state rights theme. Adequate presentation of the war as a collision between agrarian and industrial societies has demanded a load of fact and logic quite alien to the personal channels through which Civil War stories flow. Description of slavery as no more than a labor system eliminates the moral purpose and the contentious passions which render the conflict intelligible when it is reviewed in terms of individual personality. Ambition for industrial supremacy, or affection for feudal agrarianism, even when translated into personal terms, proves to be a meaner motive than the average romancer seeks for his heroes and heroines, meaner but without sufficiently personal and dramatic evil for his villains. Economic explanations of the war scene have therefore tended to appear in digressions from the primary action and movement of our romances.

Novelists still try, nevertheless, to put economic interpretations to general use; they have sensed, with many historians, the fact that economic analysis may serve as a primary weapon for the exposure of unworthy purpose. But the passion of such analysis is more likely to proceed from the anger of the author than from the real dismay of the people about whom he writes, so that economic theories prove less convincing than other patterns better fitted to fiction's explanations for the war. Generally the economic assault has been made on men and forces allied to the northern cause. Henry Morford's bitter description of *The Days of Shoddy,* published by a Northerner in wartime, reveals by its very title such a view. Yankee penury was of course a favorite topic of the southern writer, who sought the dollar sign on puritan morality. "Astonishing," remarked an Arkansas rustic, "how them Yankees always are the hardest kind of masters, though now they make out like the almighty dollar wa'n't shucks to the almighty nigger."[112] More general concepts of the economic conditions of the struggle were presented by Southerners who maintained ante-bellum arguments against commercial regulations that worked to the detriment

112. [Reeves], *Randolph Honor,* p. 136.

of the exporting sections and allowed "New England to bleed us for the benefit of her manufacturing industries. . . ."[113] Admirers of the restored union, on the other hand, have avoided economic analysis; they are upset at the threat to property and the danger to legal traditions resulting from the abolition of four billion dollars in southern slave property; this distaste apparently is an important source of northern willingness to leave uncontested the "fanatic" label attached by the South to the abolitionist groups.

Sophisticated views of the economic bases of disunion were stated as early as 1904 by both Upton Sinclair and Tom Watson, each of whom expressed his own opposition to the twentieth-century *status quo* by searching out the hidden purposes of wartime Republicans. Unionist Sinclair still traced commercial rather than industrial ambition in an explanation which is essentially a restatement of the tariff and banking arguments of ante-bellum times.[114] Watson, experienced proponent of Populist economics, believed that "Northern capital would not have allied itself to abolitionism and the policy of coercion had it not been for reasons commercial." Without such an effort, "The Northern manufacturer would have lost his best customer. Better to keep the South in the Union, where she was the helpless victim of the New England commercial system, than to allow her to set up a separate government which could build tariff walls." Loss of the rich southern provinces, "which the North exploits by federal legislation, could not be afforded." Had she not been conscious of these economic ties, Watson thought, the North would have indisputably "let the erring sisters depart in peace." Further, Watson saw in the triumph of Republicanism dramatic reversal of the basic principles which had been fixed on the American system by the repeated victories of the Democratic party over Hamiltonian ideas.

113. Floyd, *Thorns in the Flesh*, p. 54. For a contemporary Northerner's expression of the South's grievances against the commercial and industrial policies of the North, see Kettell, *Southern Wealth and Northern Profit.*
114. *Manassas*, p. 34.

The glorious old Democratic party of Jefferson and Jackson had well-nigh crushed the life out of Hamilton's creed. Federalism was at its last gasp. In spite of its subtle changes of form and name, which for a moment had deluded the people, in spite of such recruits as Henry Clay and Daniel Webster, in spite of the wily manipulators who had made political use of Andrew Jackson's power and popularity by bringing him into collision with Calhoun—in spite of all Democracy had won its fight. . . .

The Protective principle had been put under foot and the tariff was one for revenue only; the internal improvements system had received its death-blow and no longer vexed Congress with its greedy clamors; the sovereign power to create money had been taken from the banks, and the Government was lord of its own system of currency.

Could Yancey and Breckinridge and Lincoln foresee that they were tugging like blind Samsons at the very foundations of the nation's weal? Could they realize that back of the honest Abolitionist was the implacable Federalist, groping for the levers of political power? Was it within human penetration to see that slavery was the least of the issues dependent upon this fatal campaign?[115]

Watson's grasp of many facts in the economic interpretation of the Civil War did not include appreciation of the class alliances, the balanced appeal to opposing interests, which were emphasized by historian Charles A. Beard in his characterization of Republican policies. Watson's viewpoint was primarily an agrarian one, in which the issues of banks, tariffs, and internal improvements were featured to the exclusion of such factors as the promise of the Homestead Act and subsidies to enterprise. Watson was aware, nevertheless, of the "implacable Federalist, groping for the levers of political power," and his conclusions differ more in detail than in meaning from the accounts of a modern economic historian. In their half-completed views, moreover, Watson and Sinclair sounded a very unusual note for the romantic tales which composed the bulk of Civil War novels around the turn of the century. Castigation of the Yankee's love for money was a frequent feature of such works, but this phase of the average argument was a

115. Watson, *Bethany*, pp. 104-5, 294.

method for gilding the virtues of magnolia-scented belles or for providing a contrast to honest patriots of the North.

More recent novels differ but little in their avoidance of the rigid precepts of class conflict—ideas which if presented at all, are expressed in terms of colliding cultures rather than in more technical economic terminology. Even Howard Fast, in his Marxist novel of the Civil War and reconstruction, explains the coming of the war as a struggle between slavery and freedom, and he reserves his patterns of class analysis for interpretation of the post-war period.[116]

To come to terms with recent economic views the novelist would have to divorce his history from his fiction. His obligation to state arguments in terms which reflect the views of participants in the war prevents analysis of the period in the light of his knowledge of the struggle's eventual meaning. James Boyd may have understood the Civil War as a second American revolution when he published *Marching On* in 1927, but the remarks he attributes to an ante-bellum politician are probably in closer touch with the beliefs of the war period. Hear Major Cassius Pettibone, ex-congressman, on the economics of the struggle:

"The Yankee, seh, can be explained in just one word and in only one." The pause which followed was of nicely calculated length. "Money. Money, by God, seh!"
. . . "Gentlemen, who grew the cotton for this handkerchief?" He flourished it. "We did," he answered in a voice so grieved, so righteously indignant as to make that very handkerchief seem the product of his auditor's stern toil. "But do we get a fair return for our industry? No, seh. A bare pittance, seh. Just enough to keep us going." The Major's voice sank to a confidential and suspicious whisper. "But this handkerchief comes mighty high, gentlemen. You can get one in England for half as much. There must be a big profit somewhere." He raised his voice again. "There is. And who makes it? The Yankee manufacturer. Well, then, a sensible man would naturally ask, why don't you get your handkerchiefs from England, where the prices are fair? You know the answer: The tariff keeps them out. And who makes the tariff? The Yankee manufacturer." The Major replaced his handkerchief

116. *Freedom Road, passim.*

and patted his vest significantly. "Right there's the story, gentlemen. Whatever little money we make, directly we have to pay it out for Yankee goods. And on top of that he treats his own help worse than the sorriest niggers we have down here. And on top of that he preaches abolition at us." The Major dealt the gate post a flat-handed blow. "Do you know what the Yankee's motto is? It's money for himself and morality for everybody else."[117]

On a commoner level, Boyd suggested the economic understanding of 1861's man-in-the-street. A fireman in a Wilmington roundhouse based his views of abolition, Yankees, and the union on his experience with the Boston salesman who sold him an eight-pound Bible which actually weighed only five pounds and in which the illustrations of the Garden of Eden were the rankest forgeries, having earlier served to support a traveler's account of Mexican life. To such a victim of Yankee cupidity, Northerners were "the meanest folks I ever heard tell of."[118]

Translation of economic determinants into personal terms has been confined, then, to invective, to denunciation in both regions of "the profiteering gang [who] think this war is a sweet act of God."[119] Thus the Walt Whitman described by John Erskine attacked the patriots who "are the gaud and tinsel shining in people's eyes—the shoulder straps, bars and stars—all this wind and puffing and infidelity—the swarms of contractors with their endless contracts—the paper money— that's what patriots are!"[120] In the South, Clifford Dowdey explained the motives of his young Virginia fire-eater by the good faith with which his slaves had been bought. "All the money that my family has accumulated in two centuries in Virginia is invested in slaves. Now they want to wipe out our investment."[121] Holmes Alexander described Virginia's secession convention in terms of the price both North and South were willing to pay for the allegiance of the Old Dominion.

117. Boyd, *Marching On,* p. 160.
118. *Ibid.,* p. 287.
119. Griswold, *A Sea Island Lady,* p. 38.
120. *The Start of the Road,* p. 305.
121. *Bugles Blow No More,* p. 11.

Desire for stock in railroads, coal speculations, and oil develop-
ments were balanced against the appeal of cotton farms in
Texas or outside Mobile and against hint of titles of nobility
that could be won by the delegates in the new southern
empire—"There's a coronet that goes with every cotton patch
in Dixie. . . ."[122]

Recent novelists seem fully aware of the significance of class
distinctions in the Civil War North and South, but they have
failed to utilize their understanding in making a satisfactory
explanation of how men acted, or failed to act, as a result of
their economic motivations. The quality of this failure is here
analyzed at some length because in reaching for an economic
interpretation of the war's coming, the novelist was beginning
to sense the size of his role as social historian. In the contrast
he had learned to make between slavery and freedom, he
mastered the passionate terms with which war issues must be
described, if readers of another generation are to experience
them—but he shrank, for various reasons, from holding
slavery in the central place as of the sole cause for the division.
Attempting to broaden this theme, he turned to economic
analysis to demonstrate a more satisfactory basis for the conflict. The considerable ambition of this effort seems to have
fed on itself, because after his failure to personalize economic
abstractions, the novelist turned toward the imposing task of
reconstructing whole segments of culture, segments so patently
different in their separate parts that confusion and conflict
among them seemed reasonable. As his heroes emerged from
their unnatural roles as economic men, or constitutional men,
or moral men, their behavior had a depth and dimension
which gave their decisions human meaning, a fullness not
achieved by the specific arguments of their predecessors. As
spokesmen for the virtues of the North or for the values of the
South, they had served to illustrate, through the logic of their
own actions, the story of why war came between the antagonistic civilizations.

Novelists have not given a balanced account of this cultural

122. *American Nabob,* pp. 65-66.

division. Whatever their sectional affiliation, they have tended to concentrate on the South, have searched there for some complex intangible, for a whole greater than the sum of such parts as a peculiar labor system, a patterned class structure, an anachronistic political mentality, or a determined greed for wealth and power. They have tried to explain the war by showing why the South remained apart from the nation in her special hopes for a separate way of life. Concern with the unique, the strange, the archaic on the southern side led to subordination of the northern way of life. Novelists have treated northern values, victorious and permanent, as a frame of reference mutually understood between the author and his reader, a familiar ground from which the elusive southern culture can be explained. Except in contrasting definitions— which work more frequently than not to the detriment of the North—northern customs and beliefs have usually been implied, while extensive examination is reserved for the southern departure from these undefined national standards.

In the process of reporting the war as a conflict of cultures, the novelist assumed his modern stature as a social historian worth serious critical attention. His work with the separate shape of sectional values, illuminated by the detail which only fiction can furnish, became his primary contribution to our knowledge of the Civil War era. Some of the elements in this achievement are illustrated in the chapter following this one, a study of the performance of the best novelists at the task of cultural analysis. The questions posed in this chapter—the problem of why, according to fiction, the war came—are too limited to reflect fiction's broader achievements; my concern in the following paragraphs is with the place specifically assigned by the novelists to the cultural sources of conflict.

Author after author has sought a direct statement of contrast, some general characterization which, in a phrase, would illustrate the basic differences between Southerners and Northerners. Henry Ward Beecher resorted to dogmatic conclusion on this point, without effort to prove his assertions. "The people of the North and South are essentially different. There is no hope of their assimilation. Their climate, industries, political opinions, social customs, cause, and will maintain, these differences."[123] A generation later, Upton Sinclair was following the same line, basing his view of colliding civilizations on his belief in the inability of a society of farmers, mechanics, and sailors to live side by side with gentlemen "who did not work, but who owned slaves and tilled the soil."[124] Paul Laurence Dunbar, a Negro writer, expressed through his southern hero a more specific distinction, put in spiritual rather than physical terms—"It was inevitable," he said, "that the proud spirit of the South and the blind arrogance of the North would some day clash."[125] By derogation of New England manners, F. Hopkinson Smith attempted to indicate how southern sensibilities in conversation, in all dealings among equals, set the South subtly but irrevocably apart from a ruder society to the North.[126]

Thomas Dixon sought distinctions between the North and South which grew from the different degree of centralization in the two civilizations. New England, he believed, set the pattern for the North by organization with an authoritative church at its center; whereas the South's society was much more loosely knit, and depended on a free-wheeling individualism for maintenance of its institutions. The "Puritan," as a result of this confinement of his spirit, "early learned to love the pleasure of hating. He hated himself if no more promising victim loomed on the horizon."[127] In the South, on the other

123. *Norwood*, p. 382.
124. *Manassas*, p. 273.
125. *The Fanatics*, p. 33. This is essentially the view expressed by Owsley, "The Fundamental Cause of the Civil War: Egocentric Sectionalism," *Jour. So. Hist.*, VII (Feb., 1941), 3-18. Owsley emphasizes not only the difference between the two, but the contempt each section felt for the ideals and customs of the other. Recent historians, of course, have been thoroughly conscious of sectional differences outside political divisions. They have emphasized the contrast between conservative rural life in the South and the ferment of a North alive with reform movements, in the throes of its complicated adjustment to industrial living. See, for instance, Cole, *The Irrepressible Conflict*.
126. *The Fortunes of Oliver Horn*, p. 351.
127. Dixon, *The Man in Gray*, p. 101.

hand, a mannered leisure, purchased at the price of slavery, made living a thing of grace and worthy purpose. The South, according to a character described by T. S. Stribling, was "not a material nation . . . for instance we wouldn't think of going to war to pick pennies out of the pockets of the Yankees. . . . The North is concerned mainly with gaining a livelihood; the South is trying to mold something out of life itself. . . . We try to make it beautiful and courteous; we try to live gracefully; we try to talk well." Even good conversation could not be had at the North; orations and tracts paid too well to waste thought and phrase in non-commercial purposes. New England intellectuals would break off from an excited conversation, fall into complete silence, "Because the talk had given them a bright idea, and they were afraid, if they said it aloud, somebody would get to press with it before they did."[128]

The border-state observers portrayed by Joseph Hergesheimer took a different view of the relative merits of the sections. As they saw it, the South's superiority was in emotional argument, whereas the North was the victor with reason. "Emotion appears handsomer than reason," one of them explained, but "It isn't really. Only the most superior people understand and appreciate reason. . . ."[129] Another writer of the border area reduced the conflict to three words for the description of three, rather than two, distinct societies striving against each other. "Only *being* matters to the South," said Holmes Alexander. "New England does the *thinking,* and the West the *doing.* It's queer we should all be one country when we're three separate civilizations." The southern way was "fat and lazy . . . useless. . . . It's *being* that matters, they say. *Being* a gentleman, *being* cultivated, *being* this or that. But . . . America wasn't made that way. . . ."[130]

These capsule versions of the controversy have been sought by a large number of the novelists; a list of their efforts to distill the whole mass of competing ideologies into a single,

128. Stribling, *The Forge,* pp. 82-84.
129. Hergesheimer, *The Limestone Tree,* p. 202.
130. Alexander, *American Nabob,* pp. 77, 9.

cogent observation reads like the placards before a wrestling arena: proud spirit *v.* blind arrogance, regimented puritanism *v.* southern individualism, emotion *v.* reason, or being *v.* thinking and doing. In these as in most other such cases, the final division is stated on an intellectual or cultural basis, outside and beyond the separate threads of any concrete issues.

More exact definition of the proud spirit, the emotion, the "being" of the South is closely associated with the assertion that below the Mason and Dixon Line was found the "best blood in the land."[131] Early southern writers spoke without embarrassment of their superior ancestry: the young Rebel declared that "I shall fight . . . as a matter of principle, and because I am a South Carolinian, to the 'manor born. . . .' "[132] Curiously, many northern writers have accepted at face value the South's estimate of its purer blood, or at least they have admitted that in the Confederacy the blood was "hot,"[133] a word which in its usual context delineated the high-strung thoroughbred. John R. Musick, in a late nineteenth-century effort to prove the complete righteousness of the union's cause, advised that the "rebellion was brought about by a few 'hot-headed' southern politicians, of the aristocratic class, who held honest labor in contempt, and who regarded the man who toiled as no better than the negro slave. This class of southern aristocrats may be traced from the cavaliers of the Cromwellian period. . . ."[134] In the South, according to reporters from both sections, lived the "natural born" leaders. "I tell you there is nothing to equal Southern ability," wrote unionist Mary Harriott Norris. "It's bound to get what it wants before a sluggish Northerner has time to think."[135] With such testimony from the North, Southerners could declare with less consciousness of immodesty that their rule stemmed from the possession of "the ability, the birth, and breeding."[136] The bio-

131. Cruse, *Cameron Hall*, p. 80.
132. Whitson, *Gilbert St. Maurice*, pp. 49-50.
133. O. T. Beard, *Bristling with Thorns*, p. 9.
134. Musick, *Union*, p. ix.
135. *The Grapes of Wrath*, p. 114.
136. Brady, *The Patriots*, p. 12.

logical categories thus indicated were of course within the dominant race; writers of both sections ignored Negroes in their discussion of the superior southern birthright.

White southern blood has tended to thicken to a more common consistency, however, as twentieth-century novelists have taken a closer look at Confederate society. The traditional idea of aristocracy has been examined more critically and explained in terms of land and wealth rather than genetic composition. Hot blood has been reported less frequently as a quality of breeding than as a distinguishing characteristic of the newly rich.[137] "Those fellows down there," wrote Caroline Gordon of the lower South, "got rich too quick and it's gone to their heads."[138] The fire-eating Southerners described by Margaret Mitchell in her fabulous book were residents of the flush new areas, where "Wealth came out of the curving furrows, and arrogance came too—arrogance built on green bushes and the acres of fleecy white. If cotton could make them rich in one generation, how much richer they would be in the next!" Rhett Butler, agent of unwelcome truth and prophetic observation in *Gone with the Wind,* sarcastically summarized the South's aristocratic pretensions: "Why all we have," he said, "is cotton and slaves and arrogance."[139]

Recognition of the inadequacy—and the inaccuracy—of the idea of "aristocracy" as an explanation for mannered living in the South, has not halted investigation of the graceful culture ascribed by tradition to ante-bellum southern life.[140] By a

137. Historian Thomas Jefferson Wertenbaker pointed more than a generation ago to slavery and sudden prosperity as the source of haughty southern manners. He effectively disposed of the idea that the South's "aristocrats" were descended from Cavaliers who took refuge in Virginia during the troubled times of Charles I—such belief, he said, "is entirely without foundation in fact." *The Planters of Colonial Virginia,* pp. 155-61; *The First Americans,* II, 306.

138. *None Shall Look Back,* p. 8.

139. Pp. 56, 111.

140. Unanimous consent has not been attained among historians for disposal of the notion that a blooded master race ruled at the South. Hamilton J. Eckenrode concluded in 1923 that the Civil War "was, in essence, a struggle between that part of the Nordic race [Northerners] which was prepared to renounce its tradition of mastery for equality,

somewhat precious concern with the implications of the word "gentleman," certain novelists have found a way to explain social achievements which other writers, with less discrimination, have attributed to the presence of permanent rank and status at the top of southern society.

Fiction's gentleman, like its aristocrat, was the fruit of a continuity in family and custom, and of substantial economic security; he differed in that his manner was retiring rather than aggressive, and he was sensitive to, rather than brutally contemptuous of, others' feelings.[141] He had the leisure for the acquisition of polished courtesy and classical learning—and he particularly enjoyed public expression of the latter. "We listen and are compelled to admit," said N. J. W. Le Cato of southern oratory, "that whatever of calm dignity there may be in the speeches of Northern men, there is something in a Virginia orator that smacks of the ancients and carries us back to the grand old days of Demosthenes and Cicero in the Acropolis and the Roman Forum."[142] In personal affairs the notable feature of the southern gentleman's personality was an overwhelming dignity, bred of complete self-confidence. However quick he might be to anger, only the severest provocation drove him to expletive. Even in rage, he maintained a regard for personal amenities and exercised a type of self-control that the novelists regard as evidence of an inbred concern for others.

The isolation of this romantically conceived "gentleman" as the essence of southern culture appears to have governed fiction's definition of Confederate hopes. By accepting the planta-

---

modernism and material comfort and that part of the race [Southerners] which was resolved, despite modernity, to remain true to its ruling instincts." Further, the "victory of the North meant the predominance of the non-Nordic elements in American life. It meant the freeing of the slaves, the trampling of agriculture by industrialism, the rise of labor to be a great power, the overthrow of individualism. . . ." Eckenrode, *Jefferson Davis,* pp. 21, 361.

141. For more extended discussion of the preoccupation of novelists with the southern social structure and their manner in describing it, see the following section.

142. *Tom Burton,* p. 38.

tion master as the primary symbol of the way in which the life of the South moved on a different schedule and to different ends from the life of the nation at large, novelists restrict themselves to an intensely local frame of reference. The whole energy of the society they describe seems devoted to the preservation of the complete independence, the separate dignity, of the individuals who directed their plantation scenes. Their stress on the plantation master's fierce pride, and on the pretentious amenities designed to insulate that pride from the world's normal interferences, results in an anarchistic social theory. Their romantic South proves to be a design for disunity, for irresponsible indulgence of individualism irrespective of sectional needs. The idea of a cohesive southern nationalism is completely alien to the separate polished gentleman whom fiction presents as the end product of the southern culture. Patriotism in the South, as these writers see it, was confined to love of home and hearth; the idea of common sacrifice, of subordination of individual desire to the common will, is conspicuous by its absence. Southern patriotic emotions encompassed the land visible on the near side of the horizon but flamed to no urgent faith in the Confederacy, or Confederate purpose. In this context, the war developed in terms of American nationalism, opposed by southern localism.

Repeated emphasis on the reluctance with which the rebels sacrificed their love for the old union, on the sense of pain and sorrow which accompanied their action, leads to the conclusion that authors of the novels regarded southern action as primarily negative, a reverse phase linked to the positive American nationalism defended by an aroused North. A southern author "to the manner born" remembered that "the division of the country into two governments was to me a humiliation. I had loved my country, admired her greatness, gloried in her future possibilities, revered her flag."[143] Yet he went with the South, just as did the Virginian who told his friends, "you will get whipped like the devil and you will

143. W. S. Harrison, *Sam Williams,* pp. 3, 179. The quoted phrases are the author's own description of his views.

deserve it. . . ."[144] A Missouri belle who was completely
devoted to the Confederate cause still recoiled from a reading
of the plea for God's aid against rebellion that was part of the
Episcopal litany. *"Rebellion!* The girl flinched at the word
which the good gentleman had uttered in his prayers. Was she
a traitor to that flag for which her people had fought in three
wars? *Rebellion!* She burned to blot it forever from the
book."[145]

For defense of her separate and cherished institutions, the
South would fight against the invader, but her fight was without a conviction of positive creation, without any well-defined
hope of making a better nation than the one she was leaving.
So inbred and truncated were her passions and loyalties that,
in the end, they were not transferred to support of the abstraction which the Confederacy remained. The reason for this
failure is indicated in a letter DuBose Heyward's *Peter Ashley*
received from his Uncle Porcher, master of Burnt Savannah
Plantation:

Like you [Uncle Porcher told his nephew], I wanted to find out
for myself, and after wide travel I arrived at the conclusion that
of all the countries upon the globe the United States was pre-
eminently the most desirable; of all the states South Carolina stood
far in the lead; and of all sections of South Carolina the Parish of
St. John's is infinitely the most superior. It was not, however, until
my return home that it was borne in upon me that Middle St.
John's, in which God in His wisdom has seen fit to cast our lot, is
so obviously superior to the upper and lower divisions of the
parish that I have always tactfully refrained from comparisons for
fear of embarrassing our neighbors.[146]

Northern reaction to the coming of war is reported in terms
sharply different from those employed to explain the South.
There an emotional nationalism, uncomplicated by the doubts
which nagged at the southern effort, swept across the people.
"The twenty loyal millions of the North," declared John William De Forest, "shuddered with rage" at the Southerners

144. Altsheler, *In Circling Camps,* p. 26.
145. Churchill, *The Crisis,* p. 309.
146. Heyward, *Peter Ashley,* pp. 251-52.

who "proposed to destroy the grandest social fabric that Liberty ever built, the city of refuge for oppressed races, the hope of the nations."[147] The "watchword everywhere," said Mrs. Mary J. Holmes, "was 'the Union forever.'"[148] John Fox's Chad, bred in the mountains of Kentucky, was moved by the backwoods spirit which "had been caught in the hills, and was alive and unchanged at that very hour. The boy was practically born in Revolutionary days, and that was why, like all mountaineers, Chad had little love of State and only love of country—was first, last and all the time simply American. It was not reason—it was instinct."[149]

Confederate soldiers also came down from the mountains, of course, but their motives differed radically from those of the union recruit. Ellen Glasgow's "Pinetop," about to enter his first battle, was confused as to just why he was on the field, in grey uniform, and with a gun in his hand, until sudden inspiration clarified his purpose. "'Them folks have set thar feet on ole Virginny,' was what I thought. 'They've set thar feet on ole Virginny, and they've got to take 'em off damn quick.'"[150] So simple a local attachment, however, was eventually lost in the mingled confusion of the provincial faiths that separately had fed their quotas into the Confederate army. Emotional ties to a county nearby, a city in the next state, a plantation far away, had to be knotted into a common devotion, if a southern nation were to survive the pain of its birth. These separate threads of passion and devotion were never joined, according to the evidence of Civil War novels. By their direct conclusions, and by more frequent omissions, the authors indicate no consciousness at the South of common purpose, no sense of national destiny. The good fight fought by Southerners and their loyal service to the point of ultimate sacrifice were without direction, and toward no distinct ideal. Clifford Dowdey gave knowledge to his hero of these deficien-

147. *Miss Ravenel's Conversion from Secession to Loyalty*, p. 67.
148. *Rose Mather*, p. 9.
149. Fox, *The Little Shepherd of Kingdom Come*, pp. 239-40.
150. Glasgow, *The Battle-Ground*, p. 323.

cies, in his statement of the central theme of *Where My Love Sleeps*:

... we've fought through everything for something we can't even name [Blount reflected]. But we fought together. The army became a thing to have faith in. . . . I don't know, but maybe there's something . . . [Southerners] could believe in *for* their country as they now believe *in* the army. . . . No real plan of strategy was possible until there was a larger aim for the country . . . as there could be no plan for a house until the builder knew the purpose the house was to serve. What was the purpose of the Confederacy? Blount realized he did not know, that none of them knew. . . .[151]

Conclusions such as these, however useful in isolating the peculiar quality of the southern way of life, did not explain why sectional differences led to war. The best novelists early sensed the inadequacy of an interpretation which ended with demonstration of the fact that southern hopes differed from those of the nation, and they moved almost intuitively toward the explanation found most satisfactory by modern historians concerned with the differences, which are ordinary, into conflict, which is not. Long before contemporary scholars began to emphasize the irrational bases of conflict, novelists discovered that war came when "passion and crime" gained "mastery over sober counsel, equity, and justice."[152] War, according to this view, was a monument to the collapse of reason, rather than the logical effect of the southern deviation from the national purpose. From the time of the war onward, the more sensitive novelists have reported that the Americans of 1861 acted not on understanding but on ignorance of fact, that war resulted from the absence of leadership rather than from the execution of determined policy; and they portray, in the nation at large, a fatal fascination with war itself which in the end outweighed fear of its coming.

The extent to which popular passions were cynically manipulated by public men has been a source of constant speculation

151. Dowdey, *Where My Love Sleeps*, pp. 126-27, 161.
152. Dumond, *Anti-Slavery Origins of the Civil War in the United States*, p. 130.

among the novelists. The distortion of public information for unworthy ends has been seen frequently as a primary phase in the building of the conflict. William Mumford Baker, writing in 1865, under the name "George F. Harrington," denounced the irresponsibility and the ill-will of newspaper editors who relied on gullible public reception of twisted news. "Are you fool enough not to know," said Harrington's "editor," "that whatever appears in a paper today is knocked completely out of the minds of the people by what will come out in it tomorrow?" On such men depended millions of Southerners "willing to know and to do the right, yet so systematically, so awfully, so utterly blinded!"[153] A reporter working on a Charleston newspaper, according to DuBose Heyward, "was expected to be partisan," for a paper flourished according to the heat of its editorial anger. In Peter Ashley's copy, the "word 'soldiers' which appeared three times flowered gloriously into 'our gallant defenders,' 'the flower of chivalry,' 'predestined heroes of many a hard fought field.' A senator became 'that doughty defender of our honor.'"[154]

Novelists have long stressed the lesson that "arguments made in behalf of a character or a cause become the facts at last."[155] The loudest voice, rather than the wisest, dominated the final moments of the controversy. A demagogue might be known for his irresponsible and untrustworthy record, but "let him get up on a platform and tell a string of jokes, and rave about our wrongs, and the whole crowd will shout that he's the very fellow to manage the finance and the army and the navy and the post office, and everything else that the Government's got."[156] The spring days of 1861 were times when feeling was so high that "debate only fuses opinions into convictions; only fans the flames and makes the fire a conflagration."[157]

The South of fiction as well as of fact arrived at this state

153. Baker, *Inside,* pp. 20-23.
154. Heyward, *Peter Ashley,* pp. 104-5.
155. Masters, *The Tide of Time,* p. 23.
156. Altsheler, *In Circling Camps,* pp. 21-22.
157. Page, *Red Rock,* p. 12.

before the remainder of the country. Epes Sargent noted in
1863 that "the whole code and temper of the South" demanded
that "men *may not* differ, and *shall not* differ, on the subject
of slavery."[158] Stubborn rejection of reasoned argument, denial
of the right to opposing views, left Southerners, according to
John William De Forest's Dr. Ravenel, "as ill-informed as
Hottentots. They have no more idea of their relative strength
as compared to that of the United States than the Root-diggers
of the Rocky Mountains. They are doomed to perish by their
own ignorance and madness." Dr. Ravenel had been forced to
flee New Orleans because

I had to take sides. Those unhappy Chinese allow no neutrals—
nothing but themselves, the central flowery people, and outside
barbarians. They have fed on the poor blacks until they can't
abide a man who isn't a cannibal. He is a reproach to them, and
they must make away with him. They remind me of a cracker
whom I met at a cross road tavern in one of my journeys through
the north of Georgia. This man, a red-nosed, tobacco-drizzling,
whiskey-perfumed giant, invited me to drink with him, and, when
I declined, got furious and wanted to fight me. I told him that
I never drank whiskey and that it made me sick, and finally succeeded in pacifying him without touching his poison. In fact he
made a kind of apology for having offered to cut my throat.
"Wa'al, the fact is, stranger," he said, "I" (laying an accent as
strong as his liquor on the personal pronoun) "I use whiskey."—
You understand the inference, I suppose: a man who refused
whiskey was a contradiction, a reproach to his personality: such a
man he could not suffer to live. It was the Brooks and Sumner
affair over again. Brooks says, "fact is *I* believe in slavery," and
immediately hits Sumner over the head for not believing in it.[159]

To O. T. Beard, the delusions of southern faith made of the
South's "gentleman" a "cavern of echo. He sneered at the
Yankee, despised the laborer, worshipped 'king cotton,' pro-
pugned State's rights, and glibly asserted the omnipotence of
the South." He might admit that the North could make some
trifling stand for opposite views, "But, sah, you will find the

158. *Peculiar,* p. 217.
159. De Forest, *Miss Ravenel's Conversion from Secession to Loyalty,*
pp. 9-14.

resistance of the Yankee to be the kicking of a toad, sah! The squirming of a sarpent, sah, after youa heel is on them, sah. . . . The Southern gentleman is invincible, sah! Invincible! A half-dozen Southern regiments can stride over the North at will, sah! Yes, at will, sah! From the Potomac to the Passamaquoddy, sah! To the Passamaquoddy, sah!"[160]

Post-war southern writers endorsed these northern descriptions of southern delusions. Molly Elliott Seawell, for instance, observed that "there was really no liberty of conscience, much less of speech, concerning the separation of the South from the North, or the future of slavery. The minds of these people were made up and compromise was impossible."[161] Thomas Dixon saw the tragedy in such positive decision, in the southern inability to make the South's beliefs and practices known to the world. In the passionate indictment presented by *Uncle Tom's Cabin,* Dixon's Robert E. Lee saw force "As terrible as an army with banners. I heard the throb of drums through its pages." Yet for answer to so frenzied an attack, the South was able only to shut its ears, and shut the ears of all it could control. For counter-attack in the war of words, the region was without armaments. "The South has only trained swords," the Lee of this novel said. "And not so many of them as we think. We have no writers. We have no literature. We have no champions in the forum of the world's thought. We are being arraigned at the judgment bar of mankind and we are dumb."[162]

160. Beard, *Bristling with Thorns,* pp. 9-12.
161. *The Victory,* p. 14.
162. Dixon, *The Man in Gray,* pp. 68-69. Dixon himself, of course, provided a fictional answer to Mrs. Stowe in *The Leopard's Spots*—a book comparable in passion, if in little else, to *Uncle Tom's Cabin.* Dixon thus joined at least fifteen pre-war novelists of the South, and a number of post-war ones, who attempted such rebuttal. Craven, *The Coming of the Civil War,* p. 162. For an evaluation of such works as J. R. Thornton, *The Cabin and the Parlor, Or, Slaves Without Masters,* J. W. Page, *Uncle Robin in His Cabin in Virginia and Tom Without One in Boston,* Robert Criswell, *Uncle Tom's Cabin Contrasted with Buckingham Hall,* or Mary H. Eastman, *Aunt Phyllis' Cabin, Or, Southern Life As It Is,* see Gaines, *The Southern Plantation,* pp. 45-49. The last novel named was described as the most effective of the "anti-Tom" stories by Forrest Wilson, *Crusader in Crinoline,* p. 325.

The bulk of commentary describing this ante-bellum iron curtain is concerned with the South, but occasional writers referred to uncompromising dogmatism on the Civil War issues as more of a national than a southern problem. Joseph C. Lincoln translated this view into a downeast homily.

It's my experience that good folks are good folks—north, south, east, and west. The trouble is that so many of us are like the weathervane on my barn that got stuck pointing north-east last winter and now it never points any other way. I meant to have it oiled, but now it's gone so long that I'm afraid nothing will start it but a hammer, and that might not be so good for the vane. There are a lot of hammers out in this country just now, and—well if the vane holds together we're lucky.[163]

But the hammers were swung with a vengeance. They were in the hands of the mob, and the

mob never reasons. It only believes. Reason is submerged in passion. . . . The mob mind, once formed, is a new creation and becomes with amazing rapidity a resistless force. The reason for its uncanny power lies in the fact that when once formed it is dominated by the unconscious, not the conscious, forces of man's nature. Its credulity is boundless. Its passions dominate all life. The records of history are a sealed book. Experience does not exist. Impulse rules the universe. . . . For the first time in the history of the republic the mob mind had mastered the collective soul of its people. The contagion had spread both North and South. In the North by sympathy, in the South by a process of reaction even more violent and destructive of reason.[164]

Such castigation of public opinion is featured in novels written during every period since the war; from the 1860's to the 1940's there have been writers who agreed with N. J. W. Le Cato, that "the fact is, more truth has been strangled, and more justice sacrificed at the shrine of public opinion than ever fell a victim to tyranny, or ever was immolated at the altar of ignorance and superstition." The mass mind has not "even *supported* the advance guard of human thought. On the other hand, it invariably puts itself in the way, blocks up the road; and not infrequently turns away from a struggling

163. Lincoln, *Storm Signals,* p. 24.
164. Dixon, *The Man in Gray,* pp. 309-11.

Right, and makes common cause with rampant Error. . . ."[165] With the whole nation wildly excited, and while the coolest minds were in "chaos," the mob was constantly incited to new extremes by the demagogues of North and South, who "were daily making matters worse by the unyielding arrogance of their attitude."[166]

In the opinion of important novelists it was the public clamor, swollen to ungovernable and brutal proportions, which led finally to rupture of the peace. The hostile necessity festered at the fringe of rational issues, a by-product of the grievances and ambitions which bear reasonable analysis. Stripped of authority by gales of passion over the land, reason retreated to hidden places; and in its absence left no deputy to stay the coming conflict. In an effort to illustrate this aspect of the war's sources, novelists have largely ignored issues of grave national import and concentrated on simple, illuminating incidents which correctly gauged the local temper. To the characters of George Washington Cable, for instance, realization of the inevitability of war came when they witnessed an incident on the streets of New Orleans during the closing days of the presidential campaign of 1860. A vendor of campaign badges was supplied, by mistake, with a Lincoln medallion among his images of Breckinridge, Douglas, and Bell. He barely escaped lynching at the hands of the mob which swirled angrily about him. "Didn't I tell you?" said Cable's Italian laborer, wise in the ways of men. "Bound to have war; is already begin-n."[167] Author Holmes Alexander gave voice to former President John Tyler, who confessed his helplessness as an agent of compromise against such a tide of emotion. "Do you know the legend of King Canute," he said. "How he set his throne on the beach and commanded the sea to rise no more."[168]

There is a final curious element in the mass psychology which is described in the novels as a force quite unrelated to

165. Le Cato, *Tom Burton*, p. 25.
166. G. C. Eggleston, *Dorothy South*, p. 377.
167. *Dr. Sevier*, pp. 341-42.
168. Alexander, *American Nabob*, p. 69.

sectional hates and fears. Separate in its appeal was the "quick and vivifying pulse of war"[169] itself—a kind of bottomless void, tugging with an urgent and mystic attraction at the observer on its brink, promising terrible satisfaction of the "homicidal wish," the "fancy with which the human mind had toyed in times of peace in dreams and reveries. . . ."[170] Young men went joyfully into the conflict, staking their lives on the hope of finding "something exhilarating in the bravery which will dare a great danger. . . ."[171] Particularly in the South, if these works of fiction are to be believed, there was a vast supply of half-broken young animals, wild at the smell of blood, their purpose uncomplicated by the slightest division in loyalties, or by moral reflection. To such potential soldiers as the Tarleton twins, in Miss Mitchell's *Gone with the Wind,* the thought of peaceful settlement for the crisis was a shocking idea; they were indignant at the notion that their bravery might go untested.[172] George Washington Cable's young hero, trembling with the pleasure and the terror of anticipated sacrifice, nursing his daydream of a charge to the "death of . . . [his] dearest choice," with a "cheer on . . . [his] lips, red sword waving high,"[173] personifies this essential element in fiction's sense of why the war came. Sidney Lanier, who published *Tiger-Lilies* while the memory of the war was still fresh in his mind, sought to generalize about the positive fascination which lay for Americans in the promise of battle:

An afflatus of war was breathed upon us. Like a great wind, it drew on and blew upon men, women, and children. Its sound mingled with the solemnity of the church-organs and arose with the earnest words of preachers praying for guidance in the matter. It sighed in the half-breathed words of sweethearts conditioning impatient lovers with war-services. It thundered splendidly in the impassioned appeals of orators to the people. It whistled through the streets, it stole in to the firesides, it clinked glasses in barrooms, it lifted the gray hairs of our wise men in conventions, it

169. Stribling, *The Forge,* p. 98.
170. Dixon, *The Man in Gray,* p. 352.
171. Magill, *Women,* p. 5.
172. P. 5.
173. *Dr. Sevier,* pp. 366-71.

thrilled through the lectures in college halls, it rustled the thumbed book-leaves of the school-rooms. . . .

Who could have resisted the fair anticipations which the new war-idea brought? It arrayed the sanctity of a righteous cause in the brilliant trappings of military display; pleasing, so, the devout and the flippant which in various proportions are mixed elements in all men. It challenged the patriotism of sober citizen, while it inflamed the dream of the statesman, ambitious of his country or for himself. It offered test to all allegiances and loyalties; of church, of states; of private loves, of public devotion; of personal consanguinity; of social ties. To obscurity it held out eminence; to poverty, wealth; to greed, a gorged maw; to speculation, legalized gambling; to patriotism, a country; to statesmanship, a government; to virtue, purity; and to love, what all love most desires— a field wherein to assert itself by action.[174]

The peculiar virtue of the novel's capture of this spirit lies not in generalization, but rather in exhibition of mass characteristics in individual terms, through the medium of believable personality. Stephen Crane, for instance, wrote not to psychoanalyze the nation at large; he sought only an accurate statement of the traditions and illusions which sustained Henry Fleming until the youth received the "Red Badge of Courage." Henry Fleming "had, of course, dreamed of battles all his life—of vague and bloody conflicts that had thrilled him with their sweep and fire." He had seen himself at the head of contending armies, with the "peoples secure in the shadow of his eagle-eyed prowess." At this war in his own country, however, he looked with some misgiving. "It must be some sort of play affair. He had long despaired of witnessing a Greek-like struggle. Such would be no more, he had said. Men were better, or more timid. Secular and religious education had effaced the throat-grappling instinct, or else firm finance held in check the passions." He was frequently inclined to enlist and was checked only by his mother's "Henry, don't be a fool."[175]

At last, however, he had made firm rebellion against this yellow light thrown upon the color of his ambitions. The newspapers, the gossip of the village, his own picturings, had aroused him to an

174. Lanier, *Tiger-Lilies*, pp. 96-97.
175. Crane, *The Red Badge of Courage*, pp. 4-6.

uncheckable degree. They were in truth fighting finely there. Almost every day the newspapers printed accounts of a decisive victory.

One night, as he lay in bed, the winds had carried to him the clangoring of the church bell as some enthusiast jerked the rope frantically to tell the twisted news of a great battle. This voice of the people rejoicing in the night had made him shiver in a prolonged ecstasy of excitement. Later, he had gone down to his mother's room and had spoken thus: "Ma, I'm going to enlist." [176]

The same conflict faced Joseph Sumner, a southern boy who broke similarly with parental authority and calm good sense. At fifteen and at sixteen he had wanted to go; at seventeen he could be held no longer. " 'Today I am seventeen years old,' " he cried to his mother, " 'and I have but one feeling: that it is not my duty to stay at home any longer; it is my duty to go into the army. . . . Because,' he said, launching at her the last power of his soul, *'because it is right.' "* [177] From a corner of Charleston harbor, another lad witnessed the bombardment of Sumter and achieved the same decision:

This was *life*. This was seeing life. A strange cry swelled in him, chokingly. He 'hoped to God' that the damned Yankees would never 'get enough.' What did it matter who was hurt, who died? What did it matter how long the war would take? They would be wiped out, the dad-blamed Yankees, the intruders, the Abolitionists. Maybe they're too cowardly to stand it, he wondered. He was sick, wanting an opponent worthy of his mettle. They would *have* to fight, by God they would! A man like Wright—why he would *make* them fight. And there was purification in this sudden frenzy. Dickie felt 'good,' he was glad. His mother must needs acquiesce. . . . There were reasons for existence plain to a man which were not included in their vocabulary. [178]

Inchoate youthful purpose was not the only spirit gratified by the war's coming. The ambitions of world-worn men were also stirred by the conflict's promise of reward. Their decisions were more complicated, and their purposes less naive, but their actions, like those of younger men, were equally unrelated to

176. *Ibid.*, pp. 6-7.
177. J. L. Allen, *The Sword of Youth*, pp. 89, 99.
178. Evelyn Scott, *The Wave*, pp. 5-6.

the abstract "causes" which historians seek for war. Charlie, the village ne'er-do-well, was greatly relieved at the fact that "When you 'j'ined up, 'thank Pete,' you 'was taken care of.'" His constant struggle to stay out of the town jail, his cowering for years "beneath the threats of the respectable," were at an end. "When this war is over, I'll be a vet, you hayseeds back in Hutchinsville. You can't say then that Charlie didn't save the day for you."[179] Another prosaic fighter was Cat-Foot Dawsy, "small, thin and anaemic, belonging to the class called 'dirt eaters,'" who maintained the union standard in the southern mountains. Dawsy "was an important member of a secret organization vowed to resist the compulsion of Tennessee mountaineers into Southern regiments." His loyal convictions sprang from his "general aversion to authority"; the exercise of his talents on the union side resulted from the fact that "the advocates of Northern politics had made no effort to coerce him in behalf of their cause."[180] To another, the war offered redemption from a career which had held perennial failure. Thomas, the blowhard Southerner, hurried back from bankruptcy in California to offer his sword to the South. "His entrance upon a scene of action would not exactly relieve him of family responsibilities, but would, he believed, give 'scope' to his powers." In the future his life would be at the service of his country. "War, Thomas thought, as he glanced out at the ship, restored the 'moral health' of the race. But he was very uneasy."[181]

Without such varied candidates for the armies, the muster rolls would never have been filled, nor war's demands satisfied for a "most profuse and perpetual manuring with human bones. . . ."[182] Neither informed purpose nor conscious ideal

179. *Ibid.*, p. 31.
180. *Ibid.*, p. 50.
181. *Ibid.*, p. 90. The concept of war as an ennobling force was not foreign, of course, to the spirit of the times Miss Scott described. Ralph Waldo Emerson, said James G. Randall, regarded war as "an elemental, purifying force." "War," declared Emerson, "is a realist, shatters everything flimsy and shifty, sets aside all false issues . . . breaks through all that is not real." Randall, "The Blundering Generation," *Miss. Val. Hist. Rev.*, XXVII (June, 1940), 19.
182. Lanier, *Tiger-Lilies*, p. 93.

was necessary to make the soldier who made the war; these only altered slightly his quality. Peter Ashley's service to the South was no less effective because he abandoned the "course that he had cut for himself, that had led him into other lands, other levels of thought. . . ." He was a more efficient soldier, in fact, by his disregard of fact and sacrifice of principle; war satisfied his desire to belong, to drift with his people—without war he might not have been able to act at all. "It was good to lie in the sun with the deep ties of his being flowing smoothly and of their own volition into the warm and genial stream. It was a good thing to have friends, to know love, to be understood."[183]

Calculation of the relative importance of irrelevant human detail in the coming of war results in no easy generalization nor exact conclusion. It is evident, however, that the novelist makes a unique contribution by his realistic appraisal of the individual crises that were the separate factors of national calamity. Where but in fiction can be found reasonable explanation for the willingness of millions to come voluntarily to war? What other art comprehends the suicidal purpose of the masses who were neither statesmen nor philosophers, whose material stake in the conflict was negligible, whose action issued from a state of happy immunity to history, fact, and logic? It is the novelist who fashions in acceptable terms an answer for the conscript who wanted to know why, with life still dear, men *volunteer* for war. "Well," one soldier replied, "I was sick of farming, and I didn't mind getting away from my wife and chillen for a while neither." A companion sought voice for a sense of larger purpose: "You wouldn't understand," he told the draftee, "because it is clear you have no adventure in you. Wasn't everybody else going? Wasn't it new? Wouldn't you want to see what a battle was, a soldier's life? Besides, you couldn't be left behind. . . ."[184]

A search for the truth of the Civil War experience may unite the novelist and the historian in spirit, but their common

183. Heyward, *Peter Ashley,* p. 253.
184. Dowdey, *Where My Love Sleeps,* p. 86.

goal will not be attained through common methods. Novelists of the late nineteenth century who relied on slightly fictionalized statements of prevailing historical theories about the causes of the war generally failed to add personal dimension to the historical forces they described. Their versions of conspiracies, constitutional arguments, abolitionism, or competitive economies were reputable enough—at least they paralleled formal historical interpretations of the time—but these stories were better told by the historians for whom the excitement of evolving public policy was a primary interest. The readers of early Civil War novels were not misinformed, but they were very likely to be bored. It was not until the best-seller era at the turn of the century that novelists learned, as a general rule, to accept the discipline of their form and to suit their narratives to the shape of their talents.

Judgments based on chronological categories, comments on the "nineteenth-century" or the "twentieth-century" novel, are obviously flawed by the introduction of any critical standard in dealing with the mass of the novels. The fact that John William De Forest, Sidney Lanier, George Washington Cable, and Stephen Crane were offering psychological explanations for the coming of the war, while at the same time the conspiracy and state rights themes were being maintained in the mass of the novels, reveals the inadequacy of analysis of books by publication dates. Their contradiction of prevailing themes indicates also that developing or perfected art, rather than new views of old facts, are the substantial source of "new" interpretations. The considerable reputations won by recent historians through emphasis on the passions of the 1860's as a key to understanding of the period becomes testimony to the real achievement of the artists who reached the same conclusions while prejudice and partisanship were at their Reconstruction heights. By successful identification with the fundamental spirit of the war era, art discovered a short cut to conclusions that came to more pedestrian observers after generations of reflection. Praise for this achievement, however, is due as much to the form of the art as to the superior insight of the artist.

Given a problem of national importance, the novelist begins with a personal focus, which, if successful, may develop as a sound base for generalization; whereas the historian, faced with the same issues, must necessarily deal with official decisions and recorded public actions before he adds notice of personal problems and details. That a novelist should come first to a psychological interpretation of the war's causes is no surprise.

In other respects, even when he is faithful to recorded fact, the novelist is free from basic limitations on the writing of history. However profound his respect for the extreme complexity of causes that precede national decision, his task is virtually done once he provides coherent explanation for the actions of a single hero or family. His obligation to trace causes to ultimate sources, to weigh and judge all the elements of an historical movement need be no greater than he himself chooses to make it. He fixes the horizons of his created spokesmen and may confine to the briefest exposition any general historical background. He is freed thereby to pursue his single purpose with infinite care, to make very good the point he chooses to emphasize. His work is unlikely to be neutralized by objectivity, for, unlike that of the historian, his success depends on his identification with partisan characters.

Intense personality, of course, carries its own limitations. The romance and the adventure story make a poor medium for abstract argument; such doctrines as state rights, or involved economic interpretation, load with interruptions the story which is fiction's basic concern. Even efforts to resurrect the actual figures of the past are greatly restricted, for statesmen whose views are on the record fit poorly into fictional channels; characters who have existed outside the novelist's control escape the authority by which he governs his imagined creatures.

There is abundant compensation in the novels, however, to balance such difficulties, for within his own element, the novelist makes a unique contribution to an understanding of the war's coming. Dead passions are the cold gravy of history, repellent to tranquil memory; and the novelist, mixing again the ingredients, can provide a reader with the essence of reality. The one thing that recorded fact cannot supply is a fully realized personality; and it is by concentration on people rather than forces and events that the novels make findings of primary importance. Successful realization of individual character must be achieved before the curious logic of war's raw emotions can be exposed. Once such intensely personal qualities as selfless love, courage, or hate are understood within a single hero, then the reader enjoys a unique view of the era in which that hero performs. Only then can the lonely terror of fear before battle, or resignation to hopeless sacrifice, be caught with the heat of life in them. With such capture, inspired artistry, probing for the limits of the nation's spirit, recalling in sympathy and understanding the disintegration of ante-bellum society, mocks the footnote with an authority more imposing than truth itself. Sensitive readers, by such a medium, can penetrate the veil of years and experience for themselves the tortured decisions of 1861. With the youth of James Lane Allen's story, they can stand on the very edge of the "whole tumultuous disordered field of duty."

But what was duty? It was right to go, it was wrong to go. It was right to stay, it was wrong to stay. He could not be true without being false, faithful without being faithless, loyal unless he deserted—something, somebody.

And thus in a way the boy, alone there on his father's farm in the darkness of that September evening long years ago—in his way he was all of us. The nation writhed in the death-throes of a great sad war; but within him was a greater war still. It is the war we all wage between what is right within us and what is right; between one duty and another duty; between what is good and what is good. Not war between our strength and our weakness but between our strength and our strength, between our peace and our peace. When we triumphantly fight the evil within us with the good within us, we have our victory for our reward; but whenever we destroy one glorious virtue with another glorious virtue, our triumph can only be our loss. For we have driven from the battlefield of the mind a vital force which yesterday we may have relied upon to win life with; and to-morrow we may fail to win life again because we have defeated that force today. In the victorious war of good over evil we reap at least the approval of conscience; but in the warfare of our good upon our good we can only achieve the partial destruction of ourselves: we have become conquerers of our best.[185]

185. J. L. Allen, *The Sword of Youth*, p. 136.

THE ARTIST AND
THE PAST

I
Blue and Grey: The Essential
Contrast

THE CONFLICT between blue and grey in Civil War
fiction has been conducted on a shifting field, a battle-
ground where lines once drawn in terms of historical
generalizations are now abandoned. Differences in northern
and southern memories of the war are found today in the
separate artistic focus of the sections' better novelists, and in
the degree of loyalty maintained by these novelists to the institutions or individuals they recall. The enduring fiction of
the Civil War is still divided on sectional lines, but the point
of division is fixed by a process of artistic rather than historical
selection. Novelists are no longer really concerned with the
cause of the Union or of the Confederacy; they reveal their
regional origins by their adherence to the discipline of naturalism or of romanticism, by their statement of northern realities
or by their gathering of southern dreams.

Sectional contrasts in these terms are immediately evident
when the best Civil War novels are isolated for extended
analysis. Critics of the literature, however, have been so impressed with the incurably romantic quality of southern war
novels that they have attempted study of only half the contrast,

and have generally confined themselves to despairing derogation of neo-Confederate distortions. Even in this effort they
are too quick to despair, it seems to me. They lose sight of the
fact that it was on romantic thought, however logical or illogi-
cal, that the South based some of its deepest longings. Dreams
such as many Southerners had were insubstantial things, too
often doomed to wither in the harsh light of objective scholarship. When the historian sets out to define and document the
exact nature of ante-bellum southern hopes, he is compelled to
work with the facts of the Old South's achievements. So analyzed, the ambition realized most successfully, the ideal
achieved most fully, cannot but suffer the depreciation attend-
ant on all dreams come down to earth. But the essence of a
dream is in the dreaming—and for this reason, fiction's
idealization of mannered southern life may serve to hold the
substance of ambition, the element of the ideal, uncensored by
the realities of southern rural economics.

Novels about the ante-bellum South and the Confederacy
are not often taken on their own terms, however. Critics have
been governed by their suspicion of the literature's profoundly
romantic qualities. They have sifted from it certain stylized
elements prevalent in "lost cause" fiction and, scornful of the
moonlit inaccuracy they have exposed, have reached conclusions which tend to be a record of the divergence between
literary traditions and what they conceive to be historical reality.
Francis Pendleton Gaines, in the most engaging study of this
sort, indicted the South's artistic preservation of its war memories for "general inadequacy"—a failure he ascribed to the
"tacit assumption by . . . tradition that plantation society was
feudalistically tri-partite: the lordly planter, the slaves, the 'po'
white trash.' "[1]

My objection to this conclusion, it should be emphasized, is
not directed at its evident validity. The literary version of the
Civil War does suffer from a disproportionate emphasis on
idealized upper-class life; a record of fiction's southern society
would reveal a great surplus of lords and ladies, and woeful

1. *The Southern Plantation*, p. 144.

deficiencies, except during recent years, in the farmer population which was in reality the "backbone of that society."[2] Sins of omission, however, are a poor basis for condemnation of a novelist who, by definition after all, is privileged to set for himself the social and intellectual limits for his survey. His success within these limits is the only valid basis for critical evaluation. Reflection on the mass of novels, furthermore, should not eliminate comment on unusual books which reveal phases of social history absent from most war fiction. Many of the "best" Civil War novels introduced in these pages are not subject to the generalizations based on standard and traditional works.

Much critical effort has been wasted on compilation of standard casts of characters who appear in enough Civil War novels to be described as "typical" of the old South's plantation setting. Only a cursory reading of a few northern Civil War novels reveals that sectional distinctions based on such investigations are often false or non-existent. The stock figures habitually credited to the southern tradition—particularly the first old gentleman of the plantation home—confound easy generalizations by their appearance in settings and conditions quite foreign to the South. The squire of an Illinois village shares with a Virginia planter habits of quaint courtesy, a profound sense of individual dignity, and a sensitive honor. The Natchez nabob and the New York merchant take equal pride in the beauty of willful daughters, and each suffers moments of anguish with the swift maturing of hot-blooded sons. The establishments of both may be under the direction of tyrannical, comical, and faithful servants. The "typical" characters of northern and southern novels are separated by no consistent distinctions. Economic settings as the basis for cultural contrasts are scarcely more satisfying. Southern novels, for all their emphasis on plantation life, are here at fault; they are so crowded with accounts of rural entertainments that no time is left for chopping cotton. The northern merchant or the village lawyer is frequently presented at his business, but the Southerner sits for fiction's portrait while taking his ease.

2. Bassett, *Slavery in the State of North Carolina*, p. 47.

Distinct sectional identity becomes evident, however, in the degree of emphasis placed on social, as opposed to personal, relationships in the novels of the North and South. Stories of northern life are focussed on the abilities and the characters of single heroes of heroines, individuals whose society is depicted as the hostile setting for their lonely struggles and ambitions. With a southern writer, on the other hand, families or whole communities tend to divide the author's attention and stretch his canvas to cover a social rather than a personal scene. The easy assignment of various plantation personages to "type" only exposes the fact that large numbers of these characters gain purpose as players in a larger company, a company, moreover, that sustains each of its members with confidence and love. Northern and southern novels thus seem clearly separated both by the size of the social scene described, and by the relation of individuals within the scene to their society. Concentration on group ideals lends a unity, some elements of a composite sectional mind, to novels of southern life—a quality that has no counterpart in northern definition of varied and unrelated personal careers.

Northern fiction, to a much greater degree than southern, has tended to escape the "besetting weakness" which Lewis Mumford has described as the primary pitfall in the path of the regionalist. The northern authors have avoided

blind reaction against outward circumstances and disruptions, an attempt to find refuge within an old shell against the turbulent invasions of the outside world, armed with its new engines: in short, an aversion from what is, rather than an impulse toward what may be. For the merely sentimental regionalist, the past was an absolute. His impulse was to fix some definite moment in the past, and to keep on living it over and over again, holding the "original" regional customs . . . to keep these "original" customs and habits and interests fixed forever in the same mold: a neurotic retreat.[3]

The temptation to make such a sentimental retreat into the past has been powerfully attractive to southern writers. Their con-

3. Mumford, *Technics and Civilization,* pp. 292-93.

centration on an idealized parochial society has often been
part of an effort to embrace the whole of ante-bellum life. Their
society was destroyed by the war, and they have attempted to
take its death mask. Theirs is a static memory of something
complete, something finished, and they have conceived it their
duty to raise fitting monuments to selected portions of its history. Northerners, on the other hand, have set their pens to a
more complicated task. Their concern with individuals, rather
than with classes and societies, has not led them to an auto-
matic climax at an arbitrarily chosen moment in time—a
moment of final victory or defeat. War, to the individuals on
whom they focussed, provided a decisive turning, but on a
highway in time which began before the war, and, after it,
stretched on toward the future. Victory put no period to their
story, provided no leisured retirement that could be devoted to
a calmly taken inventory of coherent hopes, purposes, and
ideals. Their life, unlike that of the Southerners, was still with
them; it did not, with the passage of years, dissolve into a simple outline of the half-forgotten and the unknown. They dealt
with fragments of continuing experience; the world they described was without end. For Northerners, the words "before
the war" were devoid of the romantic content they tended to
hold for Southerners. The youth of the North, and youth's
dreams, lay perhaps in the pre-war years, but the disillusionment of maturity could not be dated from a hopeless charge in
the early afternoon up a Pennsylvania slope; and the burden
of post-war despair could not be translated into sullen resentment against an alien invader. Northern writers have felt
obligated to haul out the ashes of victory—a chore they have
undertaken with intensive and realistic self-criticism. Their
increasingly savage reinterpretations of the war years have
been concentrated on more and more limited bits of the northern experience, more intensively examined—until some of them
have reduced their story to disordered scraps of memory such
as might have constituted a union veteran's recurring nightmare. The contrast at the South could not be more complete.
An affection there for certain qualities in the southern com-

munity, a fascination with the unrealized promises of the southern past, have sustained even the realist in loyalty to the region which is his subject.

Judgment based on selection from the best Civil War novels, rather than averages run on the bulk of the literature, must be employed to reveal these substantial differences in northern and southern memories of the war. The handful of novels referred to in the following pages are by no means "representative" of all the war stories; for the most part they are built on variations from standard themes. They are distinguished by their originality, their serious purpose, and by their full measure of the degree to which passionate artistry can restore human detail to the public records that conceal the past in arbitrary outlines.

II
The North Examines Itself

A pattern for the North's sharply critical approach to its war record was laid down before the nineteenth century was done. Today, a critic who seeks to understand the North's version of the war looks to the works of John William De Forest, Harold Frederic, or Stephen Crane for the beginning of realism in reports of the region's experience—or for that matter, for the beginning of realism in the whole literature of the nation.[4] These authors completed their harsh analysis of the struggle for the union well before more amiable reunionizers—such writers as Winston Churchill or John Fox—reached the climax of their descriptions of the old Websterian ship of state, driving safely to haven without loss of a single star from the flag. At

4. Spiller, Thorp, Johnson, Canby, eds., *Literary History of the United States,* II, 881. "The first American writer to deserve the name of realist," this work concludes, "was John William De Forest. . . ."

the North, this technicolor vision of a brother's war was contradicted from the start by the disillusioned summaries of critics who calculated the costs of victory.

An able journalist filed in 1867 a minority report on the North's achievement which remains not only the first but also one of the most competent discussions of the union's moral casualty list. John William De Forest described with genuine patriotism *Miss Ravenel's Conversion From Secession to Loyalty,* but he was never blinded to what was ridiculous, stupid, or corrupt in the war effort of which he was a part. In his state of "New Barratavia," officers were appointed according to their political connections, rather than their promise of military ability; for although the "Governor would know better . . . he might be driven to it, for fear of losing the next election."[5] Young Colburne, the hero, had to be content with the captaincy of a company, while the majority for which he was fitted went to Gazaway, who "lives in a very close district, and influences a considerable number of votes." The governor pointed out that the leading members of his party "concur in urging upon me this promotion of Gazaway. . . . If we refuse it we shall probably lose the district and a member of Congress. That is a serious matter at this time when the administration must be supported by a strong house, or the nation may be shipwrecked." This consideration outweighed the fact that men in the field were put at the mercy of a malingerer and a coward; and when Major Gazaway was finally faced with charges and a court martial, he wangled a surgeon's certificate of disability, and was permitted to resign his commission. Back at home, he was reappointed a lieutenant colonel and put in charge of a conscript camp, where he could make $500 on each draftee who wished to escape service.

De Forest was no easier on characters for whom he had re-

5. The problem of state politics in the organization of the union forces is discussed by Shannon, *The Organization and Administration of the Union Army,* I, 45-46. Political appointments of officers, and corruption in general in the northern armies, are also considered by Randall, *The Civil War and Reconstruction,* pp. 425-30, and in "The Civil War Restudied," *Jour. So. Hist.,* VI (1940), 455.

spect. Colonel Carter, the hard-drinking, loyalist Virginian, an ideal fighting man, was in camp "a hard-hearted, intelligent, conscientious, beneficent tyrant." His virtues as an army administrator, and as a husband, however, did not match his qualities in the field. As chief quartermaster of the Gulf Department, he handled tremendous sums of money, a fact which turned him eventually to private speculation with the funds. Loss here forced him to declare large amounts of United States property surplus, sell them cheaply at auction, then discover new needs for the same material, and rebuy at much higher prices. Thus his earlier defalcations could be covered. Colonel Carter kept faith with his wife no better than with the government which trusted him with such responsibilities. He was delighted when the creole vamp of the piece offered him an opportunity for a casual seduction—and his conscience, after a brief and frantic affair, did not bother him when he was again in the presence of his young and loving wife, the former Miss Ravenel. The wages of sin, incidentally, went unpaid in this account; the other woman prospered, and Colonel Carter suffered discomfiture only by exposure of his affair, and not from a nagging inner spirit.

Amid personalities of such vigor, Captain Colburne, whose military career paralleled that of De Forest himself, came out second best. He ended the war with the rank which he held at its beginning, promotion having gone to those who had the proper political connections. Miss Ravenel was his second-hand; she married him as a widow with a young child. Peace found him wasted by disease, fatigue, and disillusionment—and half mad with the red tape which he, as the one surviving officer of his original company, had to untangle. Colburne's war, in other words, had little of romance about it; he fought a losing battle against politics, corruption, red tape, incompetent medical attention and his love for a woman who succumbed to the wholly physical attractions of his rival. The world seemed to conspire to block his path to success and happiness; as an honest and idealistic man, he was out of step with a society that rewarded more practical virtues.

De Forest's disillusioned report of the fact that army life had
little connection with romance, and that battles were more
barbarous than heroic, was duplicated in a few early novels
about life behind the northern lines. Harold Frederic, for instance, concentrated on the war madness illustrated in *The
Copperhead,* his story of a farming community in upstate New
York. Before the war, Abner Beach was the leading citizen of
Agrippa, New York. His wisdom was the school board's guide;
he was a supervisor of the town; his farm was a model of good
management. He declared himself unalterably opposed, however, to the new party that wished to "establish negro sovereignty in the Republic, and to compel each white girl to marry
a black man." As he gradually assumed the role of copperhead,
his standing in the community disintegrated rapidly. For when
his "church-going community had reached the conclusion that
a man couldn't be a Christian and hold such views of the slave
question as Beech held, it was only a very short step to the
conviction that such a man would water his milk." Beech had
been honored earlier for his reputation as "a great hand for
reading"; but when war came, it was said "that his opinions
were worthless because he got them from printed books instead of from his heart." The fallen leader was gradually isolated
from commercial and social intercourse within the village—
and isolation was soon followed by hatred. His hired man was
denied the ballot because Agrippa wanted no more than one
copperhead vote to mar its Republican strength. When Beech
lighted a bonfire to celebrate the Democratic party gains of
1862 in New York, his neighbors let their resentment sweep
them into hysterical retaliation that climaxed with the burning
of his house on a winter night. The crusade for human freedom included no tolerance for dissenters.

De Forest and Frederic swam against the current of nineteenth-century fiction, but their successor in the mastery of
realistic detail turned the stream and cut a channel which has
been utilized ever since. When Stephen Crane wrote *The Red
Badge of Courage,* according to Bernard De Voto, he "established a way of writing about battle that in our time has had a

decisive influence."[6] Crane made no effort to describe the whole war, or even a whole campaign. He concentrated on a two-day engagement, observed from the platoon level. His whole concern was with the emotions and reactions of a single youth under fire for the first time. The fact that his hero fought for the union at Chancellorsville was only incidental—his search was for the basic and universal elements of battle psychology. His story was complete when he showed how a man's instinctive fear of imminent death, his over-powering urge for self-preservation, even at the expense of a hero's self-esteem, could be suppressed for exercise of the irrational courage demanded by society of the young men it delivered to the cannon's mouth.

Henry Fleming, hero of the story, was very brave before the battle was fought. The first rebel assault did nothing to shake his confidence in the invincibility of the regiment of which he was a part; the opening skirmish only permitted the boy and his platoon a moment for self-congratulation. The battle was won, and they had proved themselves. This mood evaporated swiftly, however, when the enemy regrouped and came on. The youth "began to exaggerate the endurance, the skill, and the valor of those who were coming. Himself reeling from exhaustion, he was astonished beyond measure at such persistency. They must be machines of steel." Inexperienced dismay gave way to terror.

A man near him who up to this time had been working feverishly at his rifle suddenly stopped and ran with howls. A lad whose face had borne an expression of exalted courage, the majesty of he who dares to give his life, was, at an instance, a smitten abject. He blanched like one who has come to the edge of a cliff at midnight and is suddenly made aware. There was a revelation. He, too, threw down his gun and fled. There was no shame in his face. He ran like a rabbit.

Others began to scamper away through the smoke. The youth turned his head, shaken from his trance by this movement as if the regiment was leaving him behind. He saw the few fleeting forms.

6. "Fiction Fights the Civil War," *Sat. Rev. Lit.,* XVII (Dec. 18, 1937), 3.

He yelled then with fright and swung about. For a moment, in the great clamor, he was like a proverbial chicken. He lost the direction of safety. Destruction threatened him from all points.

Directly he began to speed toward the rear in great leaps. His rifle and cap were gone. His unbuttoned coat bulged in the wind. The flap of his cartridge box bobbed wildly, and his canteen, by its slender cord, swung out behind. On his face was all the horror of those things which he imagined. . . .

He ran like a blind man. Two or three times he fell down. Once he knocked his shoulder so heavily against a tree that he went headlong.

Since he had turned his back upon the fight his fears had been wondrously magnified. Death about to thrust him between the shoulder blades was far more dreadful than death about to smite him between the eyes. When he thought of it later, he conceived the impression that it is better to view the appalling than to be merely within hearing. The noises of battle were like stones; he believed himself liable to be crushed. [7]

Shame quickly engulfed him when he found himself among the wounded who were making their way to the rear. The battle, he discovered, had not been lost; and braver men still held the lines at the front. He found a wounded friend, who was more concerned with Henry's well-being than his own, who urged the boy to "leave me be," to go on to safety. The man fell in the midst of his pleas, and his jacket dropped away from his body to reveal a side that "looked as if it had been chewed by wolves. . . . The youth turned, with sudden, livid rage, toward the battlefield." He worked his way back to his company by nightfall and discovered, to his surprise, that a fumbled explanation about getting separated, about fighting on, was believed without question.

The second day of the battle brought increasing "hate for the relentless foe. Yesterday when he had imagined the universe to be against him, he had hated it, little gods and big gods; to-day he hated the army of the foe with the same great hatred." This was the emotion which swept him at the crucial moment into danger, rather than away from it. "Once he, in his intent hate, was almost alone, and was firing, when all those

7. Crane, *The Red Badge of Courage,* 67-69.

near him had ceased. He was so engrossed in his occupation
that he was not aware of a lull." His fellows murmured ad-
miringly; "they now looked upon him as a war devil." The
mood sustained him through the day; he led a charge; he
seized the colors when they fell and carried them on. The
colonel mentioned his bravery to his lieutenant.

The youth pondered the two days when it was done and
knew that he had had no better control of himself on the second
than he had had on the first day; one had been as senseless as
the other. But he "knew that he would no more quail before
his guides wherever they should point. He had been to touch
the great death, and found that, after all, it was but the great
death. He was a man." Memory, moreover, could not contain
the nightmare realities of battle, and "as he trudged from the
place of blood and wrath his soul changed. He came from hot
plowshares to prospects of clover tranquilly, and it was as if
hot plowshares were not. Scars faded as flowers."

The war outlined in these reports by Crane, Frederic, or De
Forest was more a calamity in individual lives than a national
or regional experience. Instead of a gorgeously patterned epic
of contending armies, battle was here presented as a senseless
denial of reason. Interpretations of the war's meaning became
exercises in abnormal psychology, rather than explanations
for the North's decisions. The pattern evident in these early
northern reports, moreover, has become a standard approach
for the ablest modern descriptions of the union war effort. At
the South, authors often continue to provide sense and logic for
military campaigns by placing their heroes at the side of a
Jackson or a Forrest; Northerners, on the other hand, achieve
a wholly different tone by reducing the scope of actual combat
until it lies within the sight and hearing of a central figure in
the front lines. Climaxes are moments of disordered horror,
rather than of patriotic achievement; and their conclusions
tend to be oriented toward what was lost rather than what was
won.

Joseph Stanley Pennell, for instance, when he investigated in
1944 *The History of Rome Hanks,* adopted a plot that had

already been used by De Forest—the story of promotion over the good captain of weaklings with political connections. Rome Hanks, however, scarcely spoke the same language as De Forest's Captain Colburne. A modern taste, to begin with, allowed Pennell freedom with four letter words that De Forest, for all his realism, could not have imagined. Pennell's war was composed of mountains of amputated limbs, flopping and headless bodies, the curses and screams of the damned.

Sometimes the sawbones were cauterizers; they would whack off a leg and burn the new bone-and-meat end with hot oil or irons. . . . Oh, there was plenty of sawing, all right . . . wagonloads of amputated feet, legs, arms, hands and everything that could be cut off a man, lying around loose in front of houses and cabins. . . .

Retribution for some sinners came like lightning:

Tom looked over the stretcher's edge and saw the shoe-stealer faceless on the grass, the weeds around him all spattered with blood, and the bloody pulp that had been a dirty Rebel face under a slouch-hat—it lay bloody under his head—clustered with bright little green flies.

A monster appeared for a moment in the dust and smoke of Pickett's Charge.

Below the man's nose there wasn't any face. His lower jaw was gone and you could see his open throat—there wasn't even any tongue. But the palate was there twitchin' around in a great blood-oozy hole with powdersmut on the white skin around it. From the hair and the look of what face there was left, it was a boy of about sixteen— [8]

From the slime of such obscene nightmares emerged Pennell's war hero—General Clint Belton. A craven in his first battle, Belton cowered under the bluffs at Pittsburg Landing, but his cowardice was overlooked by superiors who enjoyed his plentiful cigars, his excellent liquor, his blatant flattery. Nothing could stop his rise—least of all the contempt that his intimates felt for him. As Secretary of War he was able, even, to entertain presidential ambitions until his political future was

8. Pennell, *The History of Rome Hanks,* pp. 71-72, 203.

destroyed by the frauds and scandals that history relates to the career of W. W. Belknap. After his impeachment, however, a Radical Republican majority prevented his conviction. The form by which Pennell lent convincing force to his narrative might be described as a sort of literary cubism. Considered separately, the specimens in his chamber of horrors were scarcely more than waxwork figures, but jumbled together in a jagged frame of distorted chronology and geography, they emerged with an insane intensity which gave unity to the work, yet which preserved the author's view of the war as a thing of witless complexity, of contradictory and disordered madness.

The conception of war as a meaningless catastrophe has been an obsession with the best northern writers of the movement. Four of the six "best" novels from the northern point of view, listed on page 12, were confined by this conviction to concern with armies and battles, to the exclusion of more general social history. The best modern novel produced in the North about the war, MacKinlay Kantor's *Long Remember,* illustrates both the good and the bad in such approaches. Kantor described the descent of war on the sleepy little town of Gettysburg, Pennsylvania—not a story, from behind an army, of an approach to a battlefield, but rather the conversion of a peaceful village into a festering rage. The conflict was seen through the eyes of a completely detached observer, a man who had returned to Gettysburg after six years on the Minnesota frontier, and who looked with contemptuous amazement on the war spirit which surrounded him. "Everyone ought to know better," Dan Bale said. "But of course they don't. Human beings belie their designation every day, and have been doing so constantly for two years. The only hope is to keep on until all the fools are killed off." Bale reflected with disgust on the change in a childhood friend: "His pale eyes were narrow and expressionless . . . yes, he's the soldier, he is it, this is the right thing for him to do, he is suitable clay for them to shape and, Almighty God, they have shaped him!"

War was a silly "boy's dream" but the people of Gettysburg

were possessed by it. A mother of the town had a pat conception of the conflict in which her son was engaged:

He lived in a tent, as did all other soldiers. The tents were snow-white, they stood in even rows, mile after mile. Pennons flapped from their ridge-poles. Tyler sat at a rude desk writing letters home, writing orders, writing dispatches. Sometimes a bugle blew. He went out, then, to oversee a drill. The army filed past, rank on rank, glistening steel, garish buttons, pristine gloves. The army saluted Tyler. He sat on his horse, rigid, stern, young. . . . . Still her boy, her boy. "Captain, the rebels are advancing." "Convey my respects to General Hooker, sir, and inform him that the rebels are advancing." Cannon began to boom in measured, spaced billows of sound; there was the "roll of musketry." Smoke became thick and white. Far away sounded the rebel yell. Advance friends, and give the countersign. Forward, march! Present arms! Fire![9]

Reality descended on Gettysburg so swiftly that it paralyzed the mind with its screeching noise, its scurrying armies, first grey then blue, and death. War overnight became the smell of "decaying flesh. . . . It was the chestnut gelding beside [the] . . . front fence, now forty hours dead, a vast balloon frosted with a thousand flies." War came with the death of a yapping household pet, one moment frantically barking at the heels of the hurrying intruders on his yard, and the next dragging to the door in yelping agony with a pistol bullet in his back. War was a great moment of history, when Pickett's men moved out toward the slope just south of the town cemetery.

God, they're dressing. Lookit that—dressing—crazy as—Anyway, that's the prettiest movement ever saw executed under fire. The ramrods clattered. Gray nations straightened out and swung to the right, arching in toward the slope. The nest of guns gave out their bile, spurt by spurt . . . rapidly they began to have faces. Most of them were lugging their rifles at their sides and working the rods with their right hands as they came. Crust of smoke sped out to meet them.

They kept roaring, every throat wide open with sound. The Nationals were standing up, man by man, standing up and falling down and standing up and falling down. Pink flag dodged forward; the smoke shredded and let it through, and a struggling clay torrent screeched behind. The front runners kept flinging out

9. Kantor, *Long Remember*, pp. 81-92.

their hands and sprawling forward, and others tumbled over them
to do the same thing. The flag bobbed closer, supported by a tight-
locked mass of bare arms. Squarely in front of the rolling haze,
a row of men came out and knelt; their muskets flamed, but you
couldn't hear the sound any more. There lived a single ocean of
pulsation and wail, a bursting rattle which knit all solitary explo-
sions together. . . . Dan slipped, his feet were tangled in something
slimy. Felt like ropes: good God, they weren't ropes. . . .[10]

The storm ended as quickly as it had begun. The next day
Henry Niede, a German farmer of the neighborhood, was
scavanging on the battlefield; corpses brought three dollars each
in the Philadelphia medical school. "And maybe I should
starve to death if they make a mess by my farm?" he said. "I
never got my wheat; and now there is a hole in my house
roof costs fifty dollars. *Ja,* it costs maybe sixty. Three dollars
apiece is all I get for these here." The body of Elijah Hud-
dleston, who was to have married his daughter, lay unrecognized on his cart.

There was no purpose in the battle as Kantor described it.
Dan Bale, the narrator, observed the first two days from within
the Confederate lines and crossed over to the other ridge on
the second evening. The talk there was the same, and the
bullets proved to be without sectional enthusiasm. The tale was
one of pointless disorder, an account of a sudden collapse in
the market price for human life. Even this change in values
was without clear emphasis, because of Kantor's fixation on
the fact of war itself. His battle came so quickly, as Allen Tate
has pointed out, that for the people he described, he provided
no "well-defined background of civilized life to give their disorder significance."[11] His sacrifice of broad purpose, of meaning, was conscious, for by such sacrifice his central theme of
senseless conflict emerged with greater clarity.

Other modern Northerners, sensitive perhaps to the defici-
ency noted by Tate, have attempted more general interpretation of their culture. Even in these stories of civil life, however,
individual heroes have tended to be rebels against orthodox

10. *Ibid.,* pp. 376-78.
11. "Gettysburg," *Nation,* CXXXVIII (April 11, 1934), 420.

prejudices and customs; their lives have been keyed to the same note of denial, of criticism, which was characteristic of the battle figures cited. Out of step with their fellows, they have served as symbols of resistance to crawling ambitions, to the sinister transformation brought by the war era to their society. The extent and effectiveness of their resistance has thus become a measure of the shortcomings of their times.

There is a superficial similarity between the civilian heroes of the North and the courtly aristocrats of the South, in that both held as their ideal the maintenance of a sort of Jeffersonian individuality. Expression of the southern version of this ideal, however, tends to take the form of an agrarian hope, a search for physical self-sufficiency, which is quite apart from the quest for spiritual independence, for intellectual adventure, which is reported as the northern effort. Leonard Westerfield Atterberry, the hero of Edgar Lee Masters' *The Tide of Time,* would have seen no virtue in proud isolation from popular commotions. He was a lawyer, a meddler with other people's misfortunes. He found his role as the "natural defender of the misunderstood."[12] He was satisfied with his calling, for he thought it a noble thing to "help people to settle their quarrels," to "keep them out of quarrels." He broke a thousand lances on the windmills of village mediocrity before he came slowly to recognize the fact that idealism, like baser motivations, could be subject to distortion and misuse. He never overcame his dismay at wartime expression of the "idealistic side to human nature. The tragic thing is that whenever this side is stirred, materialism and trade use it and profit by it." A war fought in a cause however just could not have good results, for the

only God that wants wars is the God of the jungle; and the only currents of destiny are the volitions of men, and for the most part they are but the secret machinations of men who are dynastically minded; and who perceiving that they have the power to make eras, and that the time is ripe for some change, set about with conscious wills to change history and the fortunes of states.[13]

12. P. 317.
13. Masters, *The Tide of Time,* p. 577.

The repeated lesson of his life was that "Fate . . . lingers about the so called great adventures of men just to cover them with mysterious inconsistency and satire."

Masters was as skeptical of the glories of northern victory, of the virtues of post-war progress, as the most unrepentant Southerner—a point of view emphasized by the politics of his Democratic hero. He intended his book to "show how good human material can be swept up by the tide of time into shallows and onto shoals."[14] Leonard Westerfield Atterberry had the qualities of a great man, but his life ravelled out hopelessly from a tangled skein of lost causes. The war changed Ferrisburg, Illinois; "corruption seeped into" the town and hardfaced strangers walked its streets. The village reflected in its affairs the course of the nation.

The whole country was in turmoil and covered from end to end with the stench of corruption. The wicked policy of reconstruction had made all the Southern States subject to the rule of negroes, and their rascally white allies from the North. Speculators and thieves had descended upon the South, great bond issues were fastened upon the conquered South, and the money was filched by patriots like Editor Hamilton. The country was being devoured by stock gamblers. Bribery was the order of the day; and the states were being sapped of their rights and powers in order that there would be centrally located at Washington officials and bureaus who could be reached easily, and over the heads of Illinois, and every other state, by railroads and monopolists and corporations. Ulysses Grant knew how to reduce the fortress of Vicksburg; he had no skill in handling the rising forces of corruption and sinister lawlessness concerned in getting money and doing it as quickly as possible. He had said "let us have peace"; but how to have economic peace based upon equal rights and no privileges was beyond him. . . . Leonard Westerfield hated all this with passionate indignation. All the great pugnacity that was in him rose up to attack the regime of Grant and the North, and to denounce bitterly the corruption which . . . made itself evident in one way or another in every locality of the whole district.[15]

But time and again, "With great dissatisfaction and mortification he had to submit to defeat. He felt in sadness of heart

14. *Ibid.*, author's comment on dust jacket.
15. *Ibid.*, pp. 432-33.

that not only was the age changing around him; but that he was loosing strength with which to cope with the multiplying difficulties and with new antagonists."

To Masters, the frustrations of the Gilded Age contrasted sharply with the tranquility of ante-bellum years. In such books as his, the time before the war was described with an affection which became a pathetic sigh for America's lost youth. It was not a time, as it became for romantic Southerners, of a splendidly maturing civilization; the period was recalled, rather as a fragile moment of trembling innocence and unfettered hope. To Ross Lockridge, Jr., it was the land of *Raintree County,* "which had no boundaries in time and space, where lurked musical and strange names and mythical and lost peoples, and which was itself only a name musical and strange."[16] It was "not the country of the perishable fact. It is the country of the enduring fiction. The clock in the Court House Tower on page five of the *Raintree County Atlas* is always fixed at nine o'clock, and it is summer and the days are long." It was a land of country crossroads and well-kept farms, of peaceful villages surrounded by secret woodland retreats. The village of Danwebster, in the heart of the county, was but the "memory of a little town, of golden and agrarian days and sainted elders on the porches in the evening talking of the Union. Here lies the white republic, founded foursquare on the doctrine of universal law."

Danwebster was the homeplace of John Wickliff Shawnessy, "the budding bard of Raintree County, Life's eternal young American." Johnny Shawnessy came to manhood before the war, in a "season of gorgeous dreams by day and night." He "lived in a continual torment of desire—desire to know, to possess, to make."

The life of Johnny Shawnessy was a repetition of the legend of the Great Stone Face—but in his person and works he reflected not the granite of a New England mountain, but the fertility, the mystery, and the beauty of Raintree County earth. Like the hero of Hawthorne's story, he remained in the place

16. Title page.

of his birth while more famous sons of the county returned only occasionally for its praise—celebrated men like United States Senator Garwood B. Jones or railway magnate Cassius P. Carney. Johnny's old teacher, Professor Jerusalem Webster Stiles, was the worldly intellectual who returned to show him that he was the human likeness of his golden land. Teacher, poet, and lover, Johnny Shawnessy was a symbol of purity like the nakedness of Eden, which was defamed by giving it a name.

War was the voice of the serpent; war was the voice of thunder on the land. It is the voice of years and fates, crying at intersections; it is the bullhead beast, who runs on a Cretan maze of iron roads and chases the naked sacrifices hither and thither. The bull-god comes up fast out of the east, under the churning of his round rear haunches. Smell of blackened ash, odor of hot metal, the frictioning iron parts, blows across the earth of memories.

(O, sweet young days of the aching but unripped seedpurse. O, tall endeavors. O, innocent fragrant time.)

Listen! What voice is calling now, voice of the grooved wheels on the roads of the hurrying days! It is the thunder of big events. They are coming, full of malice and arrogance, they are coming on hooves of iron, wounding the earth of Raintree County. They will travel straight and far, through the light barriers of the corn-gold days. Lo! they will drive the young gods, the beautiful young gods, from the river's reedy marge.[17]

Johnny Shawnessy, in his twisted marriage to a psychopathic southern beauty, gave personal definition to the torment of the union. The destruction of his marriage, his "death" in war, and his resurrection to a life less friendly than he had known before, made his story, and that of the Republic, one of tragedy and betrayal, rather than fulfillment of early promise. The Indiana of his maturity was still a land of itinerant preachers, Fourth of July celebrations, picnics, footraces—but a world colder than he remembered, unhallowed by the pagan rites of its mythological youth. The breathless wonder of that youth was for children, and for a nation not yet out of its childhood.

17. Lockridge, *Raintree County*, pp. 232-33.

The romanticism with which Lockridge fashioned his song of praise for ante-bellum Raintree County has seldom been matched in similar glorification of southern memories. Yet for all the loving and longing in this account of Indiana folk life, the world, a hostile world, is never far distant; the cynical commentary of the "perfesser" weaves in and out of the whole myth, revealing the decay of hope from birth, the dissolution of truth at utterance. The characteristic northern note—doubt, dismay, and weariness—is thus maintained, even in the most romantic of the novels written about the union effort. Novelists find it no easier than scholars to escape one of the primary occupational hazards in dealing critically with the past. In fiction, the "realism" of the northern writers appears to be more of a literary than an historical achievement. Naturalistic detail and biting criticisms in the work of such authors as Pennell, Kantor, Masters, or Lockridge do not make their reports "true to life" in any full historical sense; their commentary, instead, is more often than not a means of subjecting the experience of the 1860's to analysis from a modern point of view. Insistence on the senselessness of war, disgust with the greed of the period's "interests," and conviction that the nation there took a wrong turning—each of these views is the result of a hindsight that does not always ring true in the mouths of the Civil War hero who expresses it. The fiction of the North has had more than its share of leading characters who spoke with the tongue of prophecy. Like that host of fictional Southerners who saw clearly that slavery was wrong and should be abolished, these Northerners who sensed impending threats to common men were not always convincing. A phrase, for instance, about war as a "capitalistic trap which waited to seize the unwary"[18] comes from the mouth of such an uncommon man that we meet him as an anachronistic adventurer in an uncongenial time.

These uncommon men, usually out of step with their society, populate a good part of the best northern fiction. The sensitive poet, the crusading lawyer, the virile pacifist, or the stub-

18. Kantor, *Long Remember,* p. 4.

bornly independent Democratic farmer have provided northern writers with their admirably detached vantage points for
observation of Civil War life; but the separation of heroes
from the passions of the era reduces their value as authentic
survivals from dead years. The figure of the dissenter, the
critic, has been the northern novelist's chief device for realistic
exposure of social deficiencies; but the use of such figures has
prevented complete and sympathetic identification with the
prevailing spirit of the times. In this respect, southern writers
who adopt in uncritical admiration the myths of their forebears may provide, for the historian, memorials which have
more nearly the character of primary source materials.

The valuable interpretations of the Civil War experience
provided by critical Northerners, however, seem to me to out-
weigh the element of anachronism in their methods. They
succeed in outlining important underlying forces of the time,
and they win respect for the accuracy with which they report
details of battle and civil life. Their efforts to understand the
war's lasting alterations of America have given their work a
vitality, a social usefulness, which is evident less frequently
in southern portrayals of the war as a catastrophic punctuation
point to the majestic phrases of an old southern litany. The
novels of the North are filled with passion, too, with emotions no less powerful than those with which Southerners
attach their loyalties to the Lost Cause. But the faith of northern authors is in man, rather than in his society, and their
sorrow a product of their fear that after the war man possessed
a little less of himself than before. The nostalgic note essential
to good historical fiction is supplied by their sensitive docu-
mentation of the fact that victory, too, is a lost cause. There
is a certain humility in their approach to this complex achievement, a sense of truth one sometimes misses from the more
coherent southern faith. Like Southerners, northern authors
sigh after a cause somehow lost, but their mourning has a very
different quality. Instead of turning to the erection of tower-
ing monuments to prove their society's past magnificence, they
grieve as a father might, standing at the grave of a dead child.

III
The South Admires Itself

Successful artists, in their search for the heart of loyalty in the South, have tended to concentrate on experiments with the chemistry of family and kinship. In a mysterious fusion of southern blood and soil they have sought the root of the passion which armed the Southerner for defense of his own. This sense of family, so persistently selected by the novelists as the key to the southern mind, is a primary reference point from which fiction's account of southern society may be considered. It is the basis of the group portraiture that is characteristic of novels about the South. The traditional "aristocracy" were no prouder of their lineage, according to the novels, than were the plainer gentry who avoided noble airs; and the middle-class farmer shared with his pioneer and poor-white neighbors a powerful sense of obligation to his kin. The trait deserves extended study both for the way it distinguishes southern fiction from the northern pattern and for its importance to the historian of the South.[19]

At "aristocratic" levels of southern life, not only possessions, but a sense of being possessed governed reactions in manorial societies like that described by Stark Young in *So Red the Rose*. In giving artistic projection to this instinct, the novelists have come very close to bridging the gap between the quick and the dead. Young's work, despite its violence to the factual record of Natchez society, resurrected with loving sympathy

19. Arthur Wallace Calhoun's conclusion that rural isolation—where "every economic and social force contributed to family solidarity"—was the dominant feature in a society marked by strong family ties, suggests that family loyalty has nothing essentially southern about it. Yet Civil War novels laid in the agrarian Northwest, or rural New York, concern themselves little with family units. *A Social History of the American Family From Colonial Times to the Present,* II, 330-31.

the core of southern faith. Ellen Glasgow, like other critics, sensed in it a consciousness, "rare in American literature, of being rooted not only in a special sense of time and place, but in some larger habit of mind, some abstract fidelity."[20] Communication of this spirit is by indirection, by implication, for the most part, but occasionally it flashes through in more exact statement. When Hugh McGehee sought words to arm his son with a faith that would sustain him at war, he was struggling for statement of his own creed. "The way I've been obliged to see it is this," he said:

Our ideas and instincts work upon our memory of these people who have lived before us, and so they take on some clarity of outline. It's not to our credit to think we began today and it's not to our glory to think that we end today. All through time we keep coming to the shore like waves—like waves. You stick to your blood, son; there's a certain fierceness in blood that can bind you up with a long community of life. . . . And think with passion, it's the only kind of thought that's worth anything.[21]

So Red the Rose is not so much a book of individuals as it is of families; Hugh and Edward McGehee, Malcolm and Sallie Bedford, their innumerable aunts, cousins, children, and neighbors—none has identity outside the group; their ideas and conversations have meaning only within the exchange of their select circle. "I always say to strangers in Natchez," remarked Agnes McGehee, "they would make a mistake trying to remember each separate person." The life of members of this society was anachronistic at the outset; no believers in slavery, they did nothing to abolish it; unmoved by the shrill hysteria of the Confederacy, they were swept to the defense of it. They were too polished for fierce anger, too honest for self-righteousness, and so much an institution that the war's harshest blows failed to shake their stability. Alteration of the union or the Confederacy, Mississippi or Natchez, scarcely interrupted the endless talk which was the chief staple of the

20. "A Memorable Novel of the Old Deep South," New York Herald Tribune Books (July 22, 1934), p. 1.
21. Young, So Red the Rose, pp. 150-51.

House of McGehee. "Mr. Mack and his crew won't consume me," Hugh McGehee said when the carpetbaggers came,

but that's only because he hasn't brains enough, and hasn't life enough behind him. If I were mean, I reckon, I'd have to laugh about that; these men just haven't enough life behind them to match me. I mean by "life" tradition, forefathers and a common system of living. Don't laugh at me for a professor or some common editor; but these people make you want to explain things you'd always taken for granted. When you begin to explain things . . . you've already begun to lose them. Still I have to laugh. It's as if I stood on the ground and they didn't.[22]

The Bedfords and the McGehees typify the virtues and the faults of the aristocratic classes conceived by certain writers to compose the only important elements of the plantation South. The central figure in novels of this tradition was the planter-patriarch, to whose service the whole of fiction's plantation society was dedicated.[23] Families took intense pride in the affectations of the gentleman-master. The protection of his dignity, the shielding of his person from unpleasantness, were welcome tasks to which the lesser figures about him were devoted. His archaic habits were honored with extravagant respect, for his very existence was proof of a praiseworthy social system. Neither the ambitions of youth, nor the services of men in their prime were followed with the interest and concern that smoothed his comfortable path. Description of this

22. *Ibid.*, p. 394.

23. The patriarchal tradition has been emphasized by historians concerned with the society of the South. They have showed that not only members of plantation society, but poor whites, farmers, and persons of every degree tried to "emulate the delusive riches of the planter." Dodd, *The Cotton Kingdom,* pp. 30-31. The plantation master was "looked up to as a superior person, a natural leader, a just arbiter, and a sympathetic friend-in-need . . . 'plain people' tipped their hats to the 'squire,' the 'colonel,' the 'cap'n' or the 'jedge.'" Kendrick and Arnett, *The South Looks at Its Past,* p. 32. Such deference should not be confused, however, with the actual allocation of political authority in the South. "By 1860," Fletcher M. Green has pointed out, "the aristocratic planter class had been shorn of its special privileges and political power . . . the great mass of the whites had been given more and more authority, and majority rule had been definitely established." "Democracy in the Old South," *Jour. So. Hist.,* XII (1946), 23.

legendary figure in the novels has usually been undertaken by revealing personal details that stand as symbols for his grace. Colonel Tremaine, master of Harrowby, in the Virginia tidewater, was the "last gentleman in Virginia who wore a ruffled shirt." He

adhered rigidly to the fashions of forty years before, when he had been in the zenith of his beauty. He wore his hair plastered down in pigeon wings on each side of his forehead and these pigeon wings were of a beautiful dark brown in spite of Colonel Tremaine's seventy-two years. The secret of the colonel's lustrous locks was known only to himself and to Hector, and even Mrs. Tremaine maintained a delicate reserve concerning it. Colonel Tremaine also held tenaciously to a high collar with a black silk stock, and his shirt front was a delicate mass of thread cambric ruffles, hemstitched by Mrs. Tremaine's own hands. His manners were as affected as his dress and he was given to genuflections, gyrations, and courtly waving of his hands in addressing persons from Mrs. Tremaine down to the smallest black child on the estate. . . .[24]

Maintenance of the pretensions of such a dignitary required all the energies of his household. In order that his calm might be ruffled by nothing less than affronts to his sensitive honor, he was careful to ride away from the mansion on holidays, for "the express purpose of being out of the way," while his wife superintended the infinite detail of preparation for a Virginia entertainment. The cost of such a system to the wife, constantly noted by the authors, was heavy. She entered middle age at thirty, having shouldered from the moment of marriage in her middle teens, the burdens of mother, wife, clothier, doctor, and disciplinarian to the whole plantation organization. Scarlett O'Hara

had never seen her mother's back touch the back of any chair on which she sat. Nor had she ever seen her sit down without a bit of needlework in her hands, except at mealtime, while attending the sick or while working at the bookkeeping of the plantation. It was delicate embroidery if company were present, but at other times her hands were occupied with Gerald's ruffled shirts, the

24. Seawell, *The Victory*, pp. 6-9.

girls' dresses or garments for the slaves. Scarlett could not imagine her mother's hands without her gold thimble or her rustling figure unaccompanied by the small negro girl whose sole function in life was to remove basting threads and carry the rosewood sewing box from room to room, as Ellen moved about the house superintending the cooking, the cleaning, and the wholesale clothes-making for the plantation.[25]

Gerald O'Hara, although not to the manner born, was typical of his estate in his comfortable ignorance of the real authority in his home. "It was a secret he would never learn, for everyone from Ellen down to the stupidest field hand, was in a tacit and kindly conspiracy to keep him believing that his word was law." Gerald, who became a planter-aristocrat on the night he showed four deuces in a Savannah poker game, embodied other virtues of his class by possession of a "choleric exterior," which concealed none too well "the tenderest of hearts." Even the poker hand that brought him Tara marked him as a member of the class apart—four of a kind, while without the vulgar display of a royal flush, was clearly in the grand style, to be associated with no commonly respectable full house or straight.

The separate concepts of aristocracy in the three works cited are representative of distinct trends in fiction's effort to explain the charm of the South's first families. Stark Young expounded a genealogical interpretation of southern leadership, whereas Molly Elliott Seawell illustrated the life of her FFV's by careful portraiture of their stylized theatrical qualities. Margaret Mitchell, in almost sacrilegious contradiction, cited wealth, and after that blustery good fellowship, as the attributes necessary for admission to the select company. By each view, however, the plantation patriarch was the outstanding product of the system. His position and person dominated all who were around him—to such a degree that only frank renegades from orthodox southern life, like Rhett Butler and Scarlett O'Hara, emerged with personalities of comparable force. The average young men of this society were no more

25. Mitchell, *Gone with the Wind,* pp. 40-41.

than an admiring audience for the first old gentleman, to
whose estate they aspired; and the unwed belle had but a brief
moment to exercise her capricious charms before she disappeared into the anonymity of married life. Her service as plantation mistress might make her the central figure of her
domestic organization, but this was a circumstance she carefully concealed, so that the brilliance of her master might
remain undimmed. In the end, according to the novels, the
whole assembly of young bloods and tender beauties, of ele-
gant ladies and admiring house servants, was but a mirror by
which the vanities of the plantation aristocrat might be
reflected and preserved.

Fiction's aristocrats were so detached from life's common
concerns that their reactions to wartime adversities were curiously neutral. They rode to death in battle with the same ges-
tures, the same words, that had served for a thrilling jump
after the hounds; and if they survived, they met defeat with
weariness, perhaps, but without any loss of essential qualities.
The mannered adaptability of these chosen few to changed
circumstances, their sacrifice of purpose to the amenities by
which life was made pleasant, left an end effect of witless
eccentricity rather than feudal arrogance. Malcolm Bedford,
tippling on the front gallery of Portobello, scribbling obitu-
aries to friends yet living, is the image that survives memory
of Hugh McGehee's proud attention to blood lines. The
retreat of such families as the McGehee's and the Bedfords
from the hardships of defeat into the mellow glow of their
virtues left a suggestion of decay. No future remained for
them—unless, of course, their sons still live at Natchez, opening their manor houses for the season, exposing to the tourist's
alien eye a glimpse of life in that day when a proper order
ruled.

In this genteel fraternity, a fiercer rage than that excited by
the invader was reserved for the local offender who brought
discredit to southern institutions. Encountering a slave who
had been abused by a newly-rich driver of the community,
Ellen Glasgow's Major Lightfoot first resolved to kill the

offending owner on sight but conquered his impulse before the two met.

So he took a different course, and merely swore a little as he threw a roll of banknotes into the road. "Don't open your mouth to me, you hell hound," he cried, "or I'll have you whipped clean out of this county, sir, and there's not a gentleman in Virginia that wouldn't lend a hand. Don't open your mouth to me, I tell you; here's the price of your property, and you can stoop in the dirt to pick it up. There's no man alive that shall question the divine right of slavery in my presence; but—but it is an institution for gentlemen, and you, sir, are a damned scoundrel!"[26]

Some observers have seen "only foppery in the punctilio of good manners, and nothing but decadence in ancestor worship."[27] To a Virginia matriarch described by Clifford Dowdey, it appeared that the men of the war period "live so much by the outward forms of the older generation that all the tales they tell give only one side. Lanny Warwick there, I know he talks about my husband's 'reform' killing him. But Odell Blackford was an ordinary man with a lot of dash, and he tried to live like the big men. That's what killed him. That's the trouble with so many of our younger men, like Lanny—they're trying to imitate a generation that's gone."[28]

Whatever this gentleman of the old South actually was—venerable reality or fatuous sham—his existence has been regarded by many novelists as evidence of a broad gulf between the cultures of the North and South. The manners of the South might be treated as "medieval trappings," for which the remainder of the country was too practical,[29] or as a sort of spiritual self-sufficiency, a withdrawal from any dependence on the union;[30] but by either view, a distinctive way of life in the section, a separate patriarchal society, was demonstrated. So complete was the isolation of the genteel South, according to Thomas Nelson Page, that a visitor to an ante-bellum plan-

26. Glasgow, *The Battle-Ground*, pp. 88-89.
27. Alexander, *American Nabob*, p. 9.
28. Dowdey, *Where My Love Sleeps*, p. 99.
29. Dowdey, *Bugles Blow No More*, p. 12.
30. Watson, *Bethany*, p. 12.

tation "would have departed with a feeling of mystification, as though he had been drifting in a counter-current and had discovered a part of the world sheltered and to some extent secluded from the general movement and progress of life."[31]

Novelists have written much more convincingly of plainer gentry who, although they shared the ideology, the manners, and much of the background of the privileged few, were not isolated from economic pressures, from fears for their personal futures. The dividing line between the gentleman, as opposed to the aristocrat, is very vague—the distinction in the novels is one of total effect, rather than of exact definition. Major Louis Buchan, of Pleasant Hill in northern Virginia, was, like the proudest of the nabobs, a believer in "honor and dignity for their own sake since all proper men knew what honor was and could recognize dignity. . . ."[32] He could make only fifteen bushels of corn to the acre on his worn land, and his twenty remaining slaves were too many for the place to support, but he was still master of "the Johnsonian diction appropriate to formal occasions, a style that he could wield in perfect sentences four hundred words long." He thought that "government is a group of high minded gentlemen who are trying to yield everything to one another" and could not "understand that reason and moderation haven't anything to do with crisis. . . ." His wife was devoted to the formal patterns on which their life was based; in the simplest habits she sought a fixed regularity. When she washed "the good china" after dinner,

she washed each piece in the suds of one basin and rinsed it in the clear water of the other, then wiped it dry with a little napkin. If this little ritual of utility—not very old to be sure but to [her] immemorial—had been questioned, she would have felt that the purity of womanhood was in danger, that religion and morality were jeopardized, and that infidels had wickedly asserted that the State of Virginia (by which she meant her friends and kin) was not the direct legatee of the civilization of Greece and Rome.[33]

31. Page, *Gordon Keith,* p. 5.
32. Tate, *The Fathers,* p. 210.
33. *Ibid.,* pp. 183-84.

Secure in the knowledge that "her small world held life in its entirety . . . through that knowledge, she knew all that was necessary of the world at large." Not unaware of the abyss yawning about a people armed only by refinement, the Buchans still lived as though "civilization [were] the agreement, slowly arrived at, to let the abyss alone." Helpless under the increasing pressure of troubled years, the family was first torn by the presence of an alien intruder within its circle, and then broken by the divided loyalties which followed secession and war.

When the outsider, George Posey, ignored the delicate indirection by which Major Buchan rejected his suit for a Buchan daughter, he slipped within defenses so long unused that they had ceased to exist. The Major's authority was of the sort that could only rule in the complete recognition of its justice by those to whom it was applied; once questioned, it was without potency. The Major was not accustomed to living among people like George Posey, who "pressed advantages," and faced by such he could only retreat in confusion and apology. The tragedy of Virginia in 1861 drove him to stubborn rejection of reality; in his refusal to be governed by the clamor of secession, he destroyed the family that was his life. Rather than compromise, he turned his own son from the house. "Semmes came in a few minutes after supper," he wrote.

I commanded him to resign from his company, saying that I would send in to John Langton a request that his name be dropped from the rolls on the ground that membership in an organization sworn to uphold disunion was inconsistent with the views of his family. Semmes stubbornly held that he was in favor of disunion, whereupon I said, reluctantly and without passion, that he was no longer a son of mine.[34]

Major Buchan scorned opportunity to declare and profit by his unionist sentiments, however, when the war swept over his plantation. When a Yankee officer "gave" him half an hour to get out, "the major looked at him. He held himself up" as he did when he did not "like folks. Polite. He . . . [came]

34. *Ibid.*, p. 177.

down to the bottom step and said, 'there is *nothing* you can give to me, sir,' and walked back into the house." He died a few moments later.

This selfless intensity with which traditional habits were asserted, the unyielding, destructive persistence with which change was resisted, gave way in the end to the yellow light of terror. Manners torn away revealed, for the Buchans, depths of violence born in blood rather than in mind, in instinct rather than habit. Tormented by the guilt she felt for introducing the Posey taint to her family's blood, Susan Buchan Posey sought absolution in a night of horror which led to the murder of her brother and the living burial of her sister-in-law. From these mounting calamities only the youngest Buchan boy escaped—and he to the cleaner fury of the battle field.

The theme of disordered passion, undermining self-respect, distorting the internal balance of normal family relationships, has proved, in the hands of recent novelists, an effective means for exposing the disintegration of southern society under the impact of war. The dissolution of manners, of group pride, or of family loyalty becomes evidence of defeat more devastating than the result of purely military action. Evelyn Scott has illustrated such psychological destruction in her story of the way simple physical hardship robbed Miss Araminta Decatur, an ancient virgin of Richmond, of the sense of status that was her most cherished possession.[35] War's privations had made impossible proper care of Miss Araminta's sister, Maude Mary, whose reflected glories had been the major source of her life's satisfactions. "Thus, she did not 'mind *small* deprivations' for herself, but it was a 'sin, a crime, a wicked outrage' that Sister Maude Mary, who had been the 'most courted' of young women in Richmond, 'in her day,' should lack 'necessities.' "

Hunger, however, "gripped like a tight fist in the pit of the stomach." Miss Araminta had "never been very bold as a bargainer," and her effort to sell household treasures had not maintained the sisters for long. She received few calls on her

35. *The Wave.*

talent for "plain sewing," because in her requests for business among her acquaintances she had obeyed Maude Mary's violent entreaty *"not* to show humility." As she walked abroad in Richmond on a morning in 1863, she reflected that "The Richmond cabinet certainly ought to be reminded that the Decatur family had a 'history,' and that the last surviving daughters of its house could not live 'like niggers.' " This was her state of mind when she encountered a muttering crowd of housewives and old men whose demands for food were transforming them into a mob. She was caught up in the moving crowd before she realized what was going on.

She was shamed. She longed to turn aside. But the flood of figures accumulated, and she was hemmed in by lines of the passive and excited. A few old men, and an occasional ragged negro varied the aspect of this progress which disgraced her sex. Miss Araminta had for a long time denied sensations of madness. Maude Mary always seemed to her, in that important matter of a ladylike example, a paragon. It was impossible to conceive of Maude Mary in such a situation as this. And if she had been trapped momentarily, she would have evaded association with this perverse group. Not a person here would have dared to 'hustle and bustle' *her* along, and to bear her forward as Miss Araminta was being borne, in sheer helplessness. Shaky, and vanquished almost beyond reflection, she doubled her small fists, and the tears of exhaustion rose beneath her lids.[36]

When the mob swept her into the shambles of a bakery, however, her sense of outrage was conquered by the tantalizing smell of fresh baked bread. "Maude Mary needs bread and decent food as much as anybody, Miss Araminta declared to herself. . . . If they were going to behave madly, they need not suppose that she would permit hoodlums like these to take *all* the bread."

She had seized her precious loaf and had almost broken free of the crowd when a path was forced through the street by a carriage, surrounded by militant outriders. When she realized that the figure in the carriage was President Davis, she was suddenly conscious of the enormity of her position.

And she had no explanation of herself. Maude Mary had 'met'

36. *Ibid.*, p. 199.

President Davis, years before. Miss Araminta's pugnacity withered, in tiny, submissive resentment to Maude Mary's opinion, Maude Mary's will and comment.

Then the crowd lurched. President Davis had opened his wallet—she realized it only tardily—and was throwing pennies, with a free, chill hand, to the prideless populace who forgot him, who reached, who grovelled, who fought in the gutters with the shrill cries of pleased children.

She could endure no more. . . . Giving us *money,* she thought. The idea! Does he consider us *beggars!*[37]

Her resentment almost preserved her from her conscience. But her consciousness of poverty could not reduce the overwhelming importance of the fact that she "had been born a lady . . . something passionately necessary to her self-respect still eluded her."

The brittle respectability of Miss Araminta, thus splintered by the war's privations, symbolized fiction's version of a somewhat precious sensitivity among purse-poor gentry to the brutalities of the era. Without the self-confidence of classes cushioned by great wealth, these genteel folk clutched desperately at status, at order, at the proprieties—even with their world turned upside down. The subtleties of their defenses were not reinforced, on the one hand, by the sense of detachment from the upheaval that was achieved by aristocratic neighbors, nor leavened on the other by the earthy resilience of farmers who were their economic equals. Their devotion to "principle" would have made it difficult for them to understand, for instance, the matter-of-fact adaptability with which Tom Watson's "grandfather" met the profound issues of the day. This old gentleman was

orthodox in politics, took his creed just as he found it; believed what the party leader proclaimed, made no independent research in any direction; and the vitality which he thus saved he expended in raising potatoes, corn, and cotton. He was a "Toombs man"; therefore . . . when Toombs quit the Whig party and joined the Democrats, whom he had so often vociferously damned . . . grandfather changed cars also.[38]

37. *Ibid.,* p. 203.
38. Watson, *Bethany,* p. 16.

It was in their ability to "change cars" with the times that such men differed from the gentry and the aristocracy. They shared with more pretentious neighbors intense pride, family loyalty, and even comfortable means, but their strength was not dissolved in the maintenance of appearances. War, to them, was simply one more natural calamity. Their society did not escape destruction, but its end came from moments of direct violence, rather than from some lingering and subtle decay. The very habit of violence, often emphasized as a trait of southern character,[39] was often the custom which destroyed them. William Faulkner, in *The Unvanquished,* took for his theme the story of violence that had lost its power to cleanse, the failure of murder as a proper instrument for the discharge of family obligations. The two little Confederates who matured in this tale of wartime disorder were one white and one black, but each was confirmed in a pattern neither could long maintain. Bayard Sartoris and Ringo, his Negro playmate, were exalted by their kinship with the Southern Cause through the person of Bayard's father, Colonel John Sartoris, a symbol of reckless leadership, who in the saddle of his claybank stallion seemed the sum of all the world's high purpose. When the war came to Jefferson, Mississippi, Bayard and Ringo had to combine their strength to steady a

39. Cash, *The Mind of the South,* pp. 42-44. "The perpetuation and acceleration of the tendency to violence" which Cash describes receives careful notice from the novelists—many of them, indeed, make their plots from a sort of philosophy of violence which they treat as primary in their description of the southern character. Allen Tate, whose work has been described, built the climax of his story from an eruption of unnatural passion, a blood drive. William Faulkner sees the quality as the source of degeneration in the Sartoris family—the novel here cited is the beginning point in his related stories of degradation among the classes and masses of his Mississippi community. Andrew Lytle, whose novel is described in subsequent paragraphs, works with violence on a more primitive basis. He is concerned less with the quality within men than with its physical application; his story is of the knife drawn for swift personal revenge, a thoughtless, purifying weapon— but a weapon, nevertheless, which unsheathed destroyed its user. Whether formalized in mincing duels, or casually included as a characteristic of frontier life, this thread of violence runs strongly through the Civil War novels identified with the South.

heavy rifle for a shot at the Yankees—but the brevity of their years was no bar to their acceptance of active homefront responsibilities. When Bayard's grandmother was murdered in a final extension of her thriving business in stealing Yankee mules, the boys shouldered without a second thought their duties of vengeance. They announced the successful pursuit of Granny's killer by pegging his body to his cabin door—except for a severed right hand, the hand that had done murder, which they laid on Granny's grave.

Yet Bayard Sartoris grown to manhood at the end of the war was incapable of maintaining this tradition of violence fostered by his blood and times; he was unable to assert for a second time his custom-fixed right of revenge when his father's tempestuous career was halted by murder. The John Sartoris who had come home from the war had cut himself off from his family in the intensity of his business career; his descent from the glory of battle had broken his grip on Bayard's dreams and loyalties. Oppressed by the futility of acting by convention that had ceased to govern, the youth left his gun behind when he went to face his father's killer. Bewildered and alone, he became The Sartoris, the master of his name and people, but without family love or confident purpose.

Certain physical specifications had to be met, in fact, if family relationships in the South were conducted with traditional courtesy and good manners. Without spacious living arrangements, education, and a certain amount of leisure, family life could be a thing of oppressive torment. Old Man Jimmie Vaiden's ten children were constitutionally dissimilar; any of the younger children "expected dissympathy and criticism from any brother or sister in the older set, quite regardless of the nature of the project it had in hand."[40] Members of this North Alabama family had the "uncomfortable habit . . . of nagging at one another's sore points. It seemed to have some connection with their religion—pointing out and correcting the sins of others." Their economic status denied them the equipment of polished living, had their natures been

40. Stribling, *The Forge*, p. 2.

adjusted to such a life; the Vaiden properties, summed up in a legal notice, made brief reading:

Three negro men called Columbus, Robinet, and George; two negro women, one black called Creasy, one light yellow called Gracie; two mules, one blind in the left eye called Lou, a horse mule called Rab; one milk cow called Sook; also sundry plows, guns, fox hounds, chickens, a set of blacksmith tools, an anvil; corn, hay, two bedsteads.[41]

The Vaidens, moreover, were rampant individualists. When Miss Cassandra, the old maid daughter who was the blue-stockinged advocate of improvement of the family's mind, decided to teach the mulatto girl, Gracie, to read, the fact that the law prohibited such training was no deterrent—"for the strictures of code and ermine no Vaiden, either man or woman, ever had the smallest regard."

As Southerners, the Vaidens believed in state's rights; as Alabamians, they believed in individual determinism on all legal and moral questions; as Primitive Baptists, they believed they were supernaturally foreordained from before the laying of the foundations of the earth to do as they damned pleased on all questions whatsoever—social, moral, legal, and religious.

Therefore one day Miss Cassandra had said to her mother, "I have decided to teach Gracie to read."

"It's against the law," said Mrs. Laura Vaiden, who was not so old then, nor was she born a Vaiden.

"I'm going to teach her to read because I think it will be convenient for her to know how," stated Miss Cassandra. "The law certainly was not intended to put anyone to any inconvenience."[42]

Each of the Vaidens was endowed with similar determination and equal capacity for self-justification—and as a result, their life as a family was a thing of hopeless cross-purposes. Old man Jimmie, for instance, was

always, always . . . moved to ride forth on the eve of the twelve o'clock meal. And always the family must wait till he returned

41. *Ibid.,* p. 250.
42. *Ibid.,* p. 251. Stribling in the quoted passage illustrated a facet of the southern character which has been variously explained. A suggestive essay on the South's reaction to authority is Sydnor, "The Southerner and the Laws," *Jour. So. Hist.,* VI (1940), 3-23.

sometime in the afternoon, when the chicken would be stiff, the biscuits cold, the gravy congealed, and nothing would be right down to the salt and pepper.[43]

Pursued by the protesting cries of his family, he would ride off with magnificent unconcern. If the dinner call actually penetrated his consciousness, it made no difference. "Don't I know it," the old man would boom in reply to a "dinnah is ready." "I'll be back!" Such haphazardness made their farming operations a minor miracle. All the planning that went on consisted of Vaiden "in the morning shouting to his two negroes any direction that came into his head, and in the evening asking them if it had been done. Usually it had not quite been done."

The dubious effectiveness of the Vaidens as a family unit was ended by the war. Their slipshod habits of work failed to support them through the hard times which followed peace. Miltiades, whose conscienceless ambition made him the most respected member of the family, threw up his chance to marry into possession of the Lacefield estate, having decided that a wedding with Ponny BeShears, daughter of the local storekeeper, was a surer route to power in the New South.[44] Pollycarp fell to an assassin's bullet, the victim of misdirected revenge. Augustus was hauled off to Florence to open a boarding house under the direction of the wife he had brought home from the war. Marcia eloped with a scallawag. Their dissolution as a family came when their money gave out. When the cash they received for their 1866 cotton crop was lost with the failure of a Florence broker, "they did not have

43. *Ibid.*, pp. 12-13.
44. Stribling's sequel to *The Forge* was *The Store,* in which he described how control of credit, dishonestly manipulated, led to storekeeper domination of the New South's rural economy. An engaging view of the importance of the country store to the South's postwar economic and social life is presented in T. D. Clark, *Pills, Petticoats and Plows.* Clark notes the power of the storekeeper as banker and bookkeeper to farmers of the region, but he concludes that the crossroads merchant was not the ogre which many writers have made him. The store as a social center, as the community town hall, as the link between farmers and the outside world, is Clark's chief interest.

enough resources to support themselves during the winter and two or three negro families necessary to make a crop the following year." The separation that followed was long overdue, of course; from the start there "was something melancholy and out of kilter about the Vaidens. They clung to life too long."

Before the war, however, the Vaidens enjoyed an assured place in their community. Their son could look to marriage with the daughter of the local planter, and old man Jimmie Vaiden, for all his eccentricities, was fully accepted in his society. Ambitious and able members of his family were not denied reward according to merit by barriers of caste and wealth.[45] There is distinct contrast between their social standing and that of the Frasers, the North Carolina family described by James Boyd. Rigid class lines divided life on the rich Cape Fear plantations from the precarious existence of farmers in the adjacent swamp and forest lands. James Fraser and his mother and father were not crackers; their descent from substantial status in Revolutionary times was the result, simply, of a "spell of bad luck."[46] This knowledge brought little comfort, however, and was poor support to pride or dignity. Mrs. Fraser was painfully conscious of their degradation.

"I wish your pa would brush his hair [she complained to James]. He don't, only on Sunday. By Sadday night he looks like one of these crackers back in the woods."

James Fraser sat down uncomfortably and brushed a dusty knee.

"Pa works hard," he ventured.

"I know," she admitted quickly, "and he always has. I'll allow

45. Southerners have generally been insistent on this point, sometimes dogmatically, as in the case of Dyer, *Democracy in the South Before the Civil War*, or more recently through reappraisal of the "newness" of southern society, particularly in the Gulf states. This fluid social structure has been appraised by Phillips, *Life and Labor in the Old South*, p. 340; Cotterill, *The Old South*, p. 279; Cash, *The Mind of the South*, pp. 1-5, 34-36; Simkins, *The South Old and New*, p. 57—and, for that matter, in that ante-bellum treatise which holds so many of the discoveries of the modern historian, Hundley, *Social Relations in Our Southern States*, p. 28.

46. James Boyd, *Marching On*.

him that." She looked out over the scrubby fields and frowned. "But where's it getting us?"[47]

The trouble was not land—"we had good land on the old place back of Halifax . . . but it was just the same. The big planters with their niggers made all the money." The elder Fraser was no hand for such a system; he had never had the knack for working Negroes, even if he could have afforded them. He was eventually trapped in the system where "if a man's got no niggers, he cain't get them, and if he has them, he keeps a-getting more and more and keeps a-branching out."

Necessary intercourse between the Frasers and the local rice planters lay as frequently in moments of bitter friction as in exchanges of mutual value. A farmer who protested angrily when he caught a slave poaching on his land was infuriated when he realized that the "colonel wouldn't whip him." Resentment against the gentry, however, did not relieve the Fraser family's need for the cash which getting out rails for Colonel Prevost would provide—but such exchange only heightened their consciousness of the contrast between their poverty and the elegance of life at Beaumont. There was little satisfaction for James Fraser in his mother's assertion that he was "the equal of any boy alive," and scarcely more in his family's fierce refusal to be "beholden to any one alive." He had no defense against the polite dismissal which greeted his effort to step from his place in dealings with the Colonel's family. He was slow to realize, at first, that a julep on the gallery was no substitute for a handshake, or an invitation into the plantation house. When he presumed, however, to call on the Prevost daughter who had fired his dreams, he was quickly disabused of his notions. "My daughter is engaged at present," the Colonel informed him, not without sympathy. "If in the future, she—she should be at leisure, she will be pleased to let you know." James Fraser did not need to be told twice. He refused the Colonel's hand, now proffered for the first time. "No, seh," he said. "Excuse me, but I don't shake hands

47. *Ibid.,* pp. 5-6.

where I'm not wanted." Simple ambition had not the power
to bridge the gulf between James Fraser and Stewart Prevost.
Their union was impossible before war hammered the Prevost society to bits. Defeat was more important than true love
in bringing the plantation belle to her cornshuck wedding bed.

The tragedy of the Frasers was that they were trapped in a
static society that had little need for their energies—and, as a
result, their vitality slowly drained away in poverty and consciousness of failure. War, of course, was not the only release
available from such a plight—in Andrew Lytle's Georgia, for
instance, "when a man was ruined, he set out for Texas." [48]
Members of the McIvor family in *The Long Night* were, like
the Frasers, proud of Scotch blood and family heritage, and
perversely independent in the face of adversity. The McIvors,
moreover, had not lost their spirit of pioneering adventure, nor
the element of optimism from their characters. When Cameron McIvor was ruined by a protracted bout with the law in
Georgia, he set out with all he owned for a new start in Texas.
Such a move took time; at the end of the first leg of his journey he settled to sharecrop five hundred acres for a season at
the fringe of Alabama's plantation belt. Separated from all but
his immediate kin, a stranger in his community, he was murdered when he identified the planter who owned his land as
the leader of the powerful band of speculators terrorizing the
country. He was not long unmourned, or unavenged, however.

It took two weeks for the kin to gather. But by that time, all
who could be reached had come in. Some arrived on horseback.
Others took the cars as far as they went and finished the journey
by stage. A few of the plainer relations who had been with Cameron in the Seminole Wars arrived in wagons, which they camped
by in the front yard. . . .

McIvors, Longs, Prichards thrust their boot heels into the rooms,
crossed them over tight kneecaps, or planted them grimly upon
the flowers in the carpets. Some were dressed in fine broadcloth,
others in butternut, and one rich old planter wore ancient gate
breeches. Rich or poor, they had all come in because they had
known and loved Cameron or because the memory of the long

48. *The Long Night,* p. 28.

years was still fresh, when, in the old country across the waters, they had stood up and fought the English who had crossed their borders.[49]

It was a gathering of the clan in a sense greater than family; like a Highland band from the pages of Sir Walter Scott, they met to avenge dismayed justice, to bring peace to the dead. The suggestion that the law be called in insulted them— "why, son, if every family difference found its way to our judiciary, the dockets would be as tangled as the tail of a free nigger's mule."

To Pleasant McIvor, the teen-aged son transfigured by hate of his father's killers, the murmur of his people's voices brought the vision which submerged his personality, his humanity, in single purpose, which gave him his role as abstract vengeance, bloodless yet covered with the blood of the men who had done injury to his family. In "strange and incorruptible calm" he assumed the burden of meeting "secret death with secret death. That's the way it must be. That's the way it will be." Riding by night and alone, he hovered like an angry spirit about the brawling society of poor whites, yeomen, and low-country gentry that included his victims. He picked them off one by one, as they left militia musters, plowed their fields, broke wild horses, swarmed bees, made love. Fifteen were dead when the war interrupted and confused his purpose. Caught up in a greater loyalty than he owed his father, he was almost turned from his vendetta by his devotion to the new cause and to his war-born friends. When continued pursuit of his private war finally brought death in battle to a comrade he had loved, Pleasant could no longer pursue either cause; he broke under the knowledge that "what he had done . . . no man in this world may do. Twice he had loved—once the dead, once the living, and each by each was consumed and he was doomed." Slipping away from his army post near Nashville, he sought the hills of Winston County, Alabama, where "in the secret coves, far away from the world and vengeance, a deserter might hide forever. . . ." There he lived out his life,

49. *Ibid.*, p. 62.

isolated from the family he had served, until, in his old age, he summoned the next of kin to hear of the legend he had been, for it was a thing that had to be told.

Andrew Lytle's tale of Pleasant McIvor's revenge provides a point as logical as any for halting this parade of families from various levels of life in the Old South. His story completes the circle which began with notice of Stark Young's novel—the two works are associated, in fact, by the commonly held agrarian conceptions of the authors. Comparison of *So Red the Rose* and *The Long Night,* however, gives striking evidence of the variety in southern authors' approaches to their society; Young attempted to catch the flavor of the Old South through stylized literary memories—his very title is drawn from a quotation which is a prediction of his attitudes:

> I sometimes think that never blows so red
> The rose as where some buried Caesar bled. . . .

Lytle, on the other hand, took for his darkly romantic folk tale the language and images of balladry. His story is related to oral rather than literary traditions; it drips with the blood of an August night's imagination. The stench of Lytle's rotting corpses almost defies comparison with the fragrance of Young's buried Caesars. Lytle's frontier South had no room for tradition's lords and ladies; one encountered, instead, Aunt Patsy puffing her pipe in the corner, describing the two husbands she had buried: "The fust one—it was sw'are, sw'are, sw'are. The last one—pra'er, pra'er, pra'er."

Novelists of power have not taken the last step in the descent down the stair of the white South's ante-bellum classes. Aunt Patsy's corner is the last point on their literary pilgrimage. The dirt eaters and resin suckers of the period have not yet been discovered by their Erskine Caldwell. No other classes have been avoided, however; and the single exception, when a general view of the novels is taken, seems minor. The various organs of the southern body politic have enjoyed a thoroughly adequate autopsy at the hands of recent novelists. These able writers have laid back the flabby fat of traditional idealizations of the Old South's life and have made intensive study of the region's interior.

This democratization of the Civil War novel has upset so many of the standard patterns and concepts of late nineteenth-century romance that easy conclusion eludes a student who has surveyed the literature through each of its modifications. The contrast and contradictions of life have been injected into the literary traditions of the war—and the result has been a vigorous and effective social history.[50] The novels have made real what Southerners were, as well as what they believed themselves to be. Ideal and reality remained mixed, as they do in the life of any society.

Effort to find a pattern through this varied writing, a conclusion that does no violence to its variety, exposes, more than any other southern trait, the importance of family. Despite separation by geography and economic standing, the people in virtually all the books cited were alike in their reliance on the cohesive force of family obligation. Once bereft of family loyalty, they were swept helpless to their assorted tragedies. Investigation of the family's role in crisis could be pursued indefinitely, for there are as many reactions as there are families—

50. Historians, like novelists, have made their descent through the classes of the ante-bellum South, yet their achievements in "social" history, important as some of them have been, have a fragmentary character which compares but poorly with the rounded portraits of fiction. Ulrich Bonnell Phillips, in a classic of the type, laments the historian's basic difficulty: "The plain folk did not make records comparable to those of the planters. The letters they wrote were few, and their significant, explicit items were fewer still." *Life and Labor in the Old South*, p. 340. The scholars proceed despite their difficulties, however, and such studies as those on the southern yeomen, referred to in note 137, pp. 63-64, are a monument to their perseverance. Pertinent to this work are Wiley's two studies, *The Life of Johnny Red* and *The Plain People of the Confederacy*. Historians have ventured, further, to fields left untouched by the historical novelist—to the story of the poor white, as in Buck, "The Poor Whites of the South," *Am. Hist. Rev.*, XXXI (1925), 41-55; Den Hollander, "The Tradition of 'Poor Whites,' " *Culture in the South;* and McIlwaine, *The Southern Poor-White from Lubberland to Tobacco Road*. Some problems in such specialized approaches to southern history are suggested by Sydnor, "The Southern Experiment in Writing Social History," *Jour. So. Hist.*, XI (1945), 455-68.

and new discoveries will be made as long as vivid imagination serves to repopulate the Civil War South. Choice of these particularly literate spokesmen is merely illustrative of the endless channels in which search for a people's character may be pursued. A few of them have recovered moments of time, fragments of society, elements of passion, which were irretrievably lost except to gifted imagination. Even dreams spun from the realm of romantic illusion have their place with such achievements, for in the artist's vision there may be captured a truth more accurate than fact, because it is conceived in the spirit which informs the fact. Stately gentlemen of unblemished honor, loyalty beyond the fear of death, unwavering conviction of righteous purpose—these qualities seem lost forever except in the pages of such books as these, which bring us again to the time before the union was divided, before blue and grey were faded, before bright hope, unrealized, collapsed in early sorrow.

THE USES OF
FICTIONAL HISTORY

CLASSROOM teachers of history are regularly confronted with the under-graduate discovery that a good monograph may "read like a novel." This critical estimate is usually offered so clumsily, and with such an element of patronage for our writings, that we are put immediately on the defensive—we urge that scholars, although normally dry, should not be considered abnormal in their moments of literacy. We thus ignore a shrewd lay judgment, a judgment that emphasizes the degree to which artistic selectivity controls success or failure in communication with the past. History that "reads like a novel" is history composed of revealing details as well as dispassionate post-mortem findings. Too often the historian, like Hamlet in his graveyard, alienates his audience by finding first in the skulls of Alexander and Yorick the fact that they are dead. The novelist begins with "the more consoling proposition that Alexander and Yorick . . . [were] once . . . as much alive as we." [1] The happier approach is a proper one, for it is more likely to generate the excitement that comes with realization of membership in a community of time as well as place. The student who discovers history that "reads like a novel" is probably typical of the general American reader, who turns more hopefully to fiction than to formal history for

1. In a different context this metaphor is used by Trevelyan, "History and Fiction," *Living Age,* CCCXIII (June, 1922), 572.

189

the union of emotion, memory, and reason that unites the past and present.

Scholars are unwise when they ignore the general reader's attention to fictional history. The statistics of Civil War novel production reveal a widespread fascination with the era which wants encouragement rather than frustration, a partial intimacy with national folklore which invites exploitation rather than sterilization through use of the overly-disciplined fact. Perception of kinship with the past waits in a large audience for the historian's nurturing, and his chores will be lighter if he appreciates the quality of the social myths he documents. Even when these myths are impassioned distortions of the public memory, they may serve the scholar's ends. "Bad" history is of course doubly bad when it is presented within a compelling illusion of reality, but a reader exposed to such a report is rarely done with history. The devotee of historical novels moves toward formal history rather than away from it; he rises from excitement at fictions to seek the truth of the matter. Novel reading, from the juvenile level onward, tends to wake curiosity, to foster desire for more precise and complete details than the artist chooses to employ. Now the historian does not write to provide reference works for readers of historical novels, but his audience is not so large that he can afford to reject even this use of his work. At any rate, he gains more readers than he loses through art's invasion of a field so increasingly specialized that many a new monograph has little more than antiquarian value.

Civil War novels have more than negative uses in the development of a true image of our public experience. They not only turn the mind of the lay audience to history; they also, on occasion, point the way to the scholar's conclusions. Historians stray but rarely from conventional attitudes toward the events they describe; their task often seems one simply of determining what the conventional attitudes are. Sometimes the artist, who is closer than the scholar to the world of the present, appears to sense more quickly some public need for a revised report of past decisions. The exceptional case in point is that of John William

De Forest, George Washington Cable, and Stephen Crane—each working during the nineteenth century with the psychological explanations for war now demanded by sophisticated students. Most exceptions of this sort seem related to radical changes in the public mind, like the reaction against war during the 1920's and 1930's, during which Civil War novels regularly denied that war was "necessary." Another example was the effort of Ellen Glasgow in 1902 to describe the democratic qualities of the Confederate effort—an approach that had become standard by the time of the appearance in the 1920's of such excellent works as *Marching On,* by James Boyd, and *The Wave,* by Evelyn Scott. Had more original talent been applied to Civil War fiction, there would be further evidences for this point, for the novelist serves more consciously than the historian the "Everyman" whom Carl Becker has credited with responsibility for continual reinterpretation of historical views to fit contemporary needs.

Originality, however, is not an outstanding trait of the historical novelist; the case must rest with the dependence of second rate novelists on the major patterns developed by historians to explain the meaning of the war. "Firsts" cannot be safely awarded anyway, for in both history and fiction, the interpretations presented through a century of writing about the conflict may be found in works which were in print before the war was over. While embarrassing comparisons are thus avoided, the scholar can take comfort in the fact that a reader dependent on fiction for his attitude toward the Civil War generally has the benefit of "modern" views.

Fictional history, then, is reasonably good history, a substantial stimulus to the scholar's search for the truth. Such a conclusion is not very important—certainly not important enough, in itself, to justify my extended sampling from the bargain basements of the literary market pláce. Academic folk avoid notice of historical fiction when they can and in any event are likely to suspect the worst of it. Reassurances for them—or warnings, if such had been my message—are offered unsought and are likely to go unheeded. My concern as I puzzled over the problems of fictional history shifted from judgment of the novelist's competence as historian to despair at the scholar's ignorance of popular literature. If Civil War novels are important, their worth lies in the needs they serve and the questions they answer for a very large public. The size and quality of this public is unknown, its needs unclassified, and its general taste unmeasured. Literary historians seem, on the whole, to be snobs—or at any rate to be tediously repetitive in their dependence on a very few samples from our literature. They casually exempt from methodical analysis the great varieties of intellectual experience oriented around the rental libraries and drug store racks of the land. They seem content to play follow-the-leader as they skip along the tops of the pyramids of taste erected by the readers and writers of successive generations. There has been no attempt to classify and summarize the literary history of the American *people,* as opposed to a literary history of critics, aesthetes, and intellectuals.

Pyramids of taste have very broad bases in a culture so variously served as ours. At these bases lie the unrefined emotions and conventional banalities by which a whole people reveals its definition of truth, of beauty, of human purpose. Until these emotions and banalities are methodically summarized, knowledge of the reader impulse satisfied by my subdivision of popular literature must remain speculative and inconclusive. The contemporary critical scene, however, permits little hope that such summary will be undertaken; the current trend in literary history appears to be more in the direction of critical than historical analysis. The formidable task of relating literature to the ruling conventions and ideas of a whole generation is left to the rare giant in the field—a Parrington works out his life mastering the general history of the United States, so that he can attempt to match ideas with realities. Even Parrington, moreover, revealed in his work the fact that literary historians, if they display ambition at all, are too ambitious: they seek intuitive definitions of the whole national experience, but they avoid the detailed measuring and categorizing that must precede systematic knowledge of the popular mind. A dose of scientism may be a grim prescription for students of literature, but it might help cover the current retreat of the new critics from the responsibility of defining the social services of literature. An historian looks with interest on the search of contemporary critics for interior meanings, for the profitable findings that follow the fondling of words and phrases for meaning their authors know not of. But he resists substitution of this critical technique for literary history.[2] He cannot help but urge that there is room in the universities for the old as well as the new criticism. The surface of American literature, if we describe the whole volume of our popular writings by this term, has only been skimmed by orthodox students of *belle lettres;* and a descent to analysis of mass reading seems an urgent task for scholarship.

My own experience with a mass of second-rate novels suggests that the effort would be more than an adventure among the Philistines. The rapid achievement of technical proficiency by historical novelists has guaranteed a certain quality to their efforts which is fairly impressive. Like many mass-produced items on which Americans rely, the standard-brand novel is quite well-constructed. Plots are efficiently executed, and action sequences reveal the skill of very competent craftsmen. Character analysis tends to be slighted, and the average novel wants dramatic unity; but the end product tends to be a very respectable exercise in story-telling. The end product also sells, which indicates some considerable service to popular emotional needs. Analysis of this service might prove to be a stimulating addition to the polishing of old bones that often passes for literary history in the United States.

Only in the context of this unwritten literary history of the American people can the peculiar place of the historical novel be explained. My digression on the need for the context does not free me from speculation about what the place will be; but my observations on the reader impulse served by Civil War romances must remain tentative suggestions rather than firm

2. A systematic version of literary history as outlined by the new critics may be found in Wellek and Warren, *Theory of Literature,* pp. 29-37, 263-82.

conclusions. This note of humility may be unwarranted, since among contemporary critics there is maintained a confident concensus about the appeal of historical fiction—a concensus, though, which ignores qualities of the *genre* common to all popular literature. Freeman Champney expressed the prevailing view when he observed that general concern with the Civil War in recent times "grew out of a period of sustained crisis and . . . reflects the individual frustrations and the erosion of social patterns" characteristic of the present.[3] From today's despair we can "escape" into the settled past. According to this theory we swap contemporary problems, unanswered, insoluble, for fresh and dramatic issues the outcomes of which are unplagued by nagging doubt. A different world may not be a better world, though its exciting events may make it seem so; but such a world will, at any rate, afford a sense of *completion* in its solution to issues of which we can see the end as well as the beginning.

A close look at the "escape" theory, however, reveals it to be more of an evasion than an explanation when it is applied to historical fiction. The theory is not specific: we also escape to attend a strip tease by one of Mickey Spillane's blonde villainesses; we escape through the high adventures of John's Other Wife; we escape to the comfortably primitive world of Lil' Abner. Any phase of popular culture that does not qualify as Literature, with a capital "L," is viewed by critics as another escape hatch through which untutored masses flee the complicated present. The theory does not explain the perennial popular appetite for Civil War novels, an appetite as frequently indulged in comfortable times as in crisis periods. The modern form of the American historical novel was fixed at the turn of the century—and early twentieth-century Americans were not seeking "escape" from the mood of rampant self-satisfaction which came then with realization of national wealth and power.

Study of the fluctuating popularity of Civil War novels suggests a more reasonable explanation for their reader appeal. The

3. "Literature Takes to the Woods," *Antioch Review,* IV (Summer, 1944), 246.

exceptional period of publication, the unusual times, were the years when Civil War novels were *not* being published. The only two events that brought a noticeable pause in the flood of war stories were our two world wars—and as soon as these were won, the perennial concern with America's most dramatic crisis was revived. The slack periods seem significant. Only in wartime, when public morale was being skillfully sustained by extravagantly emotional appeals to the nation's traditional symbols of patriotism, were the tinsel glories and romantic heroes of Civil War fiction dismissed from the public consciousness. The popular need for patriotic folklore appears to embarrass peacetime orators and writers of twentieth-century America; we tolerate unrelieved bombast and spread-eagle history only when "world" wars unite us in uncritical defense of our national record. Perhaps the social utility of the historical novelist lies in his unrecognized service to the same patriotic yearnings, submerged in normal times, which want more regular encouragement than that afforded by critical review of the romance of American life.

The quality of this fictional patriotism often distresses sophisticated readers; they sense in it a hollow tone, a false note which does less than justice to the American democratic experience. They thus confuse patriotism, an irrational and sometimes anti-intellectual emotion, with loyalty, which requires critical reference to the nation's traditions. The critic and historian of American loyalty does not really believe with Stephen Decatur in "my country, right or wrong"; he reserves his approval for its seasons of righteousness. Patriotism, though, assumes its fullest meaning in moments of misguided sacrifice and unthinking devotion to national or regional purpose. The record of past patriotic excesses tends to leave the statesman ashamed, the historian uncomfortable, and the philosopher dismayed. Not so, however, with the historical novelist. He revives with passion the sense of "partisan solidarity" that Veblen noted as the essential content of patriotism;[4] and he

4. *An Inquiry into the Nature of Peace and the Terms of Its Perpetuation,* p. 31. For a general discussion of this point see Curti, *The Roots of American Loyalty, passim.*

continues to sanctify calamity with an admiring record of the blood sacrifices that somehow justified it. Historical novels are a popular ceremonial record of the mysteries that unify us as a people.

Much of this record, prepared according to formula and read by an uncritical audience, seems shallow and sterile—repeated ceremonial observances usually have these qualities. Many readers, nevertheless, continue to depend for emotional and intellectual fare on fiction's version of the American experience. They can count on no other branch of popular literature for regular notice of the nation's symbolic inheritance. More often than the critics admit they are rewarded by a sensitive consciousness of the past from which they came, and of the future toward which the past directs them. The best Civil War novels, as Herbert Butterfield once said of good historical novels in general, are built around "objects and places; they have a basis in reality and their roots in the soil. . . . Patriotism that so often rings false is in this true, in that it becomes a consciousness of belonging to a place and a tradition."[5]

Credit for this achievement can be given generously. The mystery of memory and time commands such urgent concern that any serious effort to comprehend it merits our respect. Each of us must struggle in his own way to make a place for himself in what Proust called the "vast structure of recollection." No common cultural highway leads surely to knowledge of how we came to be what we are. The reading of historical novels is scarcely a substitute for varieties of the quest that lie in formal history, or philosophy, or religion. But neither has there yet appeared a substitute for the past recaptured by the artist dreaming, and working with the wit to share his dream.

5. *The Historical Novel*, pp. 41-42.

Bibliography

The five-hundred-odd Civil War novels listed in succeeding pages were the essential sources for this study. The nation's sub-literature, despite its volume and its wide appeal, has attracted neither systematic nor sustained attention from the critics, historians, and essayists in whose province it lies. Of the hundreds of brief opinions about the literature surveyed only the essay from which my title is borrowed combined knowledge of a number of the books with understanding of the purpose of the novelist as historian. Bernard DeVoto, in "Fiction Fights the Civil War," *Saturday Review of Literature*, XVII (December 18, 1937), introduced effectively, though briefly, some of the problems faced in this monograph. A useful summary of early Civil War novels was compiled by Rebecca Washington Smith, "The Civil War and Its Aftermath in American Fiction, 1861-1899, with a Dictionary Catalogue and Indexes" (unpublished Ph.D. dissertation, University of Chicago, 1932). An important opinion of the novels was that of Albion Winegar Tourgée, "The South as a Field for Fiction," *Forum,* VI (December, 1888), 404-13. Richard H. Wilmer, the collector of the novels used in this study, described his experience in "Collecting Civil War Novels," *Colophon,* III (New Series, Autumn, 1938), 513-18.

Uncontested authority on the historical novel in the United States has been achieved by Ernest E. Leisy, in *The American Historical Novel* (Norman, 1950), a critical catalogue of novels describing each period of American history. A reader seeking general introduction to the historical novel should begin with the preface to Sir Walter Scott's *Ivanhoe.* An intensive analysis of Scott's theory, and of subsequent variations in the application of his ideas, may be found in C. Hugh Holman, "William Gilmore Simms's Theory and Practice of Historical Fiction" (unpublished Ph.D. dissertation, University of North Carolina, 1949). The views of three British scholars, whose knowledge of the *genre* was reinforced by belief in its serious purposes, are valuable: George Saintsbury, "The Historical Novel," in *Essays in English Literature, 1780-1860* (2nd Series, London, 1895); George Peabody Gooch, "Historical Novels," *Contemporary Review,* CXVII (February, 1920), 204-12; and George Macaulay Trevelyan, "History and Fiction," *Living Age,* CCCXIII (June, 1922), 565-73. For representative opinions of historical fiction when the form was most popular in the United States, see

197

Paul Leicester Ford, "The American Historical Novel," *Atlantic Monthly,* LXXXI (December, 1897), 721-28; Brander Matthews, *The Historical Novel and Other Essays* (New York, 1901); and Ernest Bernbaum, "Views of Great Critics on the Historical Novel," *Publications of the Modern Language Association,* XLI (1926), 424-41.

The problem of "truth" in fictions from the past has attracted many essays of varying worth. Outstanding are Alastair MacDonald Taylor, "The Historical Novel as a Source in History," *Sewanee Review,* XLVI (October, 1938), 459-79; and Herbert Butterfield, *The Historical Novel, An Essay* (Cambridge, 1924). Also rewarding are Hillaire Belloc, "The Character of an Historical Novelist," *London Mercury,* IX (November, 1923), 37-42; Arthur Colton, "Gospel of Likemindedness," *Saturday Review of Literature,* IV (June 9, 1928), 941-42; George Dangerfield, "The Insistent Past," *North American Review,* CCXLIII (1937), 137-52; Bernard DeVoto, "Fiction and the Everlasting *If*: Notes on the Contemporary Historical Novel," *Harpers,* CLXXVII (June, 1938), 42-49; Edmund Fuller, "History and the Novelists," *American Scholar,* XVI (Winter, 1946-1947), 113-24; and Arthur Barron Tourtellot, "History and the Historical Novel: Where Fact and Fancy Meet and Part," *Saturday Review of Literature,* XXII (August 24, 1940), 3-4.

My debt to the historians who trained me and encouraged my pursuit of this subject cannot be discharged in specific reference here. This approach to the novelist as historian of the Civil War was first attempted under the discipline of a southern graduate school in which the war, and war issues, were mat-

ters of importance. Although the burden of the study rests on dreams and fictions, my general view of the war era is based on a voluminous historical literature; I can only hope that footnote references have given adequate evidence of my dependence on the work of professional historians. In particular, I was sustained in my generalizations about the views of historians on the coming of the war by Howard Kennedy Beale's essay, "What Historians Have Said about the Causes of the Civil War," in *Theory and Practice in Historical Study: A Report of the Committee on Historiography, Social Science Research Council Bulletin 54* (New York, 1946). Another extensive analysis of the historiography of the war is Thomas J. Pressly's recently published *Americans Interpret Their Civil War* (Princeton, 1954). Paul H. Buck's analysis of *The Road to Reunion, 1865-1900* (Boston, 1938), established the prevailing, though less than accurate, view of the war in American literature. Carl L. Becker, in *Everyman His Own Historian. Essays in History and Politics* (New York, 1935), made easier the task of explaining frequent reinterpretation of the war.

Frank Luther Mott, in *Golden Multitudes, The Story of Best Sellers in the United States* (New York, 1947), provides the only reliable estimates of the distribution of popular Civil War novels. Of the many biographical dictionaries employed the most valuable was that edited by Stanley J. Kunitz and Howard Haycraft, *Twentieth Century Authors: A Biographical Dictionary of Modern Literature* (New York, 1938), in which the sketches were contributed in part by the subjects themselves. All too rare are such works as Ellen Glasgow's book of prefaces, *A Certain*

Measure: *An Interpretation of Prose Fiction* (New York, 1943), in which the author explained her purpose and methods at the time she wrote her Civil War novel. Civil War novels are not rare at all. Titles employed in my study, listed below, include most of the war fiction published before 1949. The cutoff date was selected arbitrarily, but I have found no reason to regret omission of recent titles until MacKinlay Kantor published *Andersonville* in 1955. The continuing appearance of outstanding novels such as this gives point to my subtitle: the foregoing pages must be read as "an unfinished chapter in the literary history of the American people."

CIVIL WAR NOVELS

Adams, Julia Davis. *Remember and Forget*. New York: E. P. Dutton & Co., 1932.

Adams, William T. ("Oliver Optic"). *The Sailor Boy: Or Jack Somers in the Navy. A Story of the Great Rebellion*. Boston: Lee & Shepard, 1863.

————. *The Soldier Boy: Or, Tom Somers in the Army. A Story of the Great Rebellion*. Boston: Lee & Shepard, 1863.

————. *The Young Lieutenant: Or, The Adventures of an Army Officer. A Story of the Great Rebellion*. Boston: Lee & Shepard, 1865.

————. *Brave Old Salt: Or, Life on the Quarterdeck. A Story of the Great Rebellion*. Boston: Lee & Shepard, 1866.

————. *Fighting Joe: Or, The Fortunes of a Staff Officer. A Story of the Great Rebellion*. Boston: Lee & Shepard, 1866.

————. *The Yankee Middy: Or, The Adventures of a Naval Officer. A Story of the Great Rebellion*. Boston: Lee & Shepard, 1866.

————. *Taken by the Enemy*. Boston: Lee & Shepard. New York: Charles T. Dillingham, 1889.

————. *Within the Enemy's Lines*. Boston: Lee & Shepard, 1890.

————. *On the Blockade*. Boston: Lee & Shepard, 1891.

————. *Fighting for the Right*. Boston: Lee & Shepard, 1892.

————. *Stand by the Union*. Boston: Lee & Shepard, 1892.

————. *Brother Against Brother: Or, The War on the Border*. Boston: Lee & Shepard, 1894.

————. *A Victorious Union*. Boston: Lee & Shepard, 1894.

————. *In the Saddle*. Boston: Lee & Shepard, 1895.

————. *A Lieutenant at Eighteen*. Boston: Lee & Shepard, 1896.

————. *At the Front*. Boston: Lee & Shepard, 1897.

————. *On the Staff*. Boston: Lee & Shepard, 1897.

————. *An Undivided Union*. [Completed by Edward Stratemeyer]. Boston: Lee & Shepard, 1899.

Alcott, Louisa May. *Work: A Story of Experience*. Boston: Roberts Bros., 1873.

Aldrich, Bess Streeter. *Song of Years*. New York, London: D. Appleton-Century, 1939.

Alexander, Holmes. *American Nabob*. New York: Harper & Bros., 1939.

Alger, Horatio, Jr. *Frank's Campaign, Or, What Boys Can Do on the Farm for the Camp*. Boston: Loring, 1864.

Allen, Hervey. *Action at Aquila*. New York: Farrar & Rinehart, 1938.

Allen, James Lane. *The Sword of Youth*. New York: The Century Co., 1915.

Altsheler, Joseph A. *In Circling Camps: A Romance of the Civil War*. New York: D. Appleton & Co., 1900.

————. *The Last Rebel*. Philadelphia

and London: J. B. Lippincott & Co., 1900.

———. *Before the Dawn: A Story of the Fall of Richmond.* New York: Doubleday, Page & Co., 1904.

———. *The Guns of Bull Run: A Story of the Civil War's Eve.* New York and London: D. Appleton & Co., 1914.

———. *The Guns of Shiloh: A Story of the Great Western Campaign.* New York and London: D. Appleton & Co., 1914.

———. *The Scouts of Stonewall: The Story of the Great Valley Campaign.* New York and London: D. Appleton & Co., 1914.

———. *The Sword of Antietam: A Story of the Nation's Crisis.* New York and London: D. Appleton & Co., 1914.

———. *The Rock of Chickamauga: A Story of the Western Crisis.* New York and London: D. Appleton & Co., 1915.

———. *The Star of Gettysburg: A Story of Southern High Tide.* New York and London: D. Appleton & Co., 1915.

———. *The Shades of the Wilderness: A Story of Lee's Great Stand.* New York and London: D. Appleton & Co., 1916.

———. *The Tree of Appomattox: A Story of the War's Close.* New York and London: D. Appleton & Co., 1916.

"An American." *At Anchor: A Story of Our Civil War.* New York: D. Appleton & Co., 1865.

———. *Walter Graham, Statesman. An American Romance. By an American, Who Notwithstanding our Inordinate Desire for Political Preferment, Our Insatiable Greed for Wealth, and the Mighty Upheavings of Corruption and Perfidy Which Occasionally Astound Us,* *Still Believes in America.* Lancaster, Pa.; Fulton Publishing Co., 1891.

Appel, John W. *The Light of Parnell.* Philadelphia: The Heidelberg Press, 1916.

Arnold, Edgar. *The Young Refugees: The Adventures of Two Lads from Old Virginia.* Richmond: The Hermitage Press, 1912.

Ashley, C. B. *Luke Bennett's Hide Out. A Story of the War.* New York: John W. Lovell Co., n.d.

[Austin, Jane G.] *Dora Darling: The Daughter of the Regiment.* Boston: J. E. Tilton & Co., 1865.

Avery, Myrta A. *The Rebel General's Loyal Bride: A True Picture of Scenes in the Late Civil War.* Springfield, Mass.: W. J. Holland & Co., 1873.

Babcock, Bernie. *The Soul of Abe Lincoln.* Philadelphia and London: J. B. Lippincott & Co., 1923.

Babcock, William Henry. *Kent Fort Manor.* Philadelphia: Henry T. Coates & Co., 1903.

Bacheller, Irving Addison. *Father Abraham.* Indianapolis: Bobbs-Merrill Co., 1925.

Bacon, Eugenia J. *Lyddy: A Tale of the Old South.* New York: Continental Publishing Co., 1898.

Baker, William Mumford ("George F. Harrington"). *Inside: A Chronicle of Secession.* New York: Harper & Bros., 1866.

Barrow, Frances Elizabeth ("Aunt Fanny's Daughter"). *Colonel Freddy: Or, The March and Encampment of the Dashabed Zouaves. The Sock Stories by Aunt Fanny's Daughter. Red, White, and Blue Socks. Part Second, Being the Second Book of the Series.* New York: Leavitt & Allen, 1863.

———. ("Aunt Fanny"). *The Orphan's Home Mittens: And George's Account of the Battle of Roanoke Island. Being the Sixth and Last Book of the Series. By Aunt Fanny, Author of the Six Nightcap Books, Etc.* New York and London: D. Appleton & Co., 1865.

Bartlett, Major W. C. *An Idyl of War-Times.* New York: Lew Vanderpoole Publishing Co., 1890.

Barton, William E. *A Hero in Homespun: A Tale of the Loyal South.* Boston, New York, and London: Lamson, Wolffe & Co., 1897.

Baylor, Frances Courtenay. *Behind the Blue Ridge: A Homely Narrative.* Philadelphia: J. B. Lippincott Co., 1887.

Beard, O. T. *Bristling with Thorns: A Story of War and Reconstruction.* Detroit: The Detroit News Co., 1884.

Beatty, John. *McLean: A Romance of the Civil War.* Columbus, Ohio: Press of Fred J. Heer, 1904.

Bechdolt, Frederick Ritchie. *Bold Riders of the West.* New York: Doubleday, Doran, & Co., Inc., 1940.

Beecher, Henry Ward. *Norwood: Or, Village Life in New England.* New York: Charles Scribner & Co., 1868.

Beffel, Eulalie. *The Hero of Antietam.* New York: E. P. Dutton & Co., 1943.

Benson, B. K. *Who Goes There? The Story of a Spy in the Civil War.* New York: The Macmillan Co., 1900.

———. *A Friend with the Countersign.* New York and London: The Macmillan Co., 1901.

———. *Bayard's Courier: A Story of Love and Adventure in the Cavalry Campaigns.* New York and London: The Macmillan Co., 1902.

———. *Old Squire. The Romance of a Black Virginian.* New York and London: The Macmillan Co., 1903.

Bentley, Robert F. *Forestfield: A Story of the Old South (In Two Periods).* New York: The Grafton Press, 1903.

Blech, William James ("William Blake"). *The Copperheads.* New York: The Dial Press, 1941.

Bogue, Herbert Edwards. *Dareford.* Boston: C. M. Clark Co., 1907.

Bowles, Colonel John. *The Stormy Petrel: An Historical Romance.* New York: A. Lovell & Co.; London: Walter Scott, 1892.

Bowley, F. S. *A Boy Lieutenant.* Philadelphia: Henry Altemus Co., 1906.

Boyd, James. *Marching On.* New York: Charles Scribner's Sons, 1927.

Boyd, Thomas Alexander. *Samuel Drummond.* New York: Charles Scribner's Sons, 1925.

Boyle, Virginia Frazier. *Brokenburne: A Southern Auntie's Tale.* New York: E. R. Herrick & Co., 1897.

Boyles, Kate and Virgil D. *The Hoosier Volunteer.* Chicago: A. C. McClurg & Co., 1914.

Bradford, Roark. *Kingdom Coming.* New York and London: Harper & Bros., 1933.

Brady, Cyrus Townsend. *The Southerners: A Story of the Civil War.* New York: Charles Scribner's Sons, 1903.

———. *A Little Traitor to the South: A Wartime Comedy with a Tragic Interlude.* New York and London: Macmillan and Co., 1904.

———. *Three Daughters of the Confederacy: The Story of Their Loves and Hatreds, Their Joys and Their Sorrows, During Many Surprising Adventures on Land and Sea.* New York: G. W. Dillingham Co., 1905.

———. *The Patriots: The Story of Lee and the Last Hope.* New York: Dodd, Mead & Co., 1906.

————. *On the Old Kearsage: A Story of the Civil War.* New York: Charles Scribner's Sons, 1909.

————. *As the Sparks Fly Upward.* Chicago: A. C. McClurg & Co., 1911.

————. *Secret Service: Being the Happenings of a Night in Richmond in the Spring of 1865— Done into Book Form from the Play by William Gillette by Cyrus Townsend Brady.* New York: Dodd, Mead, & Co., 1912.

Branch, Houston and Frank Waters. *Diamond Head.* New York: Farrar, Straus & Co., 1948.

Branscom, Alexander C. *Mystic Romances of the Blue and the Grey Masks of War, Commerce, and Society. Pictures of Real Life Scenes Enacted in This Age. Rarely Surpassed in the Wildest Dreams of Fictitious Romance.* New York: Mutual Publishing Co., 1883.

Brier, Royce. *Boy in Blue: A Novel of the Civil War.* New York and London: D. Appleton-Century Co., 1937.

Bristow, Gwen. *The Handsome Road.* New York: Thomas Y. Crowell Co., 1938.

Bromfield, Louis. *Wild is the River.* New York: Harper & Bros., 1941.

Browne, Walter Scott. *Andrew Bentley: Or, How He Retrieved His Honor.* Camden, N. J.: A. C. Graw, 1900.

Buck, Charles W. *Colonel Bob and a Double Love: A Story from the Civil Side Behind the Southern Lines.* Louisville: The Standard Press, 1922.

Burchell, Sidney Herbert. *The Shepherd of the People: Abraham Lincoln.* London: Gay and Hancock, Ltd., 1924.

Burnett, W. R. *The Dark Command: A Kansas Iliad.* New York and London: Alfred A. Knopf, 1938.

Cable, George Washington. *Dr. Sevier.* Boston: James R. Osgood & Co., 1885.

————. *The Cavalier.* New York: Charles Scribner's Sons, 1901.

————. *Kincaid's Battery.* New York: Charles Scribner's Sons, 1908.

Cain, James M. *Past All Dishonor.* New York: Alfred A. Knopf, 1946.

Carr, Clark E. *The Illini. A Story of the Prairies.* Chicago: A. C. McClurg & Co., 1904.

Cavanah, Frances. *A Patriot in Hoops.* New York: Robert M. McBride & Co., 1932.

Chambers, Robert William. *The Haunts of Men.* New York: Bacheller, Johnson & Bacheller, 1898.

————. *Special Messenger.* New York: D. Appleton & Co., 1909.

————. *Alisa Page: A Novel.* New York and London: D. Appleton & Co., 1910.

————. *Whistling Cat.* New York and London: D. Appleton & Co., 1932.

————. *Secret Service Operator 13.* New York and London: D. Appleton-Century Co., 1934.

Chapin, Mrs. Sallie F. *Fitz-Hugh St. Clair: The South Carolina Rebel Boy: Or, It is No Crime to Be Born a Gentleman.* Philadelphia: Claxton, Remsen, & Heffelfinger; Charleston, S. C.: John M. Greer & Son, 1872.

Child, Lydia Maria Francis. *A Romance of the Republic.* Boston: Ticknor & Fields, 1867.

Chittenden, L. E. *An Unknown Heroine: An Hisorical Episode of the War Between the States.* New York: George H. Richmond & Co., 1894.

Churchill, Winston. *The Crisis.* New York and London: The Macmillan Co., 1901.

Clarkson, Charles Ervine. *A Rose of Old Virginia: A Romance of the War Between the States.* Fort Smith, Ark.: Calvary-McBride Printing Co., 1927.

Clemens, Jeremiah. *Tobias Wilson: A Tale of the Great Rebellion.* Philadelphia: J. B. Lippincott & Co., 1865.

Coates, Joseph Hornor ("Hornor Cotes"). *The Counterpart.* New York: The Macaulay Co., 1909.

Cobb, Irwin S. *Red Likker.* New York: Cosmopolitan Book Corporation, 1929.

Cochran, John S. *Bonnie Belmont. A Historical Romance of the Days of Slavery and the Civil War.* Wheeling: Wheeling News Co., 1907.

Coffin, Charles Carleton. *Winning His Way.* Boston: Ticknor & Fields, 1865.

Collingwood, Herbert W. *Andersonville Violets: A Story of Northern and Southern Life.* Boston: Lee & Shepard. New York: Charles T. Dillingham, 1889.

Collins, C. B. *Tom and Joe: Or Two Farmer Boys in War and Peace and Love. A Louisiana Memory.* Richmond: Everett Waddey, 1890.

Colton, Arthur. *Bennie Ben Cree, Being the Story of His Adventure Southward in the Year '62.* New York: Doubleday & McClure Co., 1900.

Colver, Ann. *Mr. Lincoln's Wife.* New York and Toronto: Farrar & Rinehart, Inc., 1943.

Conrad, Thomas N. *A Confederate Spy. A Story of the Civil War.* New York: J. S. Ogilvie Publishing Co., n.d.

Cooke, John Esten. *Surry of Eagle's Nest: Or, The Memoirs of a Staff-Officer Serving in Virginia.* New York: Bunce & Huntington, 1866.

————. *Hilt to Hilt: Or, Days and Nights on the Banks of the Shenandoah in the Autumn of 1864.* New York: G. W. Carleton, 1869.

————. *Mohun, Or, The Last Days of Lee and His Paladins. Final Memoirs of a Staff Officer Serving in Virginia. From the MSS. of Colonel Surry, of Eagle's Nest.* New York: F. J. Huntington & Co., 1869.

Corbett, Elizabeth F. *Faye's Folly.* New York: D. Appleton-Century Co., 1941.

Cox, Millard F. ("Henry Scott Clark"). *The Legionaries. A Story of the Great Raid.* Indianapolis: The Bowen-Merrill Co., 1899.

Crabb, Alfred Leland. *Dinner at Belmont. A Novel of Captured Nashville.* Indianapolis and New York: The Bobbs-Merrill Co., 1942.

————. *Lodging at the Saint Cloud. A Tale of Occupied Nashville.* Indianapolis and New York: The Bobbs-Merrill Co., 1946.

Crane, Stephen. *The Red Badge of Courage. An Episode of the American Civil War.* New York: D. Appleton & Co., 1896.

Crim, Matt. *Adventures of a Fair Rebel.* New York: Charles L. Webster & Co., 1891.

Crowell, Joseph E. *The Young Volunteer: A Record of the Experiences of a Private Soldier.* London and New York: F. Tennyson Neely, 1899.

Cruse, Mrs. Mary Ann ("M. A. C."). *Cameron Hall: A Story of the Civil War.* Philadelphia: J. B. Lippincott & Co., 1867.

Cummings, Edward. *Marmaduke of Tennessee.* Chicago: A. C. McClurg & Co., 1914.

Curtis, George Ticknor ("Peter Boylston"). *John Charaxes: A Tale of the Civil War in America.*

Philadelphia: J. B. Lippincott Co., 1889.

Dabney, Virginius. *The Story of Don Miff, As Told by His Friend John Bouche Whacker: A Symphony of Life.* Philadelphia: J. B. Lippincott Co., 1886.

Dahlinger, Charles W. *Where the Red Volleys Poured.* New York: G. W. Dillingham Co., 1907.

Danford, M. C. *The Trail of the Gray Dragoon.* New York: Harold Vinal, Ltd., 1928.

Darby, Ada Claire. *"Look Away, Dixie Land."* New York and Toronto: Frederick A. Stokes Co., 1941.

Daringer, Helen F. *Mary Montgomery, Rebel.* New York: Harcourt, Brace & Co., 1948.

Davis, John E. *Belleview: A Story of the South from 1860 to 1865.* New York: John B. Alden, Publisher, 1889.

Davis, M. E. M. *In War Times at La Rose Blanche.* Boston: D. Lathrop Co., 1888.

Davis, Samuel Hoffman. *Separated by Mountains.* Philadelphia: Dorrance & Co., 1933.

De Forest, John William. *Miss Ravenel's Conversion from Secession to Loyalty.* New York: Harper & Bros., 1867.

Deland, Margaretta Wade. *The Kays.* New York and London: Harper & Bros., 1926.

De Leon, Thomas Cooper. *John Holden, Unionist: A Romance of the Days of Destruction and Reconstruction.* St. Paul: The Price-McGill Co., 1893.

———. *Crag Nest: A Romance of the Days of Sheridan's Ride.* Mobile: The Gossip Printing Co., 1897.

Dickinson, Anna E. *What Answer?* Boston: Ticknor & Fields, 1868.

Dickson, Capers. *John Ashton: A*

Story of the War Between the States. Atlanta: The Foote & Davies Co., 1896.

Dillon, Mary. *In Old Bellaire.* New York: The Century Co., 1906.

[Dixon, S. H.]. *Robert Warren, The Texan Refugee. A Thrilling Story of Field and Camp Life during the Late Civil War.* Chicago: W. H. Harrison, Jr., Publisher and Bookseller, 1879.

Dixon, Thomas, Jr. *The Leopard's Spots: A Romance of the White Man's Burden—1865-1900.* New York: Doubleday, Page & Co., 1902.

———. *The Clansman: An Historical Romance of the Ku Klux Klan.* New York: Doubleday, Page & Co., 1905.

———. *The Southerner: A Romance of the Real Lincoln.* New York and London: D. Appleton & Co., 1914.

———. *The Victim: A Romance of the Real Jefferson Davis.* New York and London: D. Appleton & Co., 1914.

———. *The Man in Gray: A Romance of North and South.* New York and London: D. Appleton & Co., 1921.

Doneghy, Dagmar. *The Border: A Missouri Saga.* New York: William Morrow & Co., 1931.

Douglas, Amanda Minnie. *Kathie's Soldiers.* Boston: Lee & Shepard, 1877.

Dowdey, Clifford. *Bugles Blow No More.* Boston: Little, Brown & Co., 1937.

———. *Where My Love Sleeps.* Boston: Little, Brown & Co., 1945.

Driver, John Merritte. *Americans All. A Romance of the Great War.* Chicago: Forbes & Co., 1911.

Dunbar, Paul Laurence. *The Fanatics.* New York: Dodd, Mead & Co., 1901.

Dunn, Byron Archibald. *General*

Nelson's Scout. Chicago: A. C. Mc-Clurg & Co., 1898.
———. *On General Thomas's Staff.* Chicago: A. C. McClurg & Co., 1899.
———. *Battling for Atlanta.* Chicago: A. C. McClurg & Co., 1900.
———. *From Atlanta to the Sea.* Chicago: A. C. McClurg & Co., 1901.
———. *Raiding with Morgan.* Chicago: A. C. McClurg & Co., 1903.
———. *With Lyon in Missouri.* Chicago: A. C. McClurg & Co., 1910.
———. *The Courier of the Ozarks.* Chicago: A. C. McClurg & Co., 1912.
———. *Storming Vicksburg.* Chicago: A. C. McClurg & Co., 1913.
———. *The Last Raid.* Chicago: A. C. McClurg & Co., 1914.
———. *The Boy Scouts of the Shenandoah.* Chicago: A. C. McClurg & Co., 1916.
———. *With the Army of the Potomac,* Chicago: A. C. McClurg & Co., 1917.
———. *Scouting for Sheridan.* Chicago: A. C. McClurg & Co., 1918.
Dwight, Allan. *Linn Dickson, Confederate.* New York: The Macmillan Company, 1934.
Earle, Mary Tracy. *The Flag on the Hill Top.* Boston and New York: Houghton Mifflin & Co., 1902.
Edgerton, Lucile Selk. *Pillars of Gold.* New York: Alfred A. Knopf, 1941.
Eggleston, George Cary. *The Bale Marked X. A Blockade Running Adventure.* Boston: Lothrop Publishing Co., 1902.
———. *Dorothy South: A Love Story of Virginia Just before the War.* Boston: Lothrop Publishing Co., 1902.
———. *The Master of Warlock: A Virginia War Story.* Boston: Lothrop Publishing Co., 1903.
———. *A Captain in the Ranks:*

A Romance of Affairs. New York: A. S. Barnes & Co., 1904.
———. *Evelyn Byrd.* Boston: Lothrop Publishing Co., 1904.
———. *A Daughter of the South: A War's-End Romance.* Boston: Lothrop Publishing Co., 1905.
———. *The Warrens of Virginia: A Novel (Founded on the Play of William C. Demille).* New York: G. W. Dillingham Co., 1908.
Eggleston, Joseph William. *Tuckahoe: An Old Fashioned Story of an Old Fashioned People.* New York and Washington: The Neale Publishing Co., 1903.
Erskine, John. *The Start of the Road.* New York: Frederick A. Stokes Co., 1938.
Evans, Edna Hoffman. *Sunstar and Pepper: Scouting with Jeb Stuart.* Chapel Hill: University of North Carolina Press, 1947.
Everett, Lloyd I. *For Maryland's Honor: A Story of the War for Southern Independence.* Boston: The Christopher Publishing House, 1922.
Fairbank, Janet A. *The Courtlandts of Washington Square.* Indianapolis: The Bobbs-Merrill Company, 1922.
Falconer, William. *Bloom and Brier: Or, As I Saw It, Long Ago. A Southern Romance.* Philadelphia: Claxton, Remsen & Heffelfinger. Montgomery, Ala.: Joel White, 1870.
Faulkner, William. *The Unvanquished.* New York: Random House, 1938.
Ferrell, Elizabeth and Margaret. *Full of Thy Riches.* New York: M. S. Mill Co., Inc., 1944.
Fleming, A. M. *A Soldier of the Confederacy.* Boston: Meador Publishing Co., 1934.
Floyd, N. J. *Thorns in the Flesh: A*

Romance of the War and Ku Klux Periods. Philadelphia, Cincinnati, Chicago, New York, Boston, Kansas City: Hubbard Bros., Publishers, 1884.

———. *The Last of the Cavaliers: Or, The Phantom Peril.* New York: Broadway Publishing Co., 1904.

Fluker, Anne and Winifred. *Confed'ric Gol'.* Macon, Ga.: The J. W. Burke Co., 1926.

Fontaine, Francis. *Etowah: A Romance of the Confederacy.* Atlanta: Published by Francis Fontaine, 1887.

Ford, Sally Rochester. *Raids and Romance of Morgan and His Men.* New York: Charles B. Richardson, 1864.

Forrest, J. R. *The Student Cavaliers.* New York: R. F. Fenno & Co., 1908.

Fosdick, Charles ("H. C. Castlemon"). *Frank Before Vicksburg.* Cincinnati: R. W. Carroll, 1866.

———. *Frank on a Gun-Boat.* Philadelphia: Porter & Coates. Cincinnati: R. W. Carroll & Co., 1864.

———. *Frank on the Lower Mississippi.* Cincinnati: R. W. Carroll & Co., 1867.

———. *True to His Colors.* Philadelphia: Porter & Coates, 1889.

———. *Rodney the Partisan.* Philadelphia: Porter & Coates, 1890.

———. *Marcy the Blockade Runner.* Philadelphia: Porter & Coates, 1891.

———. *Marcy the Refugee.* Philadelphia: Porter & Coates, 1892.

———. *Rodney the Overseer.* Philadelphia: Porter & Coates, 1892.

———. *Sailor Jack the Trader.* Philadelphia: Porter & Coates, 1893.

Fox, John, Jr., *The Little Shepherd of Kingdom Come.* New York: Charles Scribner's Sons, 1903.

Frederic, Harold. *The Return of the O'Mahoney.* New York: Charles Scribner's Sons, 1892.

———. *The Copperhead.* New York: Charles Scribner's Sons, 1893.

French, Alice ("Octave Thanet"). *Expiation.* New York: Charles Scribner's Sons, 1890.

Gardner, Helen H. *An Unofficial Patriot.* Boston: Arena Publishing Co., 1894.

Garland, Hamlin. *Trail-Makers of the Middle Border.* New York: The Macmillan Co., 1926.

Garth, David. *Gray Canaan.* New York: G. P. Putnam's Sons, 1947.

Gilliam, David Tod. *Dick Devereux. A Story of the Civil War.* Cincinnati: Stewart & Kidd, 1915.

Gilmore, James Roberts ("Edmund Kirke"). *Among the Pines: Or. South in Secession-Time.* New York: J. R. Gilmore. Charles T. Evans, 1862.

———. *Among the Guerillas.* New York: Carleton, Publisher, 1866.

———. *On the Border.* Boston: Lee & Shepard, 1867.

Gilmore, James Roberts. *A Mountain-White Heroine.* New York and Chicago: Belford, Clark & Co., 1889.

Glasgow, Ellen. *The Battle-Ground.* New York: Doubleday, Page & Co., 1902.

Glenwood, Ida. *Lily Pearl and the Mistress of Rosedale.* Chicago: Dibble Publishing Co., 1892.

Gordon, Caroline. *None Shall Look Back.* New York: Charles Scribner's Sons, 1937.

Goss, Warren Lee. *Jed: A Boy's Adventures in the Army of '61-'65.* New York: Thomas Y. Crowell Co., 1889.

———. *Tom Clifton: Or, Western Boys in Grant and Sherman's Army. '61-'65.* New York and Boston: Thomas Y. Crowell Co., 1892.

———. *Jack Alden*: *A Story of Adventures in the Virginia Campaigns*. *'61-'65*. New York and Boston: Thomas Y. Crowell Co., 1895.

———. *In the Navy, Or, Father Against Son. A Story of Naval Adventures in the Great Civil War*. *'61-'65*. New York and Boston: Thomas Y. Crowell Co., 1898.

Greene, Homer. *A Lincoln Conscript*. Boston and New York: Houghton Mifflin Co., 1909.

Griswold, Francis. *A Sea Island Lady*. New York: William Morrow & Co., 1939.

Gunter, Archibald Clavering. *Billy Hamilton*. New York: The Home Publishing Co., 1898.

Hanaford, Mrs. P. A. *Frank Nelson*: *Or, The Runaway Boy*. Boston: William H. Hill, Jr., & Co., 1866.

Hancock, Albert Elmer. *Henry Bourland*: *The Passing of the Cavalier*. New York: The Macmillan Co., 1901.

Hancock, Sallie J. *The Montanas*: *Or, Under the Stars. A Romance*. New York: Carleton, 1866.

Hanford, C. H. *General Claxton. A Novel*. New York: The Neale Publishing Co., 1917.

Hargis, Thomas F. *A Patriot's Strategy*. Louisville, Ky.: Charles T. Dearing, 1895.

Harris, Joel Chandler. *On the Plantation*: *A Story of a Georgia Boy's Adventures during the War*. New York: D. Appleton & Co., 1892.

———. *A Little Union Scout*. New York: McClure, Phillips & Co., 1904.

———. *The Shadow Between His Shoulder-Blades*. Boston: Small, Maynard & Co., 1909.

Harrison, Constance Cary (Mrs. Burton). *Flower de Hundred*: *The Story of a Virginia Plantation*. New York: Cassell Publishing Co., 1890.

———. *The Carlyles*: *A Story of the Fall of the Confederacy*. New York: D. Appleton & Co., 1905.

Harrison, Ida Withers. *Beyond the Battle's Rim*: *A Story of the Confederate Refugees*. New York: The Neale Publishing Co., 1918.

Harrison, W. S. *Sam Williams*: *A Tale of the Old South*. Nashville: Methodist Episcopal Church, South, 1892.

Harte, Bret. *Clarence*. Boston and New York: Houghton Mifflin Co., 1895.

Hawkins, Willis B. *Andy Barr*. Boston: Lothrop Publishing Co., 1903.

Haydn, Ruff. *Pine Mountain Americans*. New York: The Hobson Book Press, 1947.

Haynes, Emory James. *A Wedding in War-Time*. Boston: James H. Earle, 1890.

Hayward, W. S. *The Black Angel*: *A Tale of the American Civil War*. London: Charles H. Clarke, 1868.

Heagney, H. J. *Blockade Running*: *A Tale of Adventure Aboard the "Robert E. Lee."* New York and Toronto: Longmans, Green & Co., 1939.

Henderson, Le Grand ("Le Grand"). *Glory Horn*. New York: Robert M. McBride & Co., 1941.

Henty, George Alfred. *With Lee in Virginia*: *A Story of the American Civil War*. London: Blackie & Son, 1890.

Hergesheimer, Joseph. *The Limestone Tree*. New York: Alfred A. Knopf, 1931.

Heyward, DuBose. *Peter Ashley*. New York: Farrar & Rinehart, 1932.

Hiatt, James M. *The Test of Loyalty*. Indianapolis: Merrill & Smith, 1864.

Hilles, Lewis Baker. *Chickens Come*

Home to Roost: A Novel. New York: Isaac H. Blanchard Co., 1899.

Hinman, Wilbur F. *Corporal Si Klegg and His "Pard": How They Lived and Talked, and What They Did and Suffered, While Fighting for the Flag.* Cleveland: N. G. Hamilton Co., 1889.

Holmes, Mary Jane Hawes. *Rose Mather: A Tale.* New York: G. W. Carleton & Co., 1868.

Hoover, Francis T. *Enemies in the Rear: Or, A Golden Circle Squared. A Story of Southeastern Pennsylvania in the Time of Our Civil War.* Boston: Arena Publishing Co., 1895.

Hosmer, G. W. *As We Went Marching On: A Story of the War.* New York: Harper & Bros., 1885.

Hosmer, James Kendall. *The Thinking Bayonet.* Boston: Walker, Fuller & Co., 1865.

Howard, John Hamilton. *In the Shadow of the Pines: A Tale of Tidewater Virginia.* New York: Eaton & Mains, Cincinnati: Jennings & Graham, 1906.

Howard, Oliver Otis. *Henry in the War: Or, The Model Volunteer.* Boston: Lee & Shepard, Publishers, 1899.

Howe, Mary Ann. *The Rival Volunteers: Or, The Black Plume Rifles.* New York: John Bradburn, 1864.

Hoy, Mrs. Frank L. *Adrienne.* New York and Washington: The Neale Publishing Co., 1906.

Hughes, Rupert. *The Whirlwind.* Boston: Lothrop Publishing Co., 1902.

Hutchens, Jane. *John Brown's Cousin.* New York: Doubleday, Doran & Co., 1940.

———. *Timothy Larkin.* Garden City: Doubleday, Doran & Co., 1942.

Ingraham, Ellen. ("Grace Lintner"). *Bond and Free: A Tale of the South.* Indianapolis: C. B. Ingraham, 1882.

Jacobs, Thornwell. *Red Lanterns on St. Michael's.* New York: E. P. Dutton & Co., 1940.

Johnson, Gerald W. *By Reason of Strength.* New York: Minton, Balch & Co., 1930.

Johnston, Mary. *The Long Roll.* Boston & New York: Houghton Mifflin Co., 1911.

———. *Cease Firing.* Boston & New York: Houghton Mifflin Co., 1912.

Jones, Alice ("John Alix"). *The Night-Hawk: A Romance of the '60's.* New York: Frederick A. Stokes Co., 1901.

Jones, Justin ("Harry Hazel"). *Virginia Graham: The Spy of the Grand Army.* Boston: Loring, 1868.

Kane, Harnet. *Bride of Fortune: A Novel Based on the Life of Mrs. Jefferson Davis.* New York: Doubleday & Co., 1948.

Kane, James J. *Ilian: Or, The Curse of the Old South Church of Boston. A Psychological Tale of the Late Civil War.* Philadelphia: J. B. Lippincott Co., 1888.

Kantor, MacKinlay. *Long Remember.* New York: Coward McCann, 1934.

———. *Arouse and Beware.* New York: Coward McCann, 1936.

Kate Morgan and Her Soldiers. Philadelphia: American Sunday-School Union, 1862.

Kaye-Smith, Sheila. *The Challenge to Sirius.* London: Nixbet & Co., Ltd., 1917.

Keenan, Harry F. *The Iron Game: A Tale of the War.* New York: D. Appleton & Co., 1891.

Kelland, Clarence Budington. *Arizona.* New York and London: Harper & Bros., 1939.

Kelly, Caroline E. *Andy Hall. The Mission Scholar in the Army.* Boston: Henry Hoyt, 1863.

Kelso, Isaac. *The Stars and Bars: Or, The Reign of Terror in Missouri.* Boston: A. Williams & Co., 1863.

Kennedy, Sara Beaumont. *Cicely. A Tale of the Georgia March.* Garden City: Doubleday, Page & Co., 1911.

Kennerly, S. J. *The Story of Sam Tag Age From Ten to Fifteen from 1860 to 1865.* New York: Cosmopolitan Press, 1911.

King, Charles. *Kitty's Conquest.* New York: Harper & Bros., 1884.

———. *Between the Lines: A Story of the War.* New York: Harper & Bros., 1888.

———. *A War-Time Wooing: A Story.* New York: Harper & Bros., 1888.

———. *The General's Double: A Story of the Army of the Potomac.* Philadelphia: J. B. Lippincott Co., 1888.

———. *Norman Holt: A Story of the Army of the Cumberland.* New York: G. W. Dillingham & Co., 1901.

———. *The Iron Brigade: A Story of the Army of the Potomac.* New York: G. W. Dillingham & Co., 1902.

———. *A Knight of Columbia: A Story of the War.* New York: The Hobart Co., 1904.

———. *A Broken Sword: A Tale of the Civil War.* New York: The Hobart Co., 1905.

Kirkland, Joseph. *The Captain of Company K.* Chicago: Dibble Publishing Co., 1891.

Knipe, Emilie Benson and Arthur Alden. *Girls of '64.* New York: The Macmillan Co., 1918.

Knox, Rose B. *Gray Caps.* Garden City: Doubleday, Doran, and Co., 1933.

Knox, Thomas W. *The Lost Army.* New York: The Merriam Co., 1894.

Krapp, George Philip. *Sixty Years Ago: A Tale of the Civil War.* Chicago and New York: Rand McNally Co., 1927.

Kroll, Harry Harrison. *The Keepers of the House.* Indianapolis and New York: The Bobbs-Merrill Co., 1940.

Krout, Caroline Virginia ("Caroline Brown"). *Knights in Fustian: A War Time Story of Indiana.* Boston and New York: Houghton Mifflin Co., 1900.

"Lady of Warrenton, Va., A." *The Princess of the Moon: A Confederate Fairy Story.* Warrenton, Va.: 1869.

Lancaster, Bruce and Lowell Brentano. *Bride of a Thousand Cedars: A Novel of Bermuda.* New York: Frederick A. Stokes Co., 1934.

Lancaster, Bruce. *The Scarlet Patch.* Boston: Little, Brown & Co., 1947.

———. *No Bugles Tonight.* Boston: Little, Brown & Co., 1948.

Lanier, Sidney. *Tiger-Lilies, a Novel.* New York: Hurd and Houghton, 1867.

Le Cato, N. J. W. *Tom Burton: Or, The Days of '61.* Chicago, New York and San Francisco: Belford, Clark & Co., 1888.

Leonard, Mary Hall. *The Days of the Swamp-Angel.* New York: The Neale Publishing Co., 1914.

Lincoln, Joseph. *Storm Signals.* New York and London: D. Appleton-Century Co., 1935.

Lloyd, John Uri. *Stringtown on the Pike. A Tale of Northernmost Kentucky.* New York: Dodd, Mead & Co., 1900.

———. *Warwick of the Knobs. A Story of Stringtown County, Kentucky.* New York: Dodd, Mead & Co., 1901.

Lockridge, Ross, Jr. *Raintree County.* Boston: Houghton Mifflin Co., 1947.

Long, John Luther. *War: Or, What Happens When One Loves One's*

Enemy. Indianapolis: The Bobbs-Merrill Co., 1913.

Long, Laura. *Without Valor.* New York and Toronto: Longmans, Green & Co., 1940.

Longstreet, Mrs. Rachel Abigail ("Mrs. C. H. Gildersleeve"). *Remy St. Remy, Or, The Boy in Blue.* New York: James O'Kane, 1866.

Lost Dispatch, The. Galesburg, Ill.: The Galesburg Printing & Publishing Co., 1889.

"Louisiana." *"Blue and Gray": Or Two Oaths and Three Warnings.* New Orleans: L. Graham & Son, 1885.

Lowden, Leone. *Proving Ground. A Novel of Civil War Days in the North.* New York: Robert M. McBride & Co., 1946.

Lytle, Andrew. *The Long Night.* Indianapolis and New York: The Bobbs-Merrill Co., 1936.

MacGowan, Alice. *The Sword in the Mountains.* New York and London: G. P. Putnam's Sons, 1910.

Mackie, Pauline Bradford. *The Washingtonians.* Boston: L. C. Page & Co., 1902.

Madison, Lucy Foster. *A Daughter of the Union.* New York: Grosset & Dunlap, 1903.

Magill, Mary Tucker. *Women: Or, Chronicles of the Late War.* Baltimore: Turnbull Bros., 1871.

Malone, Joseph S. *Guided and Guarded: Or, Some Incidents in the Life of A Minister-Soldier.* New York: The Abbey Press, 1901.

Markey, Morris. *The Band Plays Dixie.* New York: Harcourt Brace & Co., 1927.

Marriott, Crittenden. *Sally Castleton, Southerner.* Philadelphia and London: J. B. Lippincott, 1913.

Martin, Anne. *War Brides.* New York: Pegasus Publishing Co., 1940.

Martin, Ellen. *The Feet of Clay.* New York: Brown and Derby, 1882.

Martyn, Mrs. Sarah Towne Smith. *Our Village in War-Time.* New York: American Tract Society, 1864.

Mason, Benjamin F. *Through War to Peace.* Oakland: Pacific Publishing Co., 1891.

Mason, Francis Van Wyck ("Ward Weaver"). *Hang My Wreath.* New York: Wilfred Funk, Inc., 1941.

Masters, Edgar Lee. *The Tide of Time.* New York and Toronto: Farrar & Rinehart, 1937.

May, Thomas P. ("Fortis et Fidelis"). *The Earl of Mayfield: A Novel.* Philadelphia: T. B. Peterson & Bros., 1879.

McCabe, James Dabney, Jr., *The Aid-De-Camp: A Romance of the War.* Richmond: W. A. J. Smith, 1863.

McCord, Joseph. *Redhouse on the Hill.* Philadelphia: McCrae-Smith Co., 1938.

McElroy, John. *The Red Acorn.* Chicago: Henry A. Sumner & Co., 1883.

————. *Si, "Shorty" and the Boys on the March to the Sea.* Washington: The National Tribune Co., 1910.

————. *Si Klegg, His Transformation from a Raw Recruit to a Veteran.* Washington: The National Tribune Co., 1910.

McGehee, Thomasine. *Journey Proud.* New York: The Macmillan Co., 1939.

McLaughlin, N. Monroe. *The Last Man.* Washington: The Neale Publishing Co., 1900.

McLaws, Lafayette. *The Welding.* Boston: Little, Brown & Co., 1907.

McLeod, Isabella. *Westfield. A View of Home Life During the American War.* Edinburgh: Edmonston & Douglas, 1866.

McNeilly, Mildred Masterson. *Praise*

at Morning. New York: William Morrow & Co., 1947.

Medary, Marjorie. *College and Crinoline.* New York and Toronto: Longmans, Green & Co., 1937.

Meriwether, Elizabeth Avery. *The Sowing of Swords: Or, the Soul of the Sixties.* New York and Washington: The Neale Publishing Co., 1910.

Miller, Edwin J. *The Adventures of Ned Minton: A Story of Fact and Fiction.* Machias, Maine: A. R. Furbush, 1904.

Miner, Lewis S. *Pilot on the River.* Chicago: Albert Whitman & Co., 1940.

Minnigerode, Meade. *Cordelia Chantrell.* New York and London: G. P. Putnam's Sons, 1926.

Mitchel, F. A. *Sweet Revenge: A Romance of the Civil War.* New York: Harper & Bros., 1897.

Mitchell, Margaret. *Gone With the Wind.* New York: The Macmillan Co., 1936.

Mitchell, Silas Weir. *In War-Time.* Boston: Houghton Mifflin Co., 1885.

———. *Roland Blake.* Boston and New York: Houghton Mifflin Co., 1886.

———. *A Diplomatic Adventure.* New York: The Macmillan Co., 1906.

———. *Westways: A Village Chronicle.* New York: The Century Co., 1913.

Moody, Minnie Hite. *Long Meadows.* New York: The Macmillan Co., 1941

Montgomery, James Stuart. *Tall Men.* New York: Greenberg, 1927.

Moore, Virginia. *Rising Wind.* New York: E. P. Dutton & Co., 1928.

Morford, Henry. *The Days of Shoddy: A Novel of the Great Rebellion in 1861.* Philadelphia: T. B. Peterson & Bros., 1863.

———. *Shoulder Straps: A Novel of New York and the Army, 1862.* Philadelphia: T. B. Peterson & Bros., 1863.

———. *The Coward: A Novel of Society and the Field in 1863.* Philadelphia: T. B. Peterson & Bros., 1864.

Morris, Gouverneur. *Aladdin O'Brien.* New York: The Century Co., 1902.

Morrow, Honoré Willsie. *Forever Free.* New York: William Morrow & Co., 1927.

———. *With Malice Towards None.* New York: William Morrow & Co., 1928.

———. *The Last Full Measure.* New York: William Morrow & Co., 1930.

Murfree, Mary Noailles ("Charles Egbert Craddock"). *The Storm Center.* New York: Grossett & Dunlap, 1905.

Musick, John R. *Brother Against Brother: Or, The Tompkins Mystery. A Story of the Great American Rebellion.* New York and Chicago: J. S. Ogilvie & Co., 1887.

———. *Union. A Story of the Great Rebellion.* New York: Funk & Wagnalls Co., 1894.

Nichols, George Ward. *The Sanctuary: A Story of the Civil War.* New York: Harper & Bros., 1866.

Noble, Hollister. *Woman With a Sword. The Biographical Novel of Anna Ella Carroll of Maryland.* New York: Doubleday & Co., Inc., 1948.

Norris, Mary Harriott. *The Grapes of Wrath: A Tale of North and South.* Boston: Small, Maynard & Co., 1901.

Norton, Charles Ledyard. *Jack Benson's Log: Or, Afloat with the Flag in '61.* Boston: W. A. Wilde & Co., 1895.

O'Connor, Florence J. *The Heroine*

of the Confederacy: Or Truth and Justice. London: Harrison, 1865.

"Officer of the Union Army, An." Uncle Daniel's Story of Tom Anderson and Twenty Great Battles. New York: A. R. Hart & Co., 1886.

Old Flag, The. Philadelphia: American Sunday School Union, 1864.

Orpen, Adela E. The Jay-Hawkers: A Story of Free Soil and Border Ruffian Days. New York: D. Appleton & Company, 1900.

Page, Thomas Nelson. Two Little Confederates. New York: Charles Scribner's Sons, 1888.

——. Meh Lady: A Story of the War. New York: Charles Scribner's Sons, 1893.

——. Red Rock: A Chronicle of Reconstruction. New York: Charles Scribner's Sons, 1899.

——. A Captured Santa Claus. New York: Charles Scribner's Sons, 1902.

——. Gordon Keith. New York: Charles Scribner's Sons, 1903.

——. The Red Raiders. New York: Charles Scribner's Sons, 1924.

Palmer, Frederick. The Vagabond. New York: Charles Scribner's Sons, 1903.

Parkings, W. H. How I Escaped. A Novel. Edited by Archibald Clavering Gunter. New York: The Home Publishing Co., 1889.

Parrish, Randall. My Lady of the North: The Love Story of a Gray Jacket. Chicago: A. C. McClurg & Co., 1904.

——. My Lady of the South: A Story of the Civil War. Chicago: A. C. McClurg & Co., 1909.

——. Love Under Fire. Chicago: A. C. McClurg & Co., 1911.

——. The Red Mist: A Tale of Civil Strife. Chicago: A. C. McClurg & Co., 1914.

Paterson, Arthur. The Gospel Writ in Steel: A Story of the American Civil War. New York: D. Appleton & Co., 1898.

[Peck, Ellen]. Renshawe: A Novel. New York: G. W. Carleton & Co., 1867.

[Peck, George W.]. How Private George W. Peck Put Down the Rebellion Or, The Funny Experiences of a Raw Recruit. Chicago and New York: Belford, Clarke & Co., 1887.

Peck, William Henry. The McDonalds: Or, The Ashes of Southern Homes. A Tale of Sherman's March. New York: Metropolitan Record Office, 1867.

Pendleton, Louis Beauregard. In the Okefenokee. A Story of War Time and the Great Georgia Swamp. Boston: Roberts Bros., 1895.

Pennell, Joseph Stanley. The History of Rome Hanks and Kindred Matters. New York: Charles Scribner's Sons, 1944.

Penney, Kate Mayhew Speake. Cross Currents. Boston: Bruce Humphries, Inc., 1938.

Peple, Edward. The Littlest Rebel. New York: Moffat, Yard & Co., 1911.

Pickett, La Salle Corbell. The Bugles of Gettysburg. Chicago: F. G. Browne & Co., 1913.

"Private Secretary to——, etc., By the." The Fall of Fort Sumter: Or, Love and War in 1860-61. New York: Frederick A. Brady, 1887.

Quick, Herbert. Vandermark's Folly. Indianapolis: The Bobbs-Merrill Co., 1922.

Rand, Edward A. The Drummer-Boy of the Rappahannock: Or, Taking Sides. New York: Hunt & Eaton. Cincinnati: Granston & Stowe, 1889.

Reese, Lizette Woodworth. Worleys. New York: Farrar & Rinehart, 1936.

[Reeves, Marion Calhoun Legare].

Randolph Honor. New York: Richardson & Co., 1868.

Richardson, Norval. *The Heart of Hope.* New York: Dodd, Mead & Co., 1905.

Roberts, Elbridge Gerry. *A Naval Engagement. A Marine Narrative of Love and War.* Red Bank, N. J.: 1918.

Roberts, Maggie ("Eiggam Strebor"). *Home Scenes during the Rebellion.* New York: John F. Trow & Son, 1875.

Roberts, Walter Adolphe. *Brave Mardi Gras. A New Orleans Novel of the '60's.* Indianapolis and New York: Bobbs-Merrill Co., 1946.

Robertson, Constance. *Salute to the Hero.* New York-Toronto: Farrar & Rinehart, Inc., 1942.

———. *The Unterrified.* New York: Henry Holt & Co., 1946.

Robins, Edwards. *Chasing an Iron Horse: Or, A Boy's Adventures in the Civil War.* Philadelphia: George W. Jacobs & Co., 1902.

———. *With Thomas in Tennessee.* Philadelphia: George W. Jacobs & Co., 1903.

Robinson, Benjamin. *Dolores: A Tale of Disappointment and Distress. Compiled, Arranged, and Edited from the Journal, Letters, and Other MSS. of Roland Vernon, Esq., and from Contributions by and Conversations with the Vernon Family, of Rushbrook, in Carolina.* New York: E. J. Hale & Sons, 1868.

Robinson, Edward A. and George A. Wall. *The Gun-Bearer.* New York: Robert Bonner's Sons, 1894.

Robinson, Mary S. *A Household Story of the American Conflict. The Brother Soldiers.* New York: N. Tibbals, 1866.

Roe, Edward Payson. *His Sombre Rivals.* New York: Dodd, Mead & Co., 1883.

———. *An Original Belle.* New York: Dodd, Mead & Co., 1885.

———. *The Earth Trembled.* New York: Dodd, Mead & Co., 1887.

———. *"Miss Lou."* New York: Dodd, Mead & Co., 1888.

Roe, Edward Reynolds. *The Gray and the Blue. A Story Founded on Incidents Connected with the War for the Union.* Chicago: Rand McNally & Co., 1884.

Rose, George Hamlin. *Beyond the River.* Boston: Meador Publishing Co., 1938.

Rowell, Adelaide Corinne. *On Jordan's Stormy Banks. A Novel of Sam Davis, The Confederate Scout.* Indianapolis and New York: Bobbs-Merrill, 1948.

Royce, George M. *The Little Bugler.* St. Louis: G. J. Jones Co., 1880.

Rumbough, George P. C. *From Dust to Ashes: A Romance of the Confederacy.* Little Rock, Ark.: Brown Printing Co., 1895.

Runkel, William M. *Wontus Or The Corps of Observation.* Philadelphia: J. B. Lippincott & Co., 1874.

Russell, Charles Wells. *Roebuck. A Novel.* Baltimore: Henry Taylor & Co., 1868.

Ryals, J. V. *Yankee Doodle Dixie: Or, Love the Light of Life. An Historical Romance, Illustrative of Life and Love in an Old Virginia Country Home, and Also an Explanatory Account of the Passions, Prejudices, and Opinions Which Culminated in the Civil War.* Richmond, Va.: Everett Waddey Co., 1890.

Sage, William. *The Claybornes: A Romance of the Civil War.* Boston and New York: Houghton, Mifflin & Co., 1902.

Sargent, Epes. *Peculiar: A Tale of the Great Transition.* New York: Carleton, 1864.

Sass, Herbert Ravenel. *Look Back to Glory.* Indianapolis: Bobbs-Merrill Co., 1933.

Savage, Richard Henry. *In the House of His Friends: A Novel.* New York: The Home Pub. Co., 1901.

Sawyer, Susan Fontaine. *The Priestess of the Hills.* Boston: Meador Publishing Co., 1928.

Schachner, Nathan. *By the Dim Lamps.* New York: Frederick A. Stokes Co., 1941.

Scott, Evelyn. *The Wave.* New York: Jonathan Cape and Harrison Smith, 1929.

Scott, George. *Tamarack Farm: The Story of Rube Wolcott and His Gettysburg Girl.* New York: The Grafton Press, 1903.

Seabrook, Phoebe Hamilton. *A Daughter of the Confederacy: A Story of the Old South and the New.* New York and Washington: The Neale Publishing Co., 1906.

Seawell, Molly Elliott. *The Victory.* New York: D. Appleton & Co., 1906.

Seifert, Shirley. *The Wayfarer.* New York: M. S. Mill Co., Inc., 1938.

Selph, Fannie Eoline. *Texas: Or, The Broken Link in the Chain of Family Honors. A Romance of the Civil War.* West Nashville, Tenn.: 1905.

Sheehy, Julia Williams. *William Winston.* New York: Broadway Publishing Co., 1913.

Shelton, William Henry. *The Last Three Soldiers.* New York: The Century Co., 1897.

Shields, S. J. *A Chevalier of Dixie.* New York and Washington: The Neale Publishing Co., 1907.

Shuster, George Nauman. *Look Away!* New York: The Macmillan Co., 1939.

Sinclair, Harold Augustus. *The Years of Growth: 1861-1893.* New York: Doubleday, Doran & Co., 1940.

Sinclair, Upton. *Manassas: A Novel of the War.* New York: The Macmillan Co., 1904.

Singmaster, Elsie. *Emmeline.* Boston and New York: Houghton Mifflin Co., 1916.

———. *A Boy at Gettysburg.* Boston and New York: Houghton Mifflin Co., 1924.

———. *Swords of Steel: The Story of a Gettysburg Boy.* Boston and New York: Houghton Mifflin Co., 1933.

Slaughter, Frank Gill. *In a Dark Garden.* Garden City, New York: Doubleday & Co., Inc., 1946.

Smith, Chard Powers. *Artillery of Time.* New York: Charles Scribner's Sons, 1939.

Smith, Francis Hopkinson. *The Fortunes of Oliver Horn.* New York: Charles Scribner's Sons, 1902.

Smith, George C. *The Boy in Gray: A Story of the War.* Macon, Ga.: The Macon Publishing Co., 1894.

Sosey, Frank H. *Robert Devoy: A Tale of the Palmyra Massacre.* Palmyra, Mo.: Press of the Sosey Bros., 1903.

Spencer, Bella Z. *Tried and True: Or, Love and Loyalty. A Story of the Great Rebellion.* Springfield, Mass.: W. T. Holland, 1866.

Spooner, Arthur Willis. *Pauline: A Romance of the Civil War.* Boston: Sherman, French & Co., 1915.

Stables, William Gordon. *For Life and Liberty: A Story of Battle by Land and Sea.* London: Blackie & Sons, Ltd., 1896.

———. *Sweeping the Seas: A Tale of the Alabama.* London: Ernest Nister. New York: E. P. Dutton & Co., 1902.

Stanley, Caroline Abbott. *Order No. 11. A Tale of the Border.* New York: The Century Co., 1904.

Stephenson, Nathaniel. *They That Took the Sword.* London and New York: John Lane & the Bodley Head, 1901.

Stern, Philip Van Doren. *The Drums*

of Morning. New York: Doubleday, Doran & Co., 1942.

Stoddard, William O. *The Battle of New York: A Story for All Young People.* New York: D. Appleton & Co., 1892.

———. *Long Bridge Boys: A Story of 1861.* Boston: Lothrop Publishing Co., 1904.

Stratemeyer, Edward. *Defending His Flag: Or, A Boy in Blue and a Boy in Gray.* Boston: Lothrop, Lee & Shepard Co., 1907.

Street, James. *By Valour and Arms.* New York: The Dial Press, 1944.

———. *Tap Roots.* New York: The Dial Press, 1946.

Stribling, T. S. *The Forge.* Garden City and New York: Doubleday, Doran & Co., 1931.

Strohl, Paul ("Otto Reising"). *The Quarrel.* New York: Duell, Sloan & Pearce, 1947.

Swallow, James Francis. *A Romance of the Siege of Vicksburg.* Boston: The Chapple Publishing Co., Ltd., 1925.

Tate, Allen. *The Fathers.* New York: G. P. Putnam's Sons, 1938.

Terhune, Albert Payson. *Dad.* New York: W. J. Watt & Co., 1914.

Terhune, Mary Virginia Hawes ("Marion Harland"). *Sunnybank.* New York: Sheldon & Co., 1866.

Thane, Elswyth. *Yankee Stranger.* New York: Duell, Sloan & Pearce, 1944.

Thomas, Theresa. *Tall Grey Gates.* New York: Daniel Ryerson, Inc., 1942.

Thomas, W. H. *Running the Blockade: Or, U. S. Secret Service Adventures.* Boston: Lee & Shepard. New York: Lee, Shepard & Dillingham, 1875.

Thruston, Lucy Meacham. *Called to the Field: A Story of Virginia in the Civil War.* Boston: Little, Brown & Co., 1906.

Tomlinson, Everett Titsworth. *For the Stars and Stripes.* Boston: Lothrop, Lee & Shepard Co., 1909.

———. *The Young Blockaders: A Story of the Civil War.* Boston: Lothrop, Lee & Shepard Co., 1910.

———. *The Young Sharpshooters: A Story of the Peninsular Campaign in 1862.* Boston and New York: Houghton Mifflin Co., 1913.

———. *The Young Sharpshooters at Antietam.* Boston: Houghton Mifflin Co., 1914.

Tourgée, Albion Winegar ("Henry Churton"). *Toinette: A Novel.* New York: J. B. Ford & Co., 1874.

———. *Figs and Thistles: A Romance of the Western Reserve.* New York: Fords, Howard & Hulbert, 1879.

———. *A Royal Gentleman, And 'Zouri's Christmas.* New York: Fords, Howard & Hulbert, 1881.

———. *John Eax and Mamelon: Or The South without the Shadow.* New York: Fords, Howard & Hulbert, 1882.

———. *A Son of Old Harry: A Novel.* New York: Robert Bonner's Sons, 1891.

Townsend, George Alfred. *Katy of Catoctin: Or The Chain-Breakers.* New York: D. Appleton & Co., 1886.

Tracy, J. P. *Shenandoah. A Story of Sheridan's Great Ride. A Novel.* New York: Novelist Publishing Co., 1894.

Travers, Libbie Miller. *The Honor of a Lee.* New York: Cochrane Publishing Co., 1908.

Trowbridge, John Townsend. *The Drummerboy: A Story of Burnside's Expedition.* Boston: J. E. Tilton & Co., 1863.

———. *Cudjo's Cave.* Boston: J. E. Tilton & Co., 1864.

———. *The Three Scouts.* Boston: J. E. Tilton & Co., 1865.

Tyler, C. W. *The Scout: A Tale of the Civil War*. Nashville: The Cumberland Press, 1911.

Tyrrell, Henry. *Shenandoah: Love and War in the Valley of Virginia 1861-5. Based Upon the Famous Play by Bronson Howard*. New York and London: G. P. Putnam's Sons, 1912.

Vance, Wilson. *God's War*. London and New York: F. Tennyson Neely, 1899.

Van Praag, Francis W. *The Weaving of Webs*. New York: R. F. Fenno & Co., 1902.

Venable, Clarke ("Covington Clarke"). *Mosby's Night Hawk*. Chicago: The Reilly & Lee Co., 1931.

Verne, Jules. *Les Forceurs de Blocus* (With *Une ville flottante, et Adventures de 3 Russes et de 3 Anglais*). Paris: J. Hetzel et Cie, 1872.

————. *Nord Contre Sud*. Paris: J. Hetzel et Cie, 1887.

————. *Texar's Revenge: Or, North Against South (Nord Contre Sud). A Tale of the American Civil War (Complete in One Volume). Part I, Burbank the Northerner*. Chicago, New York: Rand McNally & Co., 1888.

Votaw, Clarence E. *Patriotism. A Story of the Civil War in America*. Philadelphia: Dorrance & Co., 1941.

Waldman, Emerson. *Beckoning Ridge*. New York: Henry Holt & Co., 1940.

Walworth, Mrs. Jeannette R. Haderman. *On the Winning Side. A Southern Story of Ante-Bellum Times*. New York: Peter Fenelon Collier, 1893.

Warren, Joseph. *The General: A Farcical Novel with an Historical Background Based on Buster Keaton's Comedy of the Same Name*. New York: Grosset & Dunlap, 1927.

Warren, Rose Harlow. *A Southern Home in War Times*. New York: Broadway Publishing Co., 1914.

Watson, Thomas Edward. *Bethany: A Story of the Old South*. New York: D. Appleton & Co., 1904.

Webster, Henry Kitchell. *Traitor and Loyalist; Or, The Man Who Found His Country*. New York: The Macmillan Co., 1904.

Westall, William. *The Princes of Peele*. New York: Lovell, Coryell & Co., 1892.

[Weston, Mrs. Maria]. *Bessie and Raymond: Or Incidents Connected with the Civil War in the United States*. Boston: Edward Payson Weston, 1866.

Wheeler, A. O. ("A. O. W."). *Eye-Witness; Or, Life Scenes in the Old North State, Depicting the Trials and Sufferings of the Unionists During the Rebellion*. Boston: B. B. Russell & Co., 1865.

Wheelwright, John T. *War Children*. New York: Dodd, Mead & Co., 1908.

White, Rev. Homer. *The Norwich Cadets: A Tale of the Rebellion*. St. Albans, Vt.: Albert Clarke, 1873.

Whitney, Louise M. *Goldie's Inheritance: A Story of the Siege of Atlanta*. Burlington, Vt.: Free Press Association, 1903.

Whitson, Mrs. L. D. *Gilbert St. Maurice*. Louisville: Bradley & Gilbert, printers, 1875.

Whittlesey, Sarah J. C. *Bertha the Beauty: A Story of the Southern Revolution*. Philadelphia: Claxton, Remsen & Heffelfinger, 1872.

Williams, Ben Ames. *House Divided*. Boston: Houghton Mifflin Co., 1947.

Williams, Churchill. *The Captain*. Boston: Lothrop Publishing Co., 1903.

Williams, Flora McDonald. *Who's the Patriot? A Story of the South-*

ern Confederacy. Louisville: Courier-Journal Job Printing Co., 1886.

Williams, George Forrester. *Bullet and Shell. War As a Soldier Saw It; Camp, March, and Picket; Battlefield and Bivouac; Prison and Hospital*. New York: Fords, Howard & Hulbert, 1883.

Williams, John S. *The Siege. A Novel of Love and War*. New York: The Cosmopolitan Press, 1912.

Wilson, Annie E. *Webs of War in Black and White*. New York: Broadway Publishing Co., 1913.

Wilson, Augusta Jane Evans. *Macaria: Or Altars of Sacrifice*. New York: John Bradburn, Publisher, 1864.

Wilson, C. R. *Bear Wallow Belles: A Love Story of the Civil War*. Louisville: R. J. Corothers, 1903.

Wilson, Kathryn Bemis. *Blue Horses: A Biographical Romance of the Civil War*. Kansas City, Mo.: Burton Publishing Co., 1931.

Winslow, William Henry. *Cruising and Blockading. A Naval Story of the Late War*. Pittsburg: J. R. Weldin & Co., 1885.

———. *Southern Buds and Sons of War*. Boston: The C. M. Clark Publishing Co., 1907.

Winston, J. *Cora O'Kane; Or, The Doom of the Rebel Guard. A Story of the Great Rebellion, Containing Incidents of the Campaign in Missouri under Generals Fremont and Sigel, and the Thrilling Exploits of the Unionists under Major Zagonyi*. Claremont, N. H.: Published by an association of disabled soldiers, 1868.

Wood, Benjamin. *Fort Lafayette: Or Love and Secession. A Novel*. New York: Carleton, 1862.

Wood, Lydia Collins. *The Haydock's Testimony: A Tale of the American Civil War*. London: Headley Bros., 1907.

Wyman, Levi Parker. *After Many Years*. Philadelphia: Dorrance & Co., 1941.

Yopp, William Isaac. *A Dual Role: A Romance of the Civil War*. Dallas: John F. Worley, 1902.

Young, Stark. *So Red the Rose*. New York: Charles Scribner's Sons, 1934.

SECONDARY SOURCES

Adams, Oscar Fay. *A Dictionary of American Authors*. Boston and New York: Houghton Mifflin Co., 1905.

Allen, Hervey. "History and the Novel," *Atlantic Monthly*, CLXXIII (February, 1944), 119-21.

American Authors, 1600-1900: A Biographical Dictionary of American Literature. Edited by Stanley J. Kunitz and Howard Haycraft. New York: H. W. Wilson Co., 1938.

"The American Republic of Jones," *Literary Digest*, LXIII (December 27, 1919), 56.

Auchampaugh, Philip Gerald. *James Buchanan and His Cabinet on the Eve of Secession*. Lancaster, Pa.: Privately printed, 1926.

Bassett, John Spencer. *Slavery in the State of North Carolina (Johns Hopkins University Studies in Historical and Political Science, XVII)*. Baltimore: The Johns Hopkins Press, 1899.

Beale, Howard Kennedy. "What Historians Have Said about the Causes of the Civil War," *Theory and Practice in Historical Study: A Report of the Committee on Historiography, Social Science Research Council Bulletin 54*. New York: Social Science Research Council, 1946.

Beard, Charles A. and Mary. *The Rise of American Civilization*, 2 vols. New York: The Macmillan Co., 1944 ed.

Becker, Carl L. *Everyman His Own Historian. Essays on History and*

Politics. New York: Appleton-Century-Crofts, Inc., 1935.

Beer, Thomas. *Hanna, Crane, and The Mauve Decade.* New York: Alfred A. Knopf, 1941.

Belloc, Hillaire. "The Character of an Historical Novel," *London Mercury,* IX (November, 1923), 37-42.

Bernbaum, Ernest. "Views of Great Critics on the Historical Novel," *Publications of the Modern Language Association,* XLI (1926), 424-41.

Berryman, John. *Stephen Crane.* New York: William Sloane Associates, 1950.

Biographical Directory of the American Congress, 1774-1927, The Continental Congress, September 5, 1774, to October 21, 1788, and the Congress of the United States, from the First to the Sixty-ninth Congress, March 4, 1789, to March 3, 1927, Inclusive. House Document 783, 69 Cong., 1 Sess. Washington: United States Government Printing Office, 1928.

"The Bonnie Blue Flag," *Saturday Review of Literature,* XV (December 31, 1937), 8.

Buck, Paul H. "The Poor Whites of the South," *American Historical Review,* XXXI (1925), 41-55.

———. *The Road to Reunion, 1865-1900.* Boston: Little, Brown & Co., 1938.

Burgess, John W. *The Civil War and the Constitution, 1859-1865,* 2 vols. New York: Charles Scribner's Sons, 1901.

Butterfield, Herbert. *The Historical Novel: An Essay.* Cambridge: The University Press, 1924.

Calhoun, Arthur Wallace. *Social History of the American Family from Colonial Times to the Present,* 3 vols. New York: Barnes & Noble, 1945.

Canby, Henry Seidel. "What Is Truth?" *Saturday Review of Literature,* IV (December 31, 1927), 481-82.

Cash, Wilbur J. *The Mind of the South.* New York: Alfred A. Knopf, 1941.

Champney, Freeman. "Literature Takes to the Woods," *Antioch Review,* IV (Summer, 1944), 246-56.

Clark, Blanche Henry. *The Tennessee Yeoman, 1849-1860.* Nashville: Vanderbilt University Press, 1942.

Clark, Thomas D. *Pills, Petticoats and Plows. The Southern Country Store.* New York: Bobbs-Merrill Co., 1944.

Cole, Arthur C. *The Irrepressible Conflict, 1850-1865 (A History of American Life, VII).* New York: The Macmillan Co., 1934.

———. "Lincoln's Election an Immediate Menace to Slavery in the States?" *American Historical Review,* XXXVI (1931), 740-67.

Colton, Arthur. "Gospel of Likemindedness," *Saturday Review of Literature,* IV (June 9, 1928), 941-42.

Cotterill, Robert Spencer. *The Old South.* Glendale, Cal.: The Arthur H. Clark Co., 1939.

Couch, William Terry. "The Agrarian Romance," *South Atlantic Quarterly,* XXXVI (October, 1937), 419-30.

———. (ed.). *Culture in the South.* Chapel Hill: The University of North Carolina Press, 1935.

Coulter, E. Merton. "What the South Has Done about Its History," *Journal of Southern History,* II (1936), 3-28.

Cowie, Alexander. *The Rise of the American Novel.* New York: American Book Co., 1948.

Craven, Avery O. *The Coming of the Civil War.* New York: Charles Scribner's Sons, 1942.

———. "Coming of the War between the States," *Journal of Southern History*, II (1936), 303-22.

Current Biography: Who's New and Why. Edited by Anna Bothe. New York: H. W. Wilson Co., 1940-1948.

Curti, Merle. *The Roots of American Loyalty*. New York: Columbia University Press, 1946.

Dangerfield, George. "The Insistent Past," *North American Review*, CCXLIII (1937), 137-52.

Davidson, James Wood. *The Living Writers of the South*. New York: Carleton, 1869.

Davis, Elmer. "Dealing with the Ancients," *Saturday Review of Literature*, IV (July 21, 1928), 1045-47.

Davis, Jefferson. *The Rise and Fall of the Confederate Government*, 2 vols. Richmond: Garrett & Massie, 1881.

Den Hollander, A. N. J. "The Tradition of 'Poor Whites,' " *Culture in the South*. Edited by William Terry Couch. Chapel Hill: The University of North Carolina Press, 1935.

DeVoto, Bernard. "Fiction and the Everlasting *If*: Notes on the Contemporary Historical Novel," *Harpers*, CLXXVII (June, 1938), 42-49.

———. "Fiction Fights the Civil War," *Saturday Review of Literature*, XVII (December 18, 1937), 3-4.

Dictionary of American Biography. 21 vols. Edited by Allen Johnson and Dumas Malone. New York: Charles Scribner's Sons, 1928-1937.

Dodd, William E. *The Cotton Kingdom. A Chronicle of the Old South*. (*The Chronicles of America Series*, XXVII). New Haven: Yale University Press, 1919.

Dumond, Dwight L. *Anti-Slavery Origins of the Civil War in the United States*. Ann Arbor: University of Michigan Press, 1939.

Dyer, Gustavus W. *Democracy in the South before the Civil War*. Nashville: Methodist Publishing House, 1905.

E. A. B., "The Craze for Historical Fiction in America," *Living Age*, CCXXV (May, 1900), 523-26.

Eaton, Clement. *Freedom of Thought in the Old South*. Durham: Duke University Press, 1940.

Eckenrode, Hamilton J. *Jefferson Davis, President of the South*. New York: The Macmillan Co., 1923.

Fain, John Tyree. "Hergesheimer's Use of Historical Sources," *Journal of Southern History*, XVIII (November, 1952), 497-504.

Farrar, John. "Novelists and/or Historians: The Historical Novel Poses a Difficult Problem for the New Writer," *Saturday Review of Literature*, XXVIII (February 17, 1945), 7-8.

Fast, Howard. *Freedom Road*. New York: Duell, Sloan & Pearce, Inc., 1944.

Fish, Carl Russell. *The American Civil War. An Interpretation*. William Ernest Smith, ed. New York and London: Longmans, Green & Co., 1937.

Fisher, H. A. L. "The Historical Novel," *The Nation and Athenaeum*, XXV (August 16, 1924), 616-18.

Ford, Paul Leicester. "The American Historical Novel," *Atlantic Monthly*, LXXXI (December, 1897), 721-28.

Franklin, John Hope. *From Slavery to Freedom. A History of American Negroes*. New York: Alfred A. Knopf, 1947.

Freeman, Douglas Southall. *The South to Posterity*. New York: Charles Scribner's Sons, 1939.

Fuller, Edmund. "History and the

Novelists," *American Scholar,* XVI (Winter, 1946-47), 113-24.

Gaines, Francis Pendleton. *The Southern Plantation. A Study in the Development and the Accuracy of a Tradition.* New York: Columbia University Press, 1925.

Gay, Robert M. "The Historical Novel: Walter D. Edmonds," *Atlantic Monthly,* CLXV (May, 1940), 656-58.

Gilder, Jeannette L. "The American Historical Novelists," *Independent,* LIII (September-December, 1901), 2096-2102.

Glasgow, Ellen. *A Certain Measure. An Interpretation of Prose Fiction.* New York: Harcourt, Brace & Co., 1943.

————. "A Memorable Novel of the Old Deep South, So Red the Rose, by Stark Young," New York *Herald Tribune Books,* X (July 22, 1934), 1.

Gooch, George Peabody. "Historical Novels," *Contemporary Review,* CXVII (February, 1920), 204-12.

Goss, Warren Lee. *The Soldier's Story of His Captivity at Andersonville, Belle Isle and Other Rebel Prisons.* Boston: Lee & Shepard, 1869.

Gray, Lewis Cecil. *History of Agriculture in the Southern United States to 1860,* 2 vols. Washington: Carnegie Institution, 1933.

Green, Fletcher Melvin. *Constitutional Development in the South Atlantic States, 1776-1860. A Study in the Evolution of Democracy.* Chapel Hill: The University of North Carolina Press, 1930.

————. "Democracy in the Old South," *Journal of Southern History,* XII (1946), 3-23.

Hackett, Alice Payne. *Fifty Years of Best Sellers.* New York: R. R. Bowker, 1945.

Hamilton, J. G. de Roulhac. "Lincoln's Election an Immediate Menace to Slavery in the States?" *American Historical Review,* XXXVII (1932), 700-11.

Henry, Robert Selph. *The Story of the Confederacy.* New York: Bobbs-Merrill Co., 1931.

Hesseltine, William Best. *Civil War Prisons. A Study in War Psychology.* Columbus: Ohio State University Press, 1930.

Hodder, Frank H. "Propaganda as a Source of American History," *Mississippi Valley Historical Review,* IX (1922), 3-18.

Holman, C. Hugh. "William Gilmore Simms's Theory and Practice of Historical Fiction." Unpublished Ph.D. dissertation, University of North Carolina, 1949.

Hosmer, James Kendall. *The Appeal to Arms, 1861-1863. (The American Nation: A History,* Vol. 20.) New York: Harper & Brothers, 1907.

Howells, William Dean. "The New Historical Romances," *North American Review,* CLXXI (October, 1900), 935-48.

Howes, Durward (ed.). *American Women. The Standard Biographical Dictionary of Notable Women.* Los Angeles: American Publication, Inc., 1939.

H. S. "Motion Without Progress," *Saturday Review of Literature,* XXVII (November 4, 1944), 16.

Hundley, D. R. *Social Relations in Our Southern States.* New York: Henry B. Price, 1860.

John William De Forest, A Union Officer in the Reconstruction. Edited by James M. Croushore and David Morris Potter. New Haven: Yale University Press, 1948.

Kendrick, Benjamin Burks, and Alex Mathews Arnett. *The South Looks at Its Past.* Chapel Hill: University of North Carolina Press, 1935.

Kettel, Thomas Prentice. *Southern*

Wealth and Northern Profits as Exhibited in Statistical Facts and Official Figures Showing the Necessity of Union to the Future Prosperity and Welfare of the Republic. New York: George W. and John A. Wood, 1860.

Kirk, John Foster. *Supplement to Alibone's Critical Dictionary of English Literature and British and American Authors.* 2 vols. Philadelphia: J. B. Lippincott Co., 1899.

Klingberg, Frank W. "James Buchanan and the Crisis of the Union," *Journal of Southern History,* IX (1943), 455-74.

Knight, Lucian Lamar. *Biographical Dictionary of Authors (Library of Southern Literature,* XV, Edwin Anderson Alderman, Joel Chandler Harris, Charles William Kent, eds.). New Orleans and Atlanta: Martin & Hoyt Co., 1909.

Lancaster, Bruce. "The Insides of a Novel," *Atlantic Monthly,* CLXXVII (February, 1946), 75-78.

Leisy, Ernest E. *The American Historical Novel.* Norman: University of Oklahoma Press, 1950.

————. "The American Historical Novel," *University of Colorado Studies, Series B,* Vol. II (October, 1945), 307-13.

Lonn, Ella. *Desertion during the Civil War.* New York: The Century Co., 1928.

McIlwaine, Shields. *The Southern Poor-White from Lubberland to Tobacco Road.* Norman: University of Oklahoma Press, 1939.

Major, Charles. "What Is Historic Atmosphere?" *Scribner's Magazine,* XXVII (June, 1900), 752-61.

Masters, Edgar Lee. *Lincoln the Man.* New York: Dodd, Mead & Co., 1931.

Matthews, Brander. "The Historical Novel," *The Forum,* XXIV (September, 1898), 79-92.

————. *The Historical Novel and Other Essays.* New York: Charles Scribner's Sons, 1901.

Milton, George Fort. *The Eve of Conflict. Stephen A. Douglas and the Needless War.* Boston and New York: Houghton Mifflin Co., 1934.

Millet, Fred Benjamin. *Contemporary American Authors. A Critical Survey and 219 Bio-bibliographies.* New York: Harcourt, Brace & Co., 1940.

Montgomery, Goode. "Alleged Secession of Jones County," *Publications of the Mississippi Historical Society,* VIII (1904), 13-22.

Morison, Samuel Eliot, and Henry Steele Commager. *The Growth of the American Republic.* 2 vols. New York: Oxford University Press, 1942 ed.

Mott, Frank Luther. *Golden Multitudes, The Story of Best Sellers in the United States.* New York: The Macmillan Co., 1947.

Mumford, Lewis. *Technics and Civilization.* New York: Harcourt, Brace and Co., 1934.

Myers, Walter L. "The Novel and the Past," *Virginia Quarterly Review,* XIV (October, 1938), 567-78.

National Cyclopedia of American Biography, Being the History of the United States as Illustrated. 24 vols. New York: James T. White Co., 1898.

Nichols, George Ward. *The Story of the Great March. From the Diary of a Staff Officer.* New York: Harper & Brothers, 1865.

Nichols, Roy Franklin. *The Disruption of American Democracy.* New York: The Macmillan Co., 1948.

Norris, Frank. *The Responsibilities of the Novelist and Other Essays.* New York: Doubleday, Page & Co., 1903.

Owsley, Frank L. "The Fundamental Cause of the Civil War: Egocentric

Sectionalism," *Journal of Southern History*, VII (1941), 3-18.

——, and Harriet C. Owsley. "The Economic Basis of Society in the Late Ante-Bellum South," *Journal of Southern History*, VI (February, 1940), 24-45.

Pattee, Fred Lewis. *A History of American Literature Since 1870*. New York: The Century Co., 1917.

——. *The New American Literature, 1890-1930*. New York: The Century Co., 1930.

Phillips, Ulrich Bonnell. *Life and Labor in the Old South*. Boston: Little Brown & Co., 1929.

Pressly, Thomas J. *Americans Interpret Their Civil War*. Princeton: Princeton University Press, 1954.

Quinn, Arthur Hobson. *American Fiction, An Historical and Critical Survey*. New York: D. Appleton-Century Co., 1936.

Ramsdell, Charles William. *Behind the Lines in the Southern Confederacy*. Baton Rouge: Louisiana State University Press, 1944.

——. "The Changing Interpretation of the Civil War," *Journal of Southern History*, III (1937), 3-28.

——. "Lincoln and Fort Sumter," *Journal of Southern History*, III (1937), 259-88.

——. "Some Problems Involved in Writing the History of the Confederacy," *Journal of Southern History*, II (1936), 133-47.

Randall, James G. "The Blundering Generation," *Mississippi Valley Historical Review*, XXVII (1940), 3-28.

——. *The Civil War and Reconstruction*. Boston, New York, Chicago, Atlanta, Dallas, San Francisco, London: D. C. Heath & Co., 1937.

——. "The Civil War Restudied," *Journal of Southern History*, VI (1940), 439-57.

Ransom, John Crowe. "The South

Defends Its Heritage," *Harpers*, CLIX (1929), 108-18.

Raymond, Ida. *Southland Writers. Biographical and Critical Sketches of the Living Female Writers of the South, With Extracts from their Writings*. Philadelphia: Claxton, Remsen & Heffelfinger, 1870.

Rhodes, James Ford. *History of the United States from the Compromise of 1850*. 7 vols. New York: Harper & Bros., 1893-1906.

Rutherford, Mildred Lewis. *The South in History and Literature. A Handbook of Southern Authors from the Settlement of Jamestown, 1607, to Living Writers*. Atlanta: Franklin-Turner Co., 1906.

Saintsbury, George. "The Historical Novel," *Essays in English Literature, 1780-1860*. 2nd Series. London: J. M. Dent & Co., 1895.

Scott, Sir Walter. *Ivanhoe*. Boston and New York: Houghton Mifflin Co., 1923 ed.

Shannon, Fred Albert. *The Organization and Administration of the Union Army, 1861-1865*. 2 vols. Cleveland: Arthur H. Clark, 1928.

Sheppard, Alfred Tressider. *The Art and Practice of Historical Fiction*. London: Humphrey Toulmin, 1930.

——. "The Historical Novel," *London Quarterly Review*, CCLIX (October, 1932), 245-58.

Shugg, Roger W. *Origins of Class Struggle in Louisiana. A Social History of White Farmers and Laborers during Slavery and After, 1840-1875*. Baton Rouge: Louisiana State University Press, 1939.

Sidney Lanier, Tiger-Lilies and Southern Prose, Centennial Edition, Vol. 5. Edited by Garland Greever and Cecil Abernethy. Baltimore: The Johns Hopkins Press, 1945.

Simkins, Francis Butler. *The South Old and New. A History, 1820-*

1947. New York: Alfred A. Knopf, 1947.

——, and James Welch Patton. *The Women of the Confederacy.* Richmond and New York: Garrett and Massie, Inc., 1936.

Smith, Harrison. "Motion Without Progress," *Saturday Review of Literature,* XXVII (November 4, 1944), 16.

Smith, Rebecca Washington. "The Civil War and Its Aftermath in American Fiction, 1861-1899, with a Dictionary Catalogue and Indexes." Unpublished Ph.D dissertation, University of Chicago, 1932.

——. *The Civil War and Its Aftermath in American Fiction, 1861-1899.* Chicago: University of Chicago Press, 1934.

Speare, Morris Edmund. *The Political Novel, Its Development in England and America.* New York: Oxford University Press, 1924.

Spiller, Robert E., Willard Thorp, Thomas H. Johnson, and Henry Seidel Canby (eds.). *Literary History of the United States.* 3 vols. New York: The Macmillan Co., 1948.

Stephens, Alexander H. *A Constitutional View of the Late War Between the States. Its Causes, Character, Conduct and Results.* 2 vols. Philadelphia: National Publishing Co., 1868-1870.

Stephenson, Nathaniel W. *The Day of the Confederacy. A Chronicle of the Embattled South (The Chronicles of America Series, XXX).* New Haven: Yale University Press, 1919.

Stephenson, Wendell H. "A Half-Century of Southern Historical Scholarship," *Journal of Southern History,* XI (1945), 3-32.

Sydnor, Charles S. "The Southerner

and the Laws," *Journal of Southern History,* VI (1940), 3-23.

——. "The Southern Experiment in Writing Social History," *Journal of Southern History,* XI (1945), 455-68.

Tate, Allen. "Gettysburg," *The Nation,* CXXXVIII (April 11, 1934), 420-21.

Tatum, Georgia Lee. *Disloyalty in the Confederacy.* Chapel Hill: The University of North Carolina Press, 1934.

Taylor, Alastair MacDonald. "The Historical Novel as a Source in History," *Sewanee Review,* XLVI (October, 1938), 459-79.

Teggert, John F. *Prolegomena to History: The Relation of History to Literature, Philosophy, and Science. University of California Publications in History,* IV (1916-1917), 155-292. Berkeley: University of California Press, 1916-1917.

Toulmin, Harry Aubrey, Jr. *Social Historians.* Boston: The Gorham Press, 1911.

Tourgée, Albion Winegar. *A Fool's Errand. By One of the Fools.* New York: Fords, Howard, and Hulbert, 1879.

——. "The South as a Field for Fiction," *The Forum,* VI (December, 1888), pp. 404-13.

Tourtellot, Arthur Barron. "History and the Historical Novel: Where Fact and Fancy Meet and Part," *Saturday Review of Literature,* XXII (August 24, 1940), 3-4.

Trevelyan, George Macaulay. "History and Fiction," *Living Age,* CCCXIII (June, 1922), 565-73.

Twelve Southerners. *I'll Take My Stand. The South and the Agrarian Tradition.* New York and London: Harper & Bros., 1930.

Twentieth Century Authors: A Biographical Dictionary of Modern

Literature. Edited by Stanley J. Kunitz and Howard Haycraft. New York: H. W. Wilson Co., 1942.

Van Auken, Sheldon. "The Southern Historical Novel in the Early Twentieth Century," *Journal of Southern History,* XIV (May, 1948), 157-58.

Van Doren, Carl Clinton. *The American Novel, 1789-1939.* New York: The Macmillan Co., 1940.

Veblen, Thorstein. *An Inquiry into the Nature of Peace and the Terms of Its Perpetuation.* New York: Viking Press, 1917.

Von Holst, Hermann E. *The Constitutional and Political History of the United States,* 8 vols. Chicago: Callaghan & Co., 1876-1892.

Weaver, Herbert. *Mississippi Farmers, 1850-1860.* Nashville: Vanderbilt University Press, 1945.

Webb, Walter Prescott. *The Great Plains.* Boston, New York, Chicago, London, Atlanta, Dallas, Columbus, San Francisco: Ginn & Co., 1931.

Weeks, Edward. Review of Kenneth Roberts' *Lydia Bailey, Atlantic Monthly,* CLXXIX (February, 1947), 128-30.

Wellek, Rene and Austin Warren. *Theory of Literature.* New York: Harcourt, Brace and Co., 1949.

Wertenbaker, Thomas Jefferson. *The First Americans, 1607-1690 (A History of American Life,* I). New York: The Macmillan Co., 1927.

———. *The Planters of Colonial Virginia.* Princeton: Princeton University Press, 1922.

Wesley, Charles H. *The Collapse of the Confederacy.* Washington: Associated Publishers, Inc., 1937.

Who's Who, An Annual Biographical Dictionary, 1899, 1910. London: Adam and Charles Black, 1899, 1910.

Who's Who Among North American Authors. Edited by Alberta Lawrence. Los Angeles: Golden Syndicate Publishing Co., 1921-1939.

Who's Who in America. A Biographical Dictionary of Notable Living Men and Women of the United States. Annual volumes, 1897-1948. Chicago: Albert Nelson Marquis Co., 1897-1948.

Who's Who in the South and Southwest. A Biographical Dictionary of Leading Men and Women of the Southern and Southwestern States. Chicago: Larkin, Roosevelt & Larkin, Ltd., 1947.

Who Was Who in America. 2 vols. Chicago: Albert Nelson Marquis Co., 1943.

Wiley, Bell I. *The Life of Johnny Reb, the Common Soldier of the Confederacy.* New York: Bobbs-Merrill Co., 1943.

———. *The Plain People of the Confederacy.* Baton Rouge: Louisiana State University Press, 1943.

———. *Southern Negroes, 1861-1865.* New Haven: Yale University Press, 1938.

Wilmer, Richard H. "Collecting Civil War Novels," *The Colophon,* III (New Series, Autumn, 1938), 513-18.

Wilson, Forrest. *Crusader in Crinoline: The Life of Harriet Beecher Stowe.* Philadelphia, London, New York: J. B. Lippincott Co., 1941.

Wilson, James Grant, and John Fiske (eds.). *Appleton's Cyclopedia of American Biography.* 6 vols. New York: D. Appleton & Co., 1887.

Woodward, Comer Vann. *Tom Watson, Agrarian Rebel.* New York: The Macmillan Co., 1938.

Writers' Program, Works Projects Administration. *Virginia: A Guide to the Old Dominion (American Guide Series).* New York: Oxford University Press, 1940.

Index

Abilene, 25
Abolitionism, 47-51, 106-11
Adams, William T. ("Oliver Optic"), 66n, 67
Agrarianism, 38, 62-64, 114
Alabama, 28, 39n, 56, 87, 179-81, 184, 185
Alcott, Louisa May, 32, 47, 104
Alexander, Holmes, 37n, 40n, 62, 118, 122, 134, 172
Allen, Hervey, 12, 66
Allen, James Lane, 12, 25n, 42, 62, 137, 142-43
Altsheler, Joseph Alexander, 44, 66-68, 92, 103, 127, 130
Andersonville, 31
Antietam, 33
Appomattox, 30n
Authors of Civil War novels, personal traditions, 24-26; birthplaces of, 26-28; source materials, 29-39; vocations of, 39-41; theories of history, 74-75; partisan positions, 79; learn limits of historical novel, 80-81, 140, 193. *See also* Civil War novels

Bagehot, Walter, 17-18n
Baker, William Mumford, 31-32, 56, 90, 130
Bassett, John Spencer, 64n
Baylor, Frances Courtenay, 12
Beale, Howard K., 80n
Beard, Charles A., 73n, 116

Beard, O. T., 123, 131-32
Beatty, John, 39n
Becker, Carl, 74-75, 191
Beecher, Henry Ward, 32n, 61n, 89, 110, 120-21
Belknap, W. W., 157
Bell, John, 134
Belloc, Hillaire, 39
Bernbaum, Ernest, 8
Boston, 65n, 83, 87, 101, 107, 118
Boyd, James, 12, 38, 63, 117-18, 182-84, 191
Bradford, Roark, 12, 38, 48, 54
Brady, Cyrus Townsend, 58-59, 98, 123
Breckinridge, John C., 116, 134
Bristow, Gwen, 63n
Brooks, Preston S., 131
Brown, John, 47n, 106
Brownlow, William G., 56
Buchanan, James, 90, 103
Buck, Paul, 4, 42, 60, 69
Burgess, John W., 99n
Butler, Rhett, 124
Butterfield, Herbert, 196

Cable, George Washington, 12, 24n, 25n, 60, 66, 68, 134, 135, 140, 191
Cain, James M., 59
Caldwell, Erskine, 186
Calhoun, John C., 82, 94, 103, 116
California, 29, 138
Carlyle, Thomas, 6

225

ism in, 159-64. *See also* Northern novels
North Carolina, 28, 40n, 182
Northern novels, when published, 23-24; realism in, 59-61; 147-65; most numerous, 69; critical of northern society, 83-85; fascination with South, 120; emphasize nationalism, 127-28. *See also* Civil War novels
Novel of character laid in past, 18. *See also* Historical novels

Oglethorpe University, 41n
Ohio, 27, 28, 31n, 39n
"Optic, Oliver." *See* William T. Adams
Owsley, Frank L., 37, 63n, 121n
Oxford, 38, 40n

Page, Thomas Nelson, 13, 32, 37n, 40n, 42, 48, 53, 57, 60, 66, 68, 70, 101, 109, 130
Parkman, Francis, 67
Parrington, Vernon L., 192
Parrish, Randall, 57n
Patriotism, 64, 195-96
Peck, George W., 39n
Peck, William Henry, 41n
Pendleton, Louis Beauregard, 37n
Pennell, Joseph Stanley, 12, 24, 25n, 155-57, 164
Pennsylvania, 27, 28, 157
Period romance, 17. *See also* Historical novels
Peru, 41
Philadelphia, 159
Phillips, Ulrich Bonnell, 64n, 187n
Pierce, Franklin, 93
Plutarch, 36
Populists, 115
Porcher, William L., 82
Porter, Fitz-John, 31n
Puritanism, 84, 86, 88, 102, 107, 121

Quinn, Arthur Hobson, 8
Quick, Herbert, 40n

Racism, 53-54, 123-25
Randall, James G., 91, 108
Ranke, Leopold von, 6
Red Badge of Courage, The. See Stephen Crane
Reeves, Marion Calhoun Legare, 114
Remarque, Erich Maria, 19
Rhode Island, 28
Richardson, Norval, 39-40n, 57n
Richmond, 30n, 37, 175-77
Roberts, Walter Adolphe, 37n
Robertson, Constance, 62
Robins, Edwards, 37n
Rock of Gibraltar, 41n
Roe, Edward Payson, 15, 56, 69, 91, 101, 109, 110
Russell, Charles Wells, 91, 105
Ryals, J. V., 93, 96, 100

Sage, William, 41
Saintsbury, George, 6n, 75
Sargent, Epes, 13, 47, 83, 131
Scott, Evelyn, 12, 76, 137-38, 175-77, 191
Scott, Sir Walter, influence of, 6-7; rules for historical fiction, 16-18n; mentioned, 19, 34, 185
Seawell, Molly Elliott, 13, 51, 53-54, 62, 132, 168-69, 170
Seward, William H., 58, 99, 111
Sex in Civil War novels, 57-58n
Sherman, William T., 5, 31n
Shiloh, 25, 59, 156
Shreveport, 38
Shuster, George Nauman, 41n
Simms, William Gilmore, 18n
Sinclair, Harold, 109, 111
Sinclair, Upton, 103, 111, 115, 121
Sioux City, 39, 40n
South, classes in, 35, 63-64, 119, 124-26, 146, 166-68, 173, 182-84, 186; victor in fiction, 42-43; iron curtain in, 88-89, 130-32; violence in, 122-23, 178-79, 184-86; localism in, 126-29; families in,